Marketing for Entrepreneurs

SECOND EDITION

To my wife Doreen, and to my daughters, Erinn, Jacquelyn, and Brenna, and to Ciara and Dex

Marketing for Entrepreneurs

Concepts and Applications for New Ventures

SECOND EDITION

Frederick G. Crane

Northeastern University

Los Angeles | London | New Delhi
Singapore | Washington DC

Los Angeles | London | New Delhi
Singapore | Washington DC

FOR INFORMATION:

SAGE Publications, Inc.

2455 Teller Road

Thousand Oaks, California 91320

E-mail: order@sagepub.com

SAGE Publications Ltd.

1 Oliver's Yard

55 City Road

London EC1Y 1SP

United Kingdom

SAGE Publications India Pvt. Ltd.

B 1/I 1 Mohan Cooperative Industrial Area

Mathura Road, New Delhi 110 044

India

SAGE Publications Asia-Pacific Pte. Ltd.

3 Church Street

#10-04 Samsung Hub

Singapore 049483

Acquisitions Editor: Patricia Quinlin

Editorial Assistant: Katie Guarino

Production Editor: Eric Garner

Copy Editor: Codi Bowman

Typesetter: C&M Digitals (P) Ltd.

Proofreader: Joyce Li

Indexer: Rick Hurd

Cover Designer: Anupama Krishnan

Marketing Manager: Liz Thornton

Permissions Editor: Adele Hutchinson

Copyright © 2013 by SAGE Publications, Inc.

Printed in the United States of America

A catalog record of this book is available from the Library of Congress.

978-1-4522-3004-7

This book is printed on acid-free paper.

MIX
Paper from
responsible sources
FSC
www.fsc.org   FSC® C014174

13 14 15 16 10 9 8 7 6 5 4 3 2

Contents

Preface

This book has been written for three types of potential entrepreneurs or existing entrepreneurs:

1. Potential entrepreneurs/entrepreneurs who have a marketing opportunity and are looking for advice on possible opportunity refinement and then guidance as to how to wrap an effective marketing plan around that opportunity.

2. Potential entrepreneurs/entrepreneurs who are attempting to determine the best marketing opportunity from a predetermined set of opportunity options and then need help in constructing a robust marketing plan around the chosen option.

3. Potential entrepreneurs/entrepreneurs who need guidance with regard to how to recognize, discover, or create marketing opportunity and then need a template for crafting a marketing plan to exploit the chosen opportunity.

It has been my experience that only a minority of budding entrepreneurs have well researched the marketing opportunity component of the new venture process while the majority have not done their homework and are sorely lacking a strong foundation upon which to build the venture. In other words, they may believe an opportunity exists but they have not taken the time and energy to fully vet the opportunity through insightful market and customer research.

I say that because I continue to see experts who cite many reasons for the high failure rates of entrepreneurial businesses including management incompetence, lack of industry experience, under-capitalization, lack of strategic focus, poor cash management, and uncontrolled growth. But, in my view, the primary reasons for new venture failure are the entrepreneur's inability to recognize, discover, or create the right marketing opportunity; the inability or unwillingness to fully research the opportunity; and/or an incapability to exploit that opportunity effectively. You may have great management skills, excellent industry experience, and plenty of cash. But this will not help you if you are pursuing the wrong opportunity or if you fail at market execution. In other words, wrapping a good-looking marketing plan around a bad (or wrong) opportunity or spending resources on a bad (or wrong) opportunity is akin to putting lipstick on a pig!

This book is intended to help you understand and apply entrepreneurial marketing concepts that should increase your likelihood of venture success. In Chapter 1, you will learn why marketing is different in an entrepreneurial context. It also discusses how social media is changing the entrepreneurial game. Chapter 2 discusses how you can find and evaluate the right marketing opportunity. The importance of the right business model to effectively exploit the opportunity is also discussed in Chapter 2. In short, a good opportunity can be negated by not having the right business model. Using marketing research to ensure entrepreneurial success is discussed in Chapter 3. In Chapter 4, you will gain a deep understanding of customers and competition. Chapter 5 details three very important concepts for the entrepreneur wishing to achieve business success: segmentation, targeting, and positioning. In Chapter 6, you will learn about the new product and service development process. How to build and sustain a strong entrepreneurial brand is discussed in Chapter 7, including how to build and sustain your brand in the social media marketing era. In Chapter 8 we will discuss how to effectively price your offering and avoid the trap of cost-plus price setting. Chapter 9 provides insight into entrepreneurial channel development and supply chain management. The importance of entrepreneurial promotion and how to do it cost-effectively is outlined in Chapter 10, including how to leverage social media to build and grow your venture. Chapter 11 discusses the entrepreneurial marketing plan and provides the basic anatomy of such a plan. In Appendix A, you will find a good example of an excellent entrepreneurial marketing plan developed by a team of students I have taught.

This book is based on my experience growing up in a family business, as a founder of several successful startups, as an investor in entrepreneurial businesses, as a advisory board member for several entrepreneurial firms, and as a consultant to entrepreneurs and to those who fund and support entrepreneurial enterprises. It is intended to help you better understand marketing and its application in an entrepreneurial context. My hope is that the concepts, methods, tools, and approaches outlined in this book will help you identify, create, and grow a successful new venture. Your success will be vital to the continued health of our new entrepreneurial-based economy. Therefore, this book is dedicated to all the aspiring entrepreneurs who wish to take the risk to start a new venture. It is hoped that the insight provided in this book will ensure that the risk taken will be amply rewarded.

I would like to thank my family for their love and patience while I crafted this book. I also want to thank the leadership at the College of Business at Northeastern University for supporting my entrepreneurial efforts. I would also like to thank my sponsoring editor Pat Quinlin, Katie Guarino, editorial assistant, as well as the other members of the SAGE team who contributed to the development and completion of the book. Finally, I want to express my sincere thanks to the reviewers of the text who helped me develop this new edition:

Stuart Atkins, Mihaylo College of Business and Economics, California State University, Fullerton

Jenny Darroch, The Peter F. Drucker and Masatoshi Ito Graduate School of Management, Claremont Graduate University

Diane Denslow, University of North Florida

Beth Fitz Gibbon, Case Western Reserve University, Weatherhead School of Management

Dr. John Godek, University of Washington Bothell

Peter Raven, Seattle University

Ugur Uygur, Loyola University Chicago

Frederick G. Crane, PhD

One

Marketing in an Entrepreneurial Context

So, you want to be an entrepreneur! That's great. It can be a challenging and rewarding experience. And if I asked you why you wanted to be an entrepreneur, I bet many of you would say it is because you want to make money. Well, that is the first mistake most entrepreneurs make. In fact, the actual purpose of an enterprise is not to make money. Instead, experts tell us that the actual purpose of an enterprise is the creation and retention of satisfied customers.[1] How well you perform these vital tasks will be reflected in the level of profitability of your enterprise. In other words, your profit is simply the scorecard with respect to how well you stay wedded to your real purpose.

You must understand this important point or your entrepreneurial career is likely to be truncated. Moreover, it is critical for you to understand marketing's role in creating and retaining satisfied customers. Simply put, it is marketing that enables you to discover, create, arouse, and satisfy customer needs and wants. In entrepreneurial terms, we often say that a successful enterprise is built by a smart entrepreneur who finds a source of "market pain" and creates a "unique" way to cure it!

For example, consider the young entrepreneurs who started Three Dog Bakery. Dan Dye and Mark Beckloff recognized that the dog treat category was a multibillion-dollar category in the United States and growing at a double-digit rate. They were also smart enough to recognize another key trend: dog as family member. That is, particular owners of dogs viewed themselves as "pet parents" and wanted only the very best for their dogs, including healthy, all-natural, and tasty treats. But many pet parents were unhappy ("market pain") with current products being marketed. The solution was to offer the pet parents an "innovative dog bakery" where dog owners could come (with their dogs) and buy products that they trusted and that their dogs would love.

The result was a tremendous success. The company has opened up franchise-owned stores all across America and have expanded into Canada, Japan, and Hong Kong. The company also distributes its dog treats through major retail chains, including Walgreens, Kroger, and Wal-Mart. The company has also expanded its line of product by adding cat treats and a line of premium dog food. Moreover, like many successful entrepreneurial firms, Three Dog effectively operates in a multichannel format including online, company and franchised owned retail store bakeries and in retail chain partners' outlets. Finally, like many good, socially conscious entrepreneurs, the founders of Three Dog Bakery have also started a nonprofit foundation. The Three Dog Bakery Foundation is a 501(c)(3) organization that offers financial assistance to any properly licensed, not-for-profit dog and cat groups with a focus of rescuing dogs and cats. Three Dog Bakery is an example of a successful entrepreneurial startup that was based on a key concept in marketing—discovering customer needs and satisfying them. Or, as we say, finding a source of market pain and finding a unique way to alleviate that pain! Three Dog Bakery also illustrates the need for entrepreneurs to consider how to sustain the growth for their enterprises. In this case, scaling up the business via franchise, expanding geographically, and adding new product lines (in their case, cat treats and dog food) and finding novel ways to reach customers including online.

Marketing: Defined

Many people are confused or have misconceptions about the concept of marketing. First, do not confuse marketing with advertising, selling, or common sense. Although advertising is one of the more visible forms of marketing, it is but one small element of marketing. Marketing is not selling. In fact, some experts suggest that if entrepreneurs engage in effective marketing, it can reduce the need for selling. Marketing is not simply common sense. While good entrepreneurs are often perceptive and intuitive, these traits alone are not sufficient for making successful marketing decisions. Effective marketing requires intimate knowledge and understanding of consumers and competition that goes beyond simple common sense.

Second, be wary of the many misconceptions about marketing, including many negative ones. For example, marketing is not hucksterism; it is not selling unwanted things and taking the customer's money. Nor is marketing about manipulating, fooling, or tricking the customer.[2] Instead, marketing is the activity for creating, communicating, delivering, and exchanging offerings that benefit the organization, its stakeholders, and society at large.[3] This definition stresses the importance of delivering genuine benefits (or value) in the offerings marketed to customers. As an entrepreneur, your business venture must create and deliver customer benefits or value. If not, there is absolutely no reason for customers to buy from you. Moreover, while gaining your first customers is critical for your venture you must also use marketing to retain those customers, by satisfying those customers and forging long-term relationships with them. If you do, you will find that these customers will remain loyal to your enterprise and can be a valuable resource in recommending your business to others.

The Seven Steps in the Marketing Process

As an entrepreneur, you will have to understand and follow the seven steps in the marketing process to create and sustain a successful venture:

1. Identify and understand customer needs.

2. Develop products, services, or experiences to meet those needs.

3. Price the products, services, or experiences effectively.

4. Inform customers that these products, services, or experiences exist.

5. Deliver the products, services, or experiences efficiently and conveniently for the customer.

6. Ensure customer satisfaction during and after the exchange process.

7. Build long-term relationships with the customers.

Northeastern University alumnus Reuben Taube and his brother Ari find themselves in the Entrepreneurial Marketing Spotlight by demonstrating that they have mastered many of the steps in the marketing process.

Entrepreneurial Marketing Spotlight

Reuben and Ari Taube are entrepreneurs. And, their success can be largely attributed to the fact they embraced the marketing process. First, being marketing oriented they discovered that many snack consumers were looking for a more healthy, organic, and gluten-free product. Second, they also discovered that there was a staple grain called sorghum that practically grows anywhere on the globe and is inexpensive, healthy, and gluten-free. Third, based on these discoveries they developed a unique product designed to meet the needs of this health-oriented snack consumer. It is called Mini Pops, an alternative to traditional popcorn! And, this new product is making a splash in the multibillion-dollar U.S. snack market. Mini Pops have fewer calories, less saturated fat, less sodium, and more protein, calcium, and fiber than popped corn. They are also high in iron, antioxidants, and heart-friendly policosanols. Additionally, sorghum grains have softer hulls than corn, preventing those awkward moments of sticking your fingers in your mouth trying to pry uncomfortable wedges from between your teeth. Mini Pops come in plain and seven other flavors such as the Nano Pepper & Herb and the Baby White Cheddar as well as in bags of raw kernels that you can pop and flavor yourself. The Brothers Taube were able to effectively price their offerings (a 16-ounce bag of raw kernels sells for $13 and the six-ounce flavored bags sells for $3.50). They also invested in promotion to inform consumers about the availability of the new product and successfully established distribution to get the product to the customer, both from the company's website (the Mini Pops shop) and at major retailers including Whole Foods. Only time will tell if the brothers can complete the rest of the marketing process (i.e., ensure satisfaction and build relationships with customers). But, they are off to a great start and we welcome them to the entrepreneurial marketing spotlight.[4]

Why Marketing in New Ventures Is Different

Marketing in an entrepreneurial context is different from an established corporation. As an entrepreneur, you will face different marketing issues compared to executives in a corporate environment.

For example, unlike your corporate counterparts:

- The entrepreneur must use marketing to identify new products, services, or experiences to market to new customers and not simply use it to sell existing products and services to existing customers.
- The entrepreneur must use marketing to obtain his or her "first customer" (gain the first dollar of business) and not simply manage an existing customer base.
- The entrepreneur must use marketing to build a new brand and not simply manage an existing brand.
- The entrepreneur must use marketing to establish effective marketing channels of distribution and not simply manage existing distribution methods.
- The entrepreneur must use marketing to establish initial price points for his or her offerings and not simply manage current prices for existing offerings.
- The entrepreneur must use marketing communications to persuade customers to try his or her offerings and not simply remind customers to continue to buy.
- The entrepreneur, because of resource scarcity, must find creative ways to leverage his or her marketing efforts, especially early in the venture startup phase.

Unfortunately, venture failure continues to be the rule and not the exception. But marketing can help you improve your odds of venture success. It can help provide you with a solid understanding of customers and markets, identify and validate the right opportunity, and determine how best to capitalize on that opportunity. One of the biggest problems faced by many entrepreneurs is the tendency to chase "too many rabbits." In other words, you must focus and try not to be all things to all people. Marketing can provide this focus. In short, it can help you zero in on the right customers—your **target market**—the specific group of customers toward which you direct your marketing efforts or marketing program. In the entrepreneurship world, particularly from the investor's perspective the target market is often referred to as the "addressable market." It is marketing—specifically, marketing research—that allows you to determine this target market—the addressable market—and then enables you to configure your marketing program.

Using Marketing to Discover and Satisfy Customer Needs

It is important for you to recognize that if you wish to improve your odds of venture success, you must use marketing to discover and satisfy customer needs. The discovery process sounds simple but it is not. Thousands of ventures fail every year in the United States, and in many cases, the failure is a direct result of the entrepreneur failing to carefully examine customers' needs or simply misreading those needs. Granted, it is often difficult to get a precise reading on what the customer needs. But as an entrepreneur, you have to be willing to be persistent and creative to uncover customer needs.

One of the best ways to do so is to go into the market to talk with and listen to customers. Through dialogue and active engagement with the customer, you will gain an understanding of the customer. In the entrepreneurship field, we often refer to this process as obtaining "the voice of the consumer." Voice of consumer research will be discussed later as an important part of finding and evaluating business opportunities.

After properly discovering customer needs, the entrepreneur must begin the task of designing his or her business to satisfy those needs. In fact, recent research involving 45 successful entrepreneurs revealed that delivering customer satisfaction was a key imperative for venture success.[5] But, as stated earlier, your venture cannot satisfy all consumers' needs, so you must concentrate your efforts on a specific group of potential customers—your target market. Selecting the proper target market involves the process of **market segmentation**—placing customers into groups (segments) that (1) have common needs and (2) will respond to a specific marketing offer. We will discuss segmentation in depth in Chapter 5. For now, it is sufficient that you know that you will select a given segment (or segments) to pursue—your target market(s)—and create the marketing offer, designed to appeal to the target market and satisfy its needs. This marketing offering is called your **marketing mix.** The marketing mix is what gets integrated into a tangible marketing program that your business will use to gain and keep customers. For Product-Based ventures, your marketing mix consists of five elements, or **5Ps:** product, price, promotion, place, and people. For a Service-Based venture, the marketing mix consists of eight elements, or **8Ps:** product, price, promotion, place, people, physical evidence, process, and productivity.

The 5Ps of Product-Based Ventures

A marketing program for a Product-Based venture—a venture that markets "tangible" or physical products—would consist of a combination of five marketing mix elements. The 5Ps are used to create, communicate, and deliver value to your customer:

- *Product:* The product to satisfy the customer's needs
- *Price:* The cost to the customer
- *Promotion:* The means of communication between you and the customer
- *Place:* The means of getting the product into the customer's hands
- *People:* The individuals who will work with you and your venture

Figure 1.1 shows the 5Ps for Sephora, a very successful beauty and skincare enterprise.

Figure 1.1   The 5Ps for Sephora

Product: Broad range of quality skincare, makeup, and fragrances for women and men (nationally branded and private label)

Price: Above market

Promotion: Public relations, catalogs, customer loyalty program, website, social media, and mobile marketing including an iPhone app

Place: More than 500 stores (more than 200 inside JC Penney stores) in twenty-four countries, online (www.sephora.com), and 1-877-Sephora

People: Highly trained, knowledgeable, and customer-centric consultants

---

Sephora has a unique open-sell environment with more than 200 brands plus Sephora's private label. The company emphasizes training of its people and even opened Sephora University in San Francisco to educate its personnel on both products and customer relations. The company also has one of the world's top beauty website and social media including an online beauty community as well as mobile technology including an iPhone app. The company has achieved outstanding year-over-year sales growth since its launch.

The 8Ps of Service-Based Ventures

A marketing program for a Service-Based venture—a venture that markets "intangibles"—would consist of a combination of eight marketing mix elements (8Ps):[6]

- *Product:* The product (service) to satisfy the customer's needs
- *Price:* The cost to the customer
- *Promotion:* The means of communication between you and the customer
- *Place:* The means of getting the product into the customer's hands
- *People:* The individuals who will work with you and your venture
- *Physical evidence:* The "tangibles" that surround your service
- *Process:* The way the service is created and delivered
- *Productivity:* Balancing service output with service quality

Figure 1.2 shows the 8Ps for Southwest Airlines, one of the most successful entrepreneurial airline startups in America. In fact, Southwest Airlines went from a small startup with just a few planes to a major carrier in less than 20 years. It has also been the most consistently profitable airline in the United States and has achieved high levels of customer satisfaction year after year.

Figure 1.2   The 8Ps for Southwest Airlines

Product: Low cost, no frills, convenience, point-to-point airline passenger service

Price: Low prices, below market

Promotion: Broad range of marketing communications, including broadcast television, sponsorships, and its website

Place: Major markets but often in secondary airports adjacent to major airports to keep costs down

People: Specific emphasis on training to achieve excellent customer service

Physical evidence: Keeping the planes clean and safe; allowing employees to dress casually; and strong branding, color language, etc.

Process: Using the same plane type to make it easier for employees to manage operations and making it easy and simple to fly with Southwest, including online booking

Productivity: Key emphasis on a 15-minute turnaround time (getting the plane ready after landing and getting it back in the air safely)

Market Fulfillment Versus Market Creation

It is safe to state that most new ventures are based on the concept of market fulfillment. That is, the entrepreneur enters an "existing market" and uses the conventional marketing process. But some new ventures are based on "market creation"—creating a new market that did not currently exist. In this case, the consumers generally have no idea about a need for such a new product, service, or experience.

In the case of market fulfillment, the conventional marketing process of discovering and satisfying customer needs really does work quite well. But it does not work so well when an entrepreneur is attempting to create entirely new markets.[7] Henry Ford, famous automobile pioneer, once said, "If I asked the customer what they really wanted, they'd have said a faster horse!"

Basically, Ford was telling us that when we try to discover what customers want, they will often simply ask for better versions of existing products. But this approach will not help an entrepreneur who wishes to produce breakthrough or new-to-world innovations. These concepts are radically different and are sometimes beyond the imagination of the customers. Thus, customers may not recognize that they need or want such innovative concepts. For example, FedEx created the overnight package delivery market, a market that did not previously exist and a market that customers did not know could exist. CNN created the 24/7 cable news market, and again, customers did not imagine such an offering being developed. A more recent example is the "flying car." The Terrafugia Transition is a two-seat aircraft designed to take off and land at local airports and drive on any road. According to entrepreneur and creator Carl Dietrich, this product changes the world of personal mobility. Travel can now become a hassle-free integrated land-air experience. If you want one of these new flying cars—or as the company calls it—"a roadable aircraft"—you can place a deposit of $10,000 to reserve one. After that you'll have to come up with another $269,000 to complete the purchase! [8]

So, in short, entrepreneurs of new-to-world concepts really have no market at the time of invention; they have to create one. In doing so, these entrepreneurs go beyond the conventional marketing process and often create markets with enormous potential for sustained growth.

How Social Media Is Changing the Entrepreneurial Game

An emergent concept is changing how business is done, including how consumers shop for and buy products and services. It is called *social media*. Many existing corporations are struggling as to how to harness and manage this concept. In fact, many are using social media in the wrong ways. At the same time, however, social media is opening up opportunities for entrepreneurs who would be well advised to recognize and embrace it—correctly. Importantly, this also means using social media to complement but NOT replace your traditional marketing and promotional efforts.

But, first things first, you must understand social media. In my view there are several components to social media: (1) social platforms—the social networks/communities created by individuals and/or organizations such as Facebook; (2) social content—the blogs, photo, audio, and video sharing offered on these platforms; and (3) the overall social interactions taking place among members on these platforms. The power of social media is awesome. For example, Facebook has 700 million users; on Twitter there are 2 billion tweets made per month; and on YouTube there are 2 billion views per day. Thus, what is really important for you to know is whether or not you participate and use social media, your likely target market customers probably are. In other words, social media can be exclusively online consumer-generated efforts by customers who talk about, promote, build, or hurt brands. And, you might not be able to control this activity! On the other hand, social media can also be used by you to promote your venture and brand. In doing so, while you still may not fully control what customers communicate about your venture and brand, you can certainly influence it.

Using social media, customers are empowered to communicate with organizations and other customers. It is creating a new form of economy—what Erik Qualman calls *socialnomics*—where customers no longer search for products or services but rather find them via social media. In doing so, customers are changing the rules of business and the way they shop.[9] For example, a social media platform like Facebook has 700 million users who can instantly connect and communicate about a new business or brand—either helping to build it or destroy it! Therefore, as an entrepreneur you cannot be a bystander—you must actively engage and leverage social media. However, you must do it right or you will be rejected by the customers you are intending to reach and influence. Clearly, social media allows budding entrepreneurs with scarce resources to keep marketing costs low while directly reaching potential customers 24/7 on a global basis. But, again, you must play by the new rules of the game as established by customers who are present there. For example, Three Dog Bakery makes good use of social media including Facebook, Twitter, and a blog component on their own website. It engages its customers and offers them content with good value including important information about brands and advice on pet ownership and pet health.

In addition to using social media to communicate with customers, entrepreneurs also have many dedicated social media sites to help them with their entrepreneurial efforts. For example, there are many social networks established exclusively for entrepreneurs. Some of the better ones, in my opinion are (1) Entrepreneur Connect, (2) Partnerup, (3) Startup Nation, (4) Linkedin—but only the startups group on this site, (5) Biznik, (6) The Funded, and (7) Young Entrepreneur. You should check out these sites since they offer excellent resources for the aspiring entrepreneur like you.

The External Marketing Environment

Most entrepreneurs believe they are clearly in control regarding the type of business they wish to operate and how they operate it. However, businesses do not operate in a vacuum. In fact, a host of factors or forces in the marketing environment are largely beyond the control of the entrepreneur. These forces can be placed into five groups: social, economic, technological, competitive, and regulatory forces. Examples are what consumers themselves want and need, changing technology, the state of the economy in terms of whether it is expanding or contracting, actions that competitors take, and government restrictions. These external forces may serve as accelerators or brakes on marketing, sometimes expanding a venture's marketing opportunities and at other times restricting them. Importantly, successful entrepreneurs evaluate these forces to determine what business opportunities such forces might provide. And entrepreneurs continue to monitor these forces to determine how best to adapt their businesses to survive and grow.

This is in contrast to other, typically unsuccessful, entrepreneurs who treat these external forces as rigid, absolute constraints that are entirely outside their influence. These entrepreneurs simply fail to anticipate and respond to these external forces. But successful entrepreneurs who are forward looking and action oriented do take advantage of these external forces. In other words, they find opportunities that are created by these external forces by aligning their enterprise to capitalize on these forces. For example, one entrepreneur saw the rising incidence of obesity in America, an external factor seemingly beyond his control. But by observing and analyzing this trend, he developed a "plus size" retail clothing business and became a successful entrepreneur. Another entrepreneur noticed the aging population of America, especially the growth in the grandparent population who wanted to stay connected with their grandchildren. Capitalizing on this trend, the entrepreneur rolled out a new online business called "grandparents.com."

Five Forces in the Entrepreneurial Marketing Environment

As mentioned, there are **five environmental forces** in entrepreneurial marketing: social, economic, technological, competitive, and regulatory forces.

Social Forces

Social forces include the characteristics of the population, as well as its values and its behavior. Changes in these forces can have a dramatic impact on what opportunities are available to the entrepreneur. For example, there have been some major demographic shifts in the United States, including growing ethnic diversity and an aging population. If current trends continue, niche marketing opportunities based on ethnicity and age will continue to emerge. For example, some entrepreneurs have built their businesses to appeal directly to specific generational cohorts (i.e., for age groups such as seniors, baby boomers, Generation X, Generation Y)—adult diapers for seniors and wireless communication devices for Gen Y. Other entrepreneurs have launched businesses to appeal to specific ethnic groups, particularly ethnic food businesses.

A second social force is culture, and in recent years, Americans have experienced notable cultural changes that have affected consumer attitudes and values. For example, with more working women, the number of tasks to do is expanding, while the time available to do them is shrinking. This has led to the phenomenon of *time poverty*. Entrepreneurs are responding to this trend by creating ventures that help alleviate or reduce the consumer's time poverty such as delivery services, online shopping businesses, and ready-to-eat foods. Another emerging cultural trend is that Americans are becoming more experiential. That is, they are seeking new experiences and are willing to try new things, including travel, new forms of entertainment, and dining.

Economic Forces

Another environmental force is the nature of our economy. Entrepreneurs must recognize what is happening at the macroeconomic level of the economy, such as whether the economy is growing as well as determining the state of consumer confidence in the economy, which will affect business and consumer spending. At the microeconomic level, entrepreneurs must determine if the consumer actually has the ability to buy particular products and/or services. Many Americans have seen erosion of their actual spending power, and this has led to a trend called *customer value consciousness*. Many entrepreneurs have successfully built businesses to respond to this trend such as "dollar store" retail formats.

Technological Forces

Another environmental force is dramatic technological change. In fact, new technologies are forever changing the way consumers shop and what they buy. Moreover, new technologies are enabling entrepreneurs to create unique new businesses or enhance how they can conduct their businesses. One of the most important technologies that has changed the marketing landscape is the Internet. As discussed earlier, it was technology that gave rise to social media, which has fundamentally changed the rules of the game as it pertains to how consumers behave and how business is done. Technology, including the Internet has enabled new entrepreneurial enterprises to be built and fully operationalized leveraging this important technological force—in other words, developing and managing online or pure-play e-businesses that exist only in an electronic marketplace. A good example is Craigslist with its electronic classified ad business. Other brick-and-mortar enterprises also leverage the Internet as part of their overall marketing efforts. There are many other examples of successful online businesses, many of which are entrepreneurial ventures. As mentioned earlier, many leverage social media websites as well as their own highly interactive websites to conduct their businesses.

Now, the new capability of a completely wireless world is also enabling consumers to stay connected to the Internet 24/7 regardless of where they are, and this is also providing new opportunities for entrepreneurs wishing to provide goods and services to this wireless and mobile population. The Internet has also opened up global marketing opportunities and the rise of international entrepreneurship, where entrepreneurs can serve global markets without the constraint of physical or geographic boundaries. One thing you have to remember as a budding American entrepreneur is that 95 percent of the consumer population lives outside the United States. You should not have to confine yourself to your domestic market when opportunities to reach across time and space are now available to you.

Competitive Forces

Competitive forces in the external marketing environment are very important for the entrepreneur to consider. The first thing every successful entrepreneur realizes is that there is always some form of current competition in the marketplace. So, if you seek funding for your enterprise, never go to a bank, angel, or private equity firm and state that your business has "no competition." In one way or another, it certainly does. Therefore, competition should be considered broadly as any alternative that could satisfy a specific customer's needs. This includes a variety of forms of competition ranging from pure (direct) competition— where every company offers a similar product to a similar customer—to total budget competition—where customers consider spending their scarce resources across seemingly dissimilar offerings (e.g., spend money on an MBA vs. buying a new boat). The trend in America in terms of competition is that most industries and markets are highly competitive, and the consumer has tremendous choice in terms of providers. Therefore, an entrepreneur has to determine "how to compete" and "how to differentiate" his or her business from the existing competitors. We will discuss competition in more detail in Chapter 4. But for now, you must recognize that competition is an external force that will surely affect the type of business you will build and the competitive strategy you craft. For example, most entrepreneurial startups do not have the size and scale to compete on price, so most attempt to compete on a nonprice dimension emphasizing some clearly superior performance deemed valuable to the customer (e.g., great customer service).

Regulatory Forces

Entrepreneurs must also be conscious of the fact that regulatory forces can influence the nature or scope of opportunities in the marketplace. Regulations consist of restrictions that local, state, and federal laws place on business with respect to the conduct of its activities. Regulation exists to protect companies and consumers and ensure a competitive marketplace. New regulations and deregulation can both provide opportunities for entrepreneurs. Deregulation of several industries over the past few decades has led to the emergence of new enterprises. For example, deregulation of the U.S. telecom industry allowed for the startup of new long-distance telephone companies and later on the development of numerous wireless phone companies. Similarly, deregulation of the U.S. airline industry produced opportunities for many regional airline startups, including Southwest Airlines and JetBlue. Greater regulation has also provided opportunities for entrepreneurs. For example, when the Environmental Protection Agency enacted stronger regulations to ensure cleaner air and water, many companies turned to entrepreneurs for new technologies to ensure compliance.

Environmental Scanning

Environmental scanning is the process of continually acquiring information on the external marketing environment to identify and interpret potential trends that may lead to entrepreneurial business opportunities. Entrepreneurs engage in environmental scanning to uncover opportunities that others may miss or ignore. Many refer to the environmental scanning process as "trendspotting." For some entrepreneurs, the goal is to discover "the next big thing" or at least identify market trends that might lead to the development and launching of a new enterprise.

One of the things you will have to understand as you attempt to engage in environmental scanning is determining what is a true trend. A trend is the specific or general direction that a society is headed, which transforms things from what they are today to something different in the future. A trend makes a difference in the way people live and work. Trends are enduring phenomena that are radically affecting the way consumers behave in the marketplace and/or the way we do business. Trends create major structural changes in society: sociocultural, economic, or technological. A trend is different from a fad, which comes and goes quickly. A fad does not change society, but a trend does. Environmental scanning is an important skill for entrepreneurs to possess. To become a good scanner, you will have to do the following: [10]

- *Adjust your reading, listening, and viewing habits.* This means focusing on things of substance and relevance to your goal of becoming an entrepreneur. Of particular importance is becoming a broad-based reader to discover societal trends that underpin market behavior. You need to make a commitment to scan for information that will provide clues about possible marketing opportunities.

- *Network with the right people.* This means staying engaged with knowledgeable and informed individuals and to remain open to learn from these people. One expert suggests that you "take a neuroscientist, sociologist, psychologist, or artist to lunch." These people can provide insight into human behavior, how markets develop, and how consumers think and feel about their experiences in the marketplace. Networking also involves being tapped into your community to keep in touch with trends that are affecting the people who might become your customers.
- *Be self-observant.* This means spending time discovering what makes you tick, what is important to you, and what challenges or problems you face. You might not be the typical consumer, but this is a good exercise in uncovering what possible trends are driving your behavior. You can then determine whether what affects you may also affect others.
- *Challenge your assumptions.* In many cases, there are traditions in society and/or in particular industries that may have outlived their usefulness. For example, there is an American tradition for school-age students to have a two-month summer vacation. And most people do not know why this tradition persists. Well, it is a carryover from the agrarian society when children in farming families took time off from school to help harvest the crops. Today, many educational institutions are challenging this tradition, and this has led to entrepreneurial opportunities such as private schools offering year long programs or innovative summer learning programs.
- *Spend time watching and talking with customers.* This is perhaps one of the most important steps in the environmental scanning process. Good environmental scanners focus their time on interacting with customers to determine their current and future needs. Successful entrepreneurs, in fact, pinpoint not only where customers are today (in terms of needs) but where they are heading in the future. One of the greatest insights you can glean from spending time with customers is understanding their behavior as it pertains to consumption. In other words, what types of buying behavior do they engage in—what they buy, how, when, where and why. In Chapter 4, we will discuss the concept of "ritualistic behavior"—behavior consumers engage in on a consistent and recurrent manner and how this may help you uncover opportunities to enable customers to do so in cheaper, faster, better, or more satisfying ways.

What is also important is to recognize that not all trends affect all consumers or affect them in the same way. Moreover, for each trend you might identify, there may be other "countervailing" trends that might be important for you to consider. For example, a novice environmental scanner might conclude that the United States is experiencing a health-consciousness trend. But this may be only partly true. Many Americans are more concerned about their health, and this has opened up opportunities for entrepreneurs who provide health-oriented goods and services. But clearly not all Americans have embraced health consciousness since many individuals remain overweight in this country. Accordingly, some entrepreneurs are building businesses to cater to overweight individuals, including plus-size clothing companies.

Finally, good environmental scanners not only interpret trends but also act on trends that offer the best business opportunities. This is illustrated by the Noah principle. That is, "Predicting rain doesn't count, building arks does." Thus, environmental scanning requires both market vigilance and marketing action.

An Environmental Scan of the United States

An environmental scan of the U.S. marketplace might uncover key trends, such as those listed in Figure 1.3. These trends are categorized under the five environmental forces discussed earlier.

Figure 1.3 An Environmental Scan of the United States	
Social	Growing ethnic diversity
	Aging
	Time poverty
	Value consciousness
	Eco-consciousness
Economic	Growth in electronic commerce economy
	Shift toward an experience economy
Technological	Diffusion of digital and mobile technologies
	Growth in biotechnology and nanotechnology
	Advances in medicine and medical treatments
Competitive	Increase in global competition
	Emergence of China and India as global competitors
	Mergers and acquisitions to improve competitiveness
	Emergence of entrepreneurial enterprises
Regulatory	Increased protection for intellectual property
	Increased emphasis on free trade
	Deregulation to encourage competition

Although the list of trends is far from complete, it reveals the breadth of an environmental scan—from the growing ethnic diversity of the American population to the shift to the experience economy to the increasing use of new technologies. As you examine the trends listed in Figure 1.3, you should be able to think about the implications of such trends and whether you can find opportunities that will stem from these trends.

As an entrepreneur, you have to understand marketing and its role in achieving venture success. Marketing helps you identify the right opportunity, and it plays a pivotal role in capitalizing on that opportunity. It is also critical that you understand the external marketing environment and recognize the opportunities and constraints it can place on your enterprise. Staying close to the market is the best way to ensure that you are building your enterprise on a solid foundation.

Key Takeaways

- Understand marketing and its central importance to entrepreneurial success.
- Use marketing to find a source of existing "market pain" and craft a unique way to cure it. Or, use marketing to create an entirely new market.
- Accept the reality of the social media era and learn to harness it for entrepreneurial success.
- Use marketing to zero in on the "right customer"—your target market.
- Go into the market to talk with and listen to customers (obtain the voice of consumer).
- Became an environmental scanner and discover truly sustainable marketing opportunities.

Entrepreneurial Exercise

Engage in some environmental scanning through broad-based reading or other means. Spot some trends. What are they? What type of marketing opportunities do these trends offer the potential entrepreneur? Now, make a list of two to three opportunities, and go into the market and talk to five to six potential customers to get their feedback on the opportunities. Do the customers agree there is an opportunity or not?

Key Terms

Addressable market   5

Marketing   2

Target market   5

Market segmentation   6

Marketing mix   6

Social media   9

5Ps   6

8Ps   6

Five environmental forces   12

Environmental scanning   15

Notes

1. Peter F. Drucker, *The Practice of Management* (New York: Harper & Row, 1954); George S. Day, "The Capabilities of Market-Driven Organizations," *Journal of Marketing* 58 (October 1994): 37–52.

2. Regis McKenna, "Marketing Is Everything," *Harvard Business Review* (January–February 1991): 65–79.

3. "AMA Adopts New Definition of Marketing," *Marketing News,* September 15, 2004, 1.

4. Personal Interview with Reuben and Ari Taube, March 2012.; and "Business Is Just Poppin; http://www.northeastern.edu/news/stories/2011/03/minipops.html, March 11, 2011.

5. Frederick G. Crane and Jeffrey E. Sohl, "Imperatives for Venture Success: Entrepreneurs Speak," *International Journal of Entrepreneurship and Innovation* 5, no. 2 (2004): 99–106.

6. Christopher Lovelock and Jochen Wirtz, *Services Marketing,* 5th ed. (Upper Saddle River, NJ: Pearson, 2004).

7. Frederick G. Crane and Marc H. Meyer, "Why Corporate America Cannot Innovate," Working Paper, Northeastern University, 2008.

8. Personal interview with Carl Dietrich, creator of the Terrafugia Transition, 2009.

9. Erik Qualman, *Socialnomics* (New York: Wiley, 2009).

10. Based on a speech delivered by Frederick G. Crane at the University of New Hampshire, fall 2004.

Two

Finding and Evaluating the Right Marketing Opportunity

A s you know, venture failure is the norm and venture success the exception. Why is this? Well, in most cases, the reality is that many business failures can be traced back to the fact the venture was built based on a bad or wrong **opportunity.**[1] Yes, would-be entrepreneurs are constantly coming up with so-called possible opportunities for potential businesses. But some opportunities are simply better than others. One of the problems entrepreneurs often have is that they tend to focus inwardly (often because of their backgrounds and/or experiences) on opportunities that they think are good opportunities. Another major problem is that some entrepreneurs simply fail to find out what the potential customer thinks about the possible business! For some entrepreneurs, it is the "Field of Dreams" mentality—if you build it, they will come. But the cold, hard fact is that most consumers are pretty happy with the products and services they buy from existing businesses. They are not, in fact, waiting anxiously for you to start your enterprise. Such an assumption on your part often gets in the way of truly finding and evaluating the right opportunity and generally results in venture failure. Ultimately, it is recognizing, discovering, or creating the right opportunity and exploiting it effectively that leads to entrepreneurial success. In fact, forget about what professors who never started a venture tell you about what leads to venture success or failure. A study involving 45 successful entrepreneurs—real people who started real businesses—found that the "right opportunity" was the number one imperative for venture success.[2]

Thus, your first task is to find a way to separate the good opportunities from the bad. Once you accomplish that, you must then put a plan in place that is designed to capitalize on that good opportunity.

Opportunities Can Be Recognized, Discovered, or Created

There are actually three views regarding entrepreneurial opportunities. That is, opportunities can be recognized, discovered, or created. With opportunity recognition, the entrepreneur recognizes (deduces) that supply and demand are known to exist. The entrepreneur simply matches up supply and demand through an existing firm or a new firm (e.g., a franchise). With opportunity discovery, the entrepreneur inductively determines that either supply or demand exists (not both), and the other side has to be discovered. For example, there is demand for cures for certain illnesses but no supply, and there was a supply of personal computers (when first invented), but demand had to be discovered. Finally, with opportunity creation, the process used by the entrepreneur is abductive (inference), and neither supply nor demand exists in any obvious manner and one or both may have to be created (e.g., Beanie Babies). Thus, it is entirely possible that an opportunity is something that is "out there" waiting for the entrepreneur to recognize or discover. And, at the same time, it is also possible that an opportunity can be created by the entrepreneur![3] This is consistent with our discussion of market fulfillment and market creation. Either way, some opportunities are simply better than others, and you have to understand the characteristics of a good opportunity.

Characteristics of a Good Opportunity

Some leading experts in the field of entrepreneurship suggest that a good opportunity should possesses the following characteristics:[4]

1. It creates significant value for customers by solving a significant problem or filling a significant unmet need for what the customer is willing to pay a premium price.

2. It offers significant profit potential to the entrepreneur and his or her investors—enough to meet their risk/reward expectations.

3. It represents a good fit with the capabilities of the entrepreneur and the management team—that is, you have the experience and skills to pursue it.

4. It offers sustainability over time—it is not based on a fad.

5. It can obtain financing.

Also, as you will see later, a good marketing opportunity will have validation from the intended customer. In short, the true litmus test for the marketing opportunity is whether the customer thinks it is a good idea and would be willing and able to pay for it.

One of the first things you need to do is to determine whether the opportunity offers significant value to the intended customer. And, importantly, find out if the customer will pay the price to receive the value offered.

This value can come in various forms. For example, what you offer might satisfy the customer in a much better way than established competition. For instance, perhaps you simply deliver a product or service faster or more reliably than the competitors. Another way of creating value is by offering something that meets or exceeds the needs of customers that have not been satisfied adequately.

So, for example, assume some customers are currently unhappy with their airline options flying from Boston to Miami—either the cost is too high or the schedule is too inconvenient. A new carrier could emerge offering better prices and greater convenience and might become a successful new player in the market. Finally, another way of creating value is to offer something that satisfies the "latent needs" of customers. Latent needs are needs the customer is not even consciously aware of. In other words, you attempt to offer an entirely new solution to a problem that the customer was not aware he or she had.

Remember our discussion on market fulfillment versus market creation in Chapter 1? In the first two situations above, you are simply trying to meet existing needs better or to address existing dissatisfaction with available alternatives (market fulfillment: opportunity recognition/ discovery). In the last situation, you are offering customers a novel solution to a problem they were not really aware they had. For example, you probably didn't realize that you had a need for an Apple iPod. But when Apple offered you this solution, you realized it was something valuable and something for which you would pay a premium price. In this case, Apple created a new market (opportunity creation).

Another characteristic of a good opportunity is that it also offers the potential for significant profit. Clearly, the notion of *significant* would vary depending on the entrepreneur. For example, for some of you wishing to own and operate a lifestyle business, the amount of profit you would deem significant is an amount that allows you to live a comfortable life. However, for those who wish to build a high-growth venture, a business that has financial investors, significant profit might mean a 20 percent profit margin on a $10 million business.

With a good opportunity, there is also a good "fit" between the opportunity and the entrepreneur (management team) in terms of industry experience and knowledge, as well as managerial, financial, and technical capabilities. Importantly, there is a good fit if you are passionate about the opportunity and are prepared to make a high level of personal commitment to capitalize on the opportunity.

A good opportunity is also one that offers sustainability over time. In other words, the opportunity is durable and will last over the long term. Many ventures are built on fads that come and go quickly, and thus the business itself may have a short life span. But a venture built on an enduring trend is more likely to produce sustained profitability over time. However, you must also recognize that sustainability in terms of customer demand is not enough. Sustainability also means you are offering something valuable to the customer that a competitor would find hard to copy. If what you offer is easily imitated by competitors, you do not have a sustainable opportunity.

Finally, another important dimension of a good opportunity is that it can obtain financing. If you seek out financing, your backers or investors must have confidence in the business venture and be willing to make the cash injection. If the backers or investors do not believe you have a solid opportunity, they will not financially support the venture.

Now, because Jeff Timmons, a leading entrepreneurship expert, has contributed so much to our understanding of entrepreneurial opportunities, he deserves a place in the Entrepreneurial Marketing Spotlight!

Entrepreneurial Marketing Spotlight

Jeff Timmons (now deceased) was the Franklin W. Olin Distinguished Professor of Entrepreneurship at Babson College. For more than four decades, Jeff was a pioneer in entrepreneurship education and entrepreneurial research. He published more than 100 articles and more than a dozen books on entrepreneurship. As a professor, he practiced what he taught and was directly involved in the real world of entrepreneurship as an investor, director, and adviser to private companies. Perhaps one of Jeff's greatest contributions to the field of entrepreneurship was his work that focused on entrepreneurial opportunities. Jeff believed that a superior opportunity has the qualities of being attractive, durable, and timely and is anchored in a product/service that creates or adds value for the customer, usually by solving a "painful" problem. He also stressed that successful entrepreneurs are opportunity focused. And he always emphasized that the best opportunities often do not start out that way. They are crafted, shaped, molded, and reinvented in real time and market space. Importantly, he always stressed that at the heart of the entrepreneurial process is the opportunity! And successful entrepreneurs know the difference between a good opportunity and a bad one. For his dedication to entrepreneurship and for his contribution to our understanding of entrepreneurial opportunities, Jeff deserves to be in the Entrepreneurial Marketing Spotlight.[5]

Finding Marketing Opportunities: Where to Look

I have argued for many years that environmental scanning may be one of the best ways to find optimal opportunities for your venture. In fact, a study of successful entrepreneurs revealed that these individuals engaged in environmental scanning.[6] And as you read in Chapter 1, environmental scanning includes not only examining trends/changes in the marketplace but also watching and talking to consumers. Closely looking for structural changes in society and determining how these changes will affect the needs of consumers (their "pain") is vital if you wish to pinpoint the right opportunities for your business. The major categories of environmental forces discussed in Chapter 1 that are assessed through environmental scanning were social, economic, technological, competitive, and regulatory.

Social Change

Numerous social changes (demographic and cultural) are having a dramatic impact on the types of entrepreneurial opportunities available in the marketplace. In Chapter 1, we discussed a few of these changes, including the growing ethnic population of America, the aging population, and time poverty. Each of these changes offers potential opportunities for the entrepreneur.

Another notable social change is eco-consciousness or going green. Many Americans are more sensitive about the impact their consumption has on the natural environment. This has led to demand for more environmentally safe or more environmentally friendly products, buying products that can be reused or recycled, or actually reducing consumption altogether. The trend toward eco-consciousness has opened up opportunities to a new breed of entrepreneurs called *ecopreneurs:* entrepreneurs who see opportunities through an environmental lens. For example, one entrepreneurial startup, Earthcycle Packaging, created an eco-friendly package made from a renewable resource called *palm fiber,* which composts in less than 90 days and provides a healthy contribution to the soil.

Finally, Americans are becoming more experiential. We are more willing to try new things and to seek out new experiences. Spending on foreign travel is up, and spending on entertainment and dining outside the home is up, particularly at ethnic restaurants. Some have referred to these experiential consumers as "trysumers"—consumers who are daring in how and what they consume. They are enabled by mobile communications technologies such as wireless phones and personal navigation devices. They can travel off the beaten path and still feel safe and in touch.

Since many of these trysumers want to try new things and not buy, new venture startups have emerged to cater to this group. For example, British Fractional Life is a venture that offers consumers a variety of asset-sharing options from luxury handbags, cars, and even helicopters, all available in shares or time slots. Some trysumers are even "trysexuals." In response, Match.com and other dating sites offer "try before you buy/rate before you date" services as well as casual encounters and speed dating.[7]

Economic Change

One of the major structural changes in our economy is the fact that we are now part of a globally interconnected marketplace and networked marketspace. This might present competitive challenges for you given that your competitors for your venture may no longer be simply down the street from you but in Korea, China, or India. On the other hand, this new economy also offers you access to the 95 percent of the population that lives outside of the United States. All too often, young entrepreneurs see opportunities only within the confines of America, and this is myopic thinking in the new economy.

Another key structural change in our economy is the shift from a manufacturing economy to a services, even experience-based, economy. We are building fewer things for people, and we are "doing" more things for people. In fact, 70 cents out of every consumer dollar is being spent on services, not tangible products. Therefore, it is not surprising to see why so many business startups are service based or experience based because that's where the money is!

Technological Change

Rapid and ongoing technological change is one of most important triggers of entrepreneurial opportunity. Nanotechnology (super-small, mini-electronics), biotechnology (e.g., implantable health monitoring systems), intelligent robots, and smart cars that can park themselves are all part of our consumer and competitive landscape. Technology is changing how we live and work and allowing us to do things that we simply could not do before. Information and communications technologies (ICTs), including the Internet, have become widespread, and entirely new business concepts have emerged as a result. For example, the Internet has given rise to Voice over Internet Protocol telephone services that now compete with traditional telecom providers. There is even IPTV, where you can watch television over the Internet, and there is commercial-free satellite radio. In addition, the emergence of social media is creating opportunities for some tech-oriented entrepreneurs looking to start their own social media sites or working on social media applications.

Some things the aspiring entrepreneur must do when assessing technological change and the possible opportunities it provides are to (1) determine the magnitude of the change, (2) examine the generality of the change, and (3) assess the commercial viability of the change. In short, the larger the technological change, the greater the opportunity. Technology that is general purpose (e.g., laser) will offer more opportunities than single-purpose technologies. And some technologies, while bringing about change, may not be commercially viable to build a business around.[8]

Competitive Change

The competitive nature of the economy is also evolving. There is both intense local and globalized competition in almost every industry sector. Moreover, mergers and acquisitions have also changed the competitive dynamic by either opening up or closing down opportunities for entrepreneurial firms. For example, the airline industry has seen a consolidation and an application of a hub-and-spoke design. This has allowed for entrepreneurial startups to enter the industry with point-to-point air travel design. Large consolidated companies that now focus on serving large business customers have also opened up opportunities for small entrepreneurial firms, which can cater to the overlooked small- to medium-sized enterprises (SMEs).

Another major competitive shift in the competitive landscape has been toward intertype competition. This means competition between seemingly dissimilar businesses. For example, the local bakery now must compete with the supermarket, the department store, the discount outlet, the local gas station, and even an online provider hundreds of miles away that will guarantee overnight delivery of custom cakes! Traditional brick-and-mortar companies are also now staking out a presence in the new online world as the number of pure-play online competitors increases.

Regulatory Change

Deregulation of industries often provides entrepreneurial opportunities, as was the case with the deregulation of the telecommunications and airline industries. On the other hand, increased regulation can also provide entrepreneurial opportunities. For example, one former student was an environmental engineer working in a corporate environment. When the Environmental Protection Agency (EPA) introduced new regulations on industries pertaining to waste water, she started a small company to provide consulting and testing to keep those industries in compliance. Similarly, new regulations on automobile emissions have given rise to new technology-based companies that work for or with automobile manufacturers to meet those requirements.

One key area of regulatory change involves the Internet and cable television market, where pro-market changes are leading to new opportunities for entrepreneurs. California, for example, has eliminated the municipality-by-municipality franchising requirement in favor of a statewide permit for companies seeking to deliver Internet and television services to homes and businesses. This will open up numerous opportunities for startups to enter the market at reduced costs and to do so more quickly.[9]

Finally, a recent study revealed that 80 percent of companies surveyed said they will increase their clean-tech spending over the next five years in light of current and future regulations pertaining to climate change. This will give rise to numerous opportunities for entrepreneurs who provide clean technologies.[10]

Veiled/Niche Opportunities

In many cases, entrepreneurs can find veiled or niche opportunities often overlooked or ignored by large corporations. A **veiled opportunity** (hidden, or not easily seen) is often uncovered (discovered) by smart entrepreneurs who stay in touch with the marketplace. For example, after conducting an environmental scan, one of my students discovered a strong trend in pet ownership. Most people could have easily determined this trend. But he drilled a little deeper and discovered a "veiled" trend— pet as family member. In this case, some pet owners viewed their cats or dogs as valued members of the family. Because of this, many pet owners wanted to protect their pets and would spend enormous amounts of money to keep them happy and healthy. Pet health insurance was a business opportunity that unveiled itself, and he built a successful business around this opportunity.

In other cases, smaller niche opportunities may emerge when you conduct your environmental scan. A **niche opportunity** is one that many large corporations deem simply too small to invest in. For example, one of my former students became a successful entrepreneur after he left his large corporate employer, which had refused to capitalize on an opportunity he identified. The value of the market for this product/ business was around $50 million. But this particular company had an internal policy of not pursuing market opportunities that were less than $100 million in market potential. In this case, the large company believed this opportunity was a niche business and was uninterested in pursuing it. But this opportunity was certainly large enough for my student to pursue, and he did so successfully.

In many cases, veiled or niche opportunities surface by going into the marketplace and seeking out the unhappy, the underserved, or the overlooked customers. Many larger corporations simply fail to do so, and this provides a window of opportunity for you as an aspiring entrepreneur.

Evaluating Marketing Opportunities

After finding or identifying "possible" marketing opportunities, your job now is to evaluate those opportunities to determine which ones might really be the "right" opportunity for you and your venture. There are a variety of criteria one could use to assess the nature and scope of any given marketing opportunity.

Figure 2.1 provides an overview of some of the most important criteria that should be used to make this evaluation. For example, market size and market growth rate are important to consider. Typically, many entrepreneurs focus single-mindedly on seemingly large aggregate markets. Yes, market size should be considered, but the rate of growth in a market is also an important criterion. For example, the soft drink category in the United States is a multibillion-dollar market, but it is basically a flat market (no growth). On the other hand, the bottled water category is a smaller market but is growing at a rapid pace.

A very important evaluative criterion when screening opportunities is whether the opportunity creates significant customer value. This value can come in the form of a lower (better) price or some added-value dimension that the customer is prepared to pay for (e.g., better quality). Another key criterion is whether you have a well-defined target market. Who is the customer? If you cannot describe and define that customer, then your opportunity lacks focus.

Customer-felt need is also an important criterion. If consumers already have a strong felt need for the product/service, it will be much easier to build and grow your venture. On the other hand, if you have to educate the customer and create felt need, your time to first dollar may take more time. If customers are currently satisfied with alternatives available in the market, this might also be a show-stopper for your venture. Of course, the customer might not be "ideally" satisfied, and if so, this may provide you with some opportunity. To determine felt need and satisfaction, you must engage the customer and get his or her feedback. We will discuss an approach to doing so later in this chapter and again in Chapter 3 when we examine marketing research.

Figure 2.1   Marketing Opportunity Evaluation Criteria

Market size	Small..........Large
Market growth rate	Low..........High
Creates significant customer value	No..........Yes
Well-defined target market	No..........Yes
Customer-felt need	Weak..........Strong
Customer satisfaction with current alternatives	Happy..........Unhappy
Access to customers	Difficult..........Easy
Ability to command a premium price	No..........Yes
Sustainable competitive advantage	No..........Yes
Ability to build and sustain the brand	No..........Yes
Presence of valuable intellectual property	No........Yes
Competitors	Many..........Few
Barriers to entry	Yes..........No
Cost to enter market	High..........Low
Cost to scale up	High..........Low
Time to first dollar	Slow..........Quick
Red ocean or blue ocean	Red ocean..........Blue ocean
Profit potential	Low..........High
What does the customer think?	Hates it..........Loves it
Voice of consumer (% who will buy)	0%..........100%
Personal fit	No..........Yes
Can the opportunity obtain financing?	No..........Yes

Another screening criterion is access to customers. This is a two-dimensional construct: physical access (can you get the product/service to the customer—a channel issue?) and communications access (are you able to talk to the customer about your product service?).

The ability to command a premium price is also part of the evaluation process. There is no question that it is possible to start and grow a venture by being a "low-cost" provider. However, my bias for entrepreneurial startups is to avoid competing on the basis of price. I stress this because you might not simply have the cost structure that allows you to compete on price. If you feel you can do so and wish to pursue the "low-cost" provider route, then that is your decision. But most entrepreneurial ventures compete by offering significant value (superiority based on a nonprice dimension) and command a premium price, which is perhaps the best option for you to consider.

Another important criterion is whether or not your venture possesses a sustainable competitive advantage. A *sustainable competitive advantage* is a unique strength relative to your competitors. It can come in the form of higher-quality products, higher-quality customer service, speed of performance, lowest-cost, or customer intimacy. More and more often, we are seeing that a sustainable competitive advantage is coming in the form of the branding. **Branding** is an activity in which an enterprise uses a name, phrase, design, symbols, or combination of these and other intangible elements to identify the products or services of one marketer and to differentiate them from those of the competition. A **brand name** is a name, sign, symbol, design, or combination of these elements intended to identify the products or services of one marketer and to differentiate them from those of the competition. Brand building is going to be critical to the success of your venture, and an entire chapter in this book (Chapter 7) is devoted to this topic. The reason why branding is so important is that most forms of competitive advantage can be easily matched by competitors. Advantages such as price, product quality, and locational convenience tend not to be sustainable. But a good brand can be sustained and may, in fact, be the last bastion for sustainable competitive advantage.

Another critical evaluation criterion is whether or not there is a presence of valuable intellectual property. One common dimension of successful ventures is that they tend to have a valuable intellectual property. **Intellectual property (IP)** is defined as creations of the mind: inventions, literary and artistic works, and symbols, names, images, and designs used in commerce. IP is divided into two categories: (1) industrial property, which includes patents, trademarks, industrial designs, and geographic indications of source; and (2) copyright, which includes literary and artistic works such as novels, poems and plays, films, musical works, artistic works such as drawings, paintings, photographs and sculptures, and architectural designs. Rights related to copyright include those of performing artists in their performances, producers of phonograms in their recordings, and those of broadcasters in their radio and television programs.

An important piece of IP for many new ventures is a **patent**—an exclusive right granted for an **invention**, which can be a **product** or a **process** that provides a new way of doing something, or offers a new technical solution to a problem. To receive a patent your invention must meet certain requirements. For example, it must be of practical use; it must show an element of novelty (a new characteristic not previously known or discovered), it must show an inventive step which would not normally be deduced by the average person. A patent provides **protection** for the invention to the **owner** of the patent and this protection is granted for a limited period, generally 20 years. Many investors want to see that your venture has a patent(s).

If your venture does not hold/own a patent, another valuable piece of IP your venture could have is a **trademark**—a **distinctive sign** which identifies certain goods or services as those produced or provided by a specific person or enterprise. The origins of a trademark dates back to ancient times, when craftsmen reproduced their signatures, or "marks" on their creations or products. Trademarks may be one or a combination of words, letters, and numerals. They may consist of drawings, symbols, three-dimensional signs such as the shape and packaging of goods, audible signs such as music or vocal sounds, fragrances, or colors used as distinguishing features. A trademark provides protection for your enterprise (assuming you file to register the trademark—and it is approved) since you are given the exclusive right to use it to identify your products or services. The period of protection varies, but a trademark can be renewed indefinitely beyond the time limit on payment of additional fees. Trademark protection is enforced by the courts, which in most countries have the authority to block trademark infringement. Now, many people use the term *trademark* interchangeably with the term *brand*. However, consider the concept of a brand as a broader notion in that it includes both tangible and intangible components such as a trademark, design, logo, the name of the concept, as well as the activity of branding— attempting to differentiate your venture and its products and/or services from competitors by focusing on building and promoting the brand per se. In my view, branding is perhaps the most important asset for a venture. Yes, I think patents are important, too. But, a brand is a special type of intangible that enhances the business value of an enterprise to a greater extent than a patent. In fact, studies have shown that an average brand accounts for more than one-third of the value of an enterprise while very strong brands may account for two-thirds of the value of a business. Thus, the branding of your new venture and its products and services is going to be critical and that is why an entire chapter is devoted to this topic (Chapter 7).[11]

The number and strength of competitors currently in the market as well as any possible barriers to entry must also be considered. Low barriers to entry, for example, may make it easier for you to enter the market but at the same time also afford others that same opportunity. Your costs to enter the market, cost to scale up the business, and time to first dollar are other important factors to consider.

Whether or not you are entering a "red ocean" or "blue ocean" is also part of your analysis.[12] A **red ocean** is characterized by existing markets with established competition where the goal is simply to outperform rivals to steal share and grow. The red ocean is typically crowded, and profit and growth are difficult to achieve. Invariably, the red ocean is a place of cutthroat competition, which turns the ocean bloody (red).

In contrast, the **blue ocean** is a new market space where demand is being created and not fought over. The blue ocean is created by new value and innovation. For example, Cirque du Soleil created a blue ocean by offering customers a combination of opera, ballet, and circus entertainment. NetJets also created a blue ocean by offering fractional jet ownership to customers wishing to avoid the hassles of flying commercially. Entering a red or blue ocean will have a dramatic impact on your potential profitability (another screening factor).

Perhaps the most important criterion to use when evaluating opportunities is finding out what the customers think and whether they will buy from you. This requires you to "talk" with your potential customers and to get validation from them. If they hate your idea and are unprepared or unwilling to buy from you, then perhaps you have the wrong opportunity. This **voice of consumer (VOC)** feedback is, in my view, the most important aspect of the evaluation process. VOC is a research technique that is designed to uncover customer wants and needs; assess customer satisfaction with existing product/service solutions; obtain feedback on new venture concepts and the products/services offered by the ventures including likelihood of purchase; and other key input regarding the nature, scope and configuration of proposed venture and/or its new products/services. VOC can be both qualitative and quantitative in nature. But, either way it involves interacting with customers in the real world (in the field) in an in-depth manner. The goal is to extract valuable customer-centric information that leads to validation of your proposed venture and its products/service, or allow for refinement of such, or killing the proposed venture. There are many VOC methods and they will be discussed in Chapter 3, including but not limited to depth interviews, focus groups, and ethnography. The value of VOC information should be judged based on its credibility, reliability, validity, and its predictability. Granted, as we discussed in Chapter 1, the voice of consumer may not work well for discontinuous, new-to-world innovations, but it will work for almost all other proposed ventures. We will discuss voice of consumer in more detail a little later in the chapter as it pertains to assessing consumers' likelihood of purchase vis-à-vis your new venture.

The last two criteria (personal fit and ability to obtain financing) are not strictly marketing related, but we include them here because they are important considerations when evaluating opportunities. Also, other important non-marketing-related evaluation criteria that you should use to assess given opportunities include, for example, the quality of the management team you could put together. Finally, it is important to remember that a given opportunity is not an opportunity for everyone; it is just an opportunity for "someone," and it might not be you. Industry experience, market knowledge, or personal fit may make an identified opportunity appropriate for one entrepreneur but not for another.

Determining the Extent of the Opportunity: Making Some Market Estimates Using Voice of Consumer Feedback

Many entrepreneurs have difficulty quantifying the extent of the opportunity under consideration. But knowing the market potential for the venture is critical before one makes an investment in the business. Typically, an entrepreneur discovers the aggregate size of a given market and then makes a revenue projection based on capturing a particular percentage of market share. For example, assume the market size for product category X is $1,000,000. Some entrepreneur will forecast capturing a particular percentage of market share, say, 20 percent. In this case, the market estimate for the enterprise would be $200,000.

Furthermore, the entrepreneur may also use three different levels of market share (e.g., 10, 15, and 20 percent) to represent pessimistic, realistic, and optimistic projections. But, when pressed, most entrepreneurs cannot validate why they are using such percentages, and few have confidence in the predictive value of their estimates.

One simple way to overcome this problem is to go to the market and talk with potential customers and get their input—voice of consumer or VOC. What you would do is develop a short venture concept statement describing what the business is, the value you provide, and the price the customer will pay. You then ask the customer, given the presented-venture concept statement, "How likely is it that you would buy from my business?" Typically, a Likert scale is used ranging from 1 to 5 with 1 being *very unlikely*, 2 being *unlikely*, 3 being *neither unlikely nor likely*, 4 being *likely*, and 5 being *very likely*. What you do then is determine the percentage of customers who answer "likely or very likely," and this gives you what is called the "voice of consumer 2-box score."

Here is an example of how it works. When I was planning on opening a gourmet food store, I knew the average expenditure on gourmet food by families in my trade area at that time was $1,000 per family per year.

I presented my venture concept to 100 potential customers and asked how likely it was that they would shop at my gourmet food store. Twenty percent said that were likely or very likely to do so. I also knew the trade area for my store had 10,000 families. So, my market estimate for my gourmet food store was as follows:

10,000 families (in trade area) × 20% (voice of consumer 2-box score) × $1,000 (annual expenditure) = $2,000,000

Of course, I made the assumption that I would obtain the entire $1,000 annual expenditure by those 20 percent of families who said they were likely/very likely to buy from me. But I was pretty comfortable with this assumption since there was no other gourmet food store in my trade area, and people had to travel more than 30 minutes to the nearest competitor. How accurate was the forecast? I did more than $1.8 million in the first year and exceeded $2 million in Year 2.

Now, of course, using voice of consumer input to make projections is not an exact science. Moreover, the measure (likelihood of purchase) is an only a "surrogate" indicator (it measures purchase intent only) and does not measure real purchase behavior. But I would argue it is a better way of quantifying the extent of your marketing opportunity compared to making market share guesstimates based on personal judgment. In essence, you are allowing the consumer to provide validation of the opportunity. And this validation is very important, especially when you seek financing for your business.

Also, if you are going to use "voice of the consumer" to validate the opportunity, you also have a unique chance of asking the consumer to help further shape and refine your business venture. In other words, you can present your concept to potential customers and then ask what else they might like the business to do for them. You will be surprised at how willing customers are to offer additional input and input that may lead to a better business for you.

Opportunities and the Business Model

Once you have identified and well screened your opportunity, the next step is to determine how you will make money from this opportunity. This is where your **business model decision** comes in. In short, a business model is a framework for making money. It outlines the set of activities that the enterprise will perform, how it will perform them, and when it will perform them to create customer value and earn a profit. I have argued for many years that a good opportunity also requires a good business model. And, importantly, a bad business model can, in fact, negate your ability to make money from a good opportunity.

However, even though the enterprise's business model is central to the firm's success, there really is little consensus in terms of exactly defining the term *business model*. Still, most experts do agree that the business model should answer the following questions:[13]

1. How will the enterprise make money?
2. How will the enterprise create value?
3. For whom will the enterprise create value?
4. What is the enterprise's internal source of sustainable competitive advantage?
5. How will the enterprise position itself in the marketplace?

Successful entrepreneurs also ask themselves the following questions with regard to the business model:[14]

1. Where is the money?
2. Who has the money?

3. How do I get the money?

4. What do I need to provide to get the money?

5. How do I get it faster than anyone else?

6. How do I get it time and time again from the same customer?

7. How can I add other revenue streams later?

It is critical for you to target the right customers with the right value. Thus, your "value proposition" is a central aspect of your business model. With your value proposition, you recognize the customer's problem, create the product/service that addresses the problem, and communicate its value to the customer.

You must focus your efforts and determine which customers you wish to serve (target market/segment) and how much of each customer's needs you want to serve. What is also very important for you to consider is not only creating recurring revenue but also obtaining incremental revenue. In fact, many customers can produce more than one source of revenue (e.g., buying a car and having it serviced). Moreover, some customers might wish to buy a product, but others might wish to lease, rent, or rent-to-own a product. An enterprise that only wishes to "sell" its product may be losing out on other potential lucrative revenue streams!

Finally, another important aspect of the business model is determining your position in the value chain (e.g., do you want to be a manufacturer, wholesaler, or retailer?). Importantly, for some of you, your enterprise may lend itself to "licensing" and not manufacturing, distributing, and marketing. In fact, one of my companies simply created innovations and then sold the rights to those innovations because I did not want to be in the manufacturing business. Thus, do not forget that licensing can be a very good way to make money without the headaches of running a more complex business.

Now, let me give you an example of how a good business model saved a business that discovered a good opportunity and produced a very superior product to capitalize on that opportunity. This little enterprise developed a self-sharpening de-heading machine used in commercial fish processing plants. Up until that point, all current de-heading machines had to be taken off-line so their blades could be sharpened.

Every time this occurred, the processing lines would be idle and the plants would lose money. This new machine allowed the lines to continue to work because the machine had a built-in sharpening mechanism. The fish processors loved the product. The problem was there was no product obsolescence built into the machine. It simply did not break down, and once the machines were sold to the processors, there would be no recurrent revenue.

The solution? The company sold an annual service maintenance package with each unit. This provided peace of mind to the processors, but because the machines were so durable and reliable, rarely did the company have to go out and service the units. Thus, while the initial business model was based on building and selling a better piece of equipment, the sustainable business model was actually selling the service maintenance packages! This example clearly illustrates the relationship between a good opportunity and a good business model.

In summary, it is critical that you develop a robust business model for your venture. In fact, without one you are not very likely to attract venture financing since investors really scrutinize ventures to ensure that the business model is strong enough to sustain the venture. And, just like you would vet your opportunity with your potential customers you also want feedback from those potential customers about your proposed business model. Does the model make sense to them? Is this how they want to do business with you? This input will help you determine how to best configure your venture to create value for your target market as well as select the best strategy for making money and sustaining the growth of your enterprise.

Key Takeaways

- Remember that opportunities can be recognized, discovered, or created.
- Always evaluate your opportunities against the known characteristics that define a "good opportunity," including whether it creates significant value for the customer.
- Be certain to look for opportunities that result from "change" in the marketing environment.
- Always properly screen your identified opportunities using objective criteria such as customer-felt need and voice of consumer feedback.
- Always make some market estimates to determine the extent of your opportunity.
- Remember that a good opportunity also requires a good business model—how you will make your money, how you will configure your venture, and what strategy you will use to guide the venture to sustained growth.

Entrepreneurial Exercise

Come up with three possible marketing opportunities. Now, using Figure 2.1, go through the process of evaluating those opportunities. What are the results? Which opportunity, if any, appears to have some potential? If none survive the process, what were the major showstoppers?

Key Terms

Branding   32
Brand   32
Intellectual property   32
Patent   33
Trademark   33
Opportunity   21

Veiled opportunity   29
Niche opportunity   29
Red ocean/blue ocean   34
Voice of consumer   34
Business model decision   37

Notes

1. Frederick G. Crane and Jeffrey E. Sohl, "Imperatives for Venture Success: Entrepreneurs Speak," *International Journal of Entrepreneurship and Innovation* 5, no. 2 (2004): 99–106.

2. Ibid.

3. Saras Saravathy, N. Dew, R. Velamuri, and S. Venkataraman, *Handbook of Entrepreneurial Research* (London: Kluwer, 2003). Also see J. Schumpeter, *Theory of Economic Development: An Inquiry Into Profits, Capital, Credit, Interest and the Business Cycle* (Cambridge, MA: Harvard University Press, 1934); I. M. Kirzner, *Perception, Opportunity and Profit* (Chicago, IL: University of Chicago Press, 1979).

4. J. Timmons and S. Spinella, *New Venture Creation*, 7th ed. (Burr Ridge, IL: McGraw-Hill, 2008); A. Osborne, *Entrepreneur's Toolkit* (Boston, MA: Harvard Business School Press, 2005).

5. Timmons and Spinelli, *New Venture Creation.*

6. Crane and Sohl, "Imperatives for Venture Success."

7. This section is based on Frederick G. Crane, Roger Kerin, Steve Hartley, and William Rudelius, *Marketing*, 7th Canadian ed. (Toronto: McGraw-Hill Ryerson, 2008).

8. Scott A. Shane, *Finding Fertile Ground* (Upper Saddle River, NJ: Wharton School Publishing, 2005).

9. Karen Kerrigan and Raymond Keating, "Telecommunications Policy Choices and Entrepreneurs," Small Business and Entrepreneurship Council's 21st Century Small Business Policy Series, Oakton, VA, 2007.

10. Ernst & Young, "Transformation. Cleantech: Enabling the Business Response to Climate Change," Global Cleantech Insights and Trends Report, 2008.

11. This section was contributed to by Erinn C. Crane, IP Attorney, Boston, MA, February 2012.

12. W. Chan Kim and Renee Mauborgne, *Blue Ocean Strategy* (Boston, MA: Harvard Business School Press, 2005).

13. Marc H. Meyer, *FastPath to Corporate Growth* (New York: Oxford University Press, 2007).

14. Ibid.

Three

Using Marketing Research to Ensure Entrepreneurial Success

In my experience, the most successful entrepreneurs tend to be the most informed! They know their industry, they know their customers, and they know their competitors. Most important, they crave information and always want to know more. And when they acquire new information, they put it to use wisely. Yes, intuition is also an important characteristic of a successful entrepreneur, but the entrepreneur is always conscious of the need to couple that intuition with good information. Successful entrepreneurs will tell you that access to information and the keen ability to interpret it are central to recognizing opportunities and determining how best to capitalize on those opportunities. It is also important that you understand that marketing research need not be expensive or complicated. In fact, there are many quick and low-cost methods of obtaining critical information that will help you build your enterprise on a solid foundation.

In this chapter, we will discuss the role marketing research plays in ensuring entrepreneurial success. We will define marketing research and outline methods you can use to obtain and apply the information you need when making decisions about your venture. Importantly, you will see that marketing research can play an important role in reducing your venture risk while increasing your chance of venture success.

Marketing Research: Defined

Marketing research is the process of defining a marketing problem or opportunity, collecting and interpreting information, and acting on the information to improve the chances of enterprise success. One of the central purposes of marketing research is to help uncover viable marketing opportunities for the entrepreneur. Marketing research is also used to assess the needs and wants of customers and to provide information that helps shape the venture's marketing program. Although marketing research can provide few answers with complete assurance, when conducted properly, it can solve most marketing-related problems that an entrepreneur might have. However, good marketing research should not be designed to simply replace your good sense, experience, or intuition but rather should be used in conjunction with those skills and as a way of taking out some of the guesswork in the marketing decision-making process.

Types and Methods of Marketing Research

In this section, we will discuss types of marketing information and several methods to obtain meaningful and relevant marketing information that will be critical to your venture success. The two major types of marketing data are **secondary data** and **primary data.**

Secondary Data

As a rule, successful entrepreneurs always gather secondary data before collecting primary data. **Secondary data** are existing data already collected and available to the entrepreneur. **Primary data**, on the other hand, are new data gathered by you. In general, secondary data can be obtained more quickly and at a lower cost compared with primary data. Moreover, secondary data can often provide answers to many of the questions you might have concerning possible marketing opportunities. However, there can be problems with secondary data. The required information may not exist, and if it does, it may not be current or particularly pertinent to your venture. Still, most researchers agree that investigating secondary data sources can save researchers from "reinventing the wheel."

Sources of secondary data are wide and varied. One key source of marketing data is available through USA.gov (www.usa.gov). This is the portal to all U.S. government websites, including the Bureau of the Census (www.census.gov). The Bureau of the Census is a federal government agency that provides census data as well as numerous other reports on American households and businesses, all available through its searchable online database. The American Factfinder (http://factfinder .census.gov) from the Bureau of the Census provides even easier access to U.S. census information.

In addition to the U.S. Bureau of the Census, there are numerous other sources of secondary data, including business directories, business periodicals, newspapers, magazines, and trade associations. Finally, numerous online databanks provide specialized data services. Figure 3.1 provides some key sources of secondary data available to the aspiring entrepreneur.

Primary Data

After you have exhausted all sources of secondary data, you may still have questions that need to be answered concerning your possible opportunities and/or the proper configuration of your venture. You can then turn to primary data—new data collected specifically for this purpose—for some answers. There are a variety of ways to generate primary data. This primary data can come on the form of voice of consumer (VOC) feedback. We briefly introduced you to this concept in Chapter 2. In this section, we will discuss the following primary data or VOC methods: depth interviews, focus groups, observation, fuzzy front-end methods, surveys, experiments, and conjoint research.

Depth Interviews

If you want to uncover what makes customers tick, what problems they have, and how you might solve them, the **depth interview** (sometimes called in-depth interviews or IDIs) is a very useful VOC technique. Depth interviews are detailed individual interviews with

Figure 3.1   Sources of Secondary Data

Reference Books

- *Market Share Reporter*
- *Sourcebook of ZIP Code Demographics*
- *Standard & Poor's Industry Surveys*
- *World Consumer Lifestyles Databook*
- *D&B Industry Norms and Key Business Ratios*

Selected Electronic Databases

- Business Source Premier
- Business and Company ASAP
- Lexis-Nexis Academic Universe
- STAT-USA
- ProQuest
- EU Country Intelligence

Web Resources and websites

- Ameristat (www.prb.org): Population data on the United States and other countries
- Bureau of the Census (www.census.gov)
- ClickZ Stats (www.clickz.com): News on trends, demographics, or other stats
- Eurostat (http://epp.eurostat.cec.eu.int): Stats from the European Union
- FedStats (www.fedstats.gov): Gateway to stats from over 100 U.S. federal agencies
- OECD (www.oced.org): International data
- Google Directory (www.google.com/Top/Business/Associations): Associations by industry
- United Nations (http://unstats.un.org): Stats from the United Nations
- List of Lists (www.specialissues.com/lol)
- Fortune.com: Top Industries (http://money.cnn.com/magazines/fortune/fortune/500)
- Statistical Abstract of the United States (http://www.census.gov/statab/www)
- *The Wall Street Journal* (www.wsj.com)
- Bloomberg (www.bloomberg.com)
- Yahoo Finance (www.yahoofinance.com)

potential customers. The entrepreneur questions the individual at length in a free-flowing conversational style to obtain relevant information. Sometimes these interviews can take a few hours, and they are often recorded on audio- or videotape. It is best for the entrepreneur to craft a discussion guide but to also allow for some flexibility so the customer can have the freedom to provide as much information pertaining to possible opportunities or the proposed venture. What you want to accomplish with depth interviews is to be able to draw some basic themes from the research that you might wish to further investigate through more quantitative approaches.

As an entrepreneur, you will find that depth interviews provide a good opportunity for you to explore and compare differences and similarities among prospective target customers. Depth interviews also allow you to spend valuable one-on-one time with target customers exploring single individual's responses without the contamination of others being present. For example, if you want to test responses to your website, depth interviews are a good choice. Typically, entrepreneurs will use depth interviews in the following situations: (1) when it is easier to reach target customers, (2) when there is a better cost-benefit compared to other methods, (3) when it is preferable to collect responses without group influence, (4) when probing is part of the information collection process, and (5) when a product, service or process is being tested for usability. Additionally, if the topics you are investigating are highly sensitive (e.g., illnesses, diseases) and/or highly personal (like finances), depth interviews are a good choice. Furthermore, if you wish to probe experts and get feedback on your venture concept, depth interviews are also particularly helpful.[1]

Focus Groups

Another very popular method to obtain primary data or VOC is the use of **focus groups—FGs).** FGs are informal interview sessions in which six to ten potential customers are brought together in a room with the entrepreneur/moderator to discuss the customers' needs/wants and types of products/services they might be interested in. While the general range of participants in FGs is six to ten, here is some research to suggest that you should probably keep your FGs to no more than eight respondents. This smaller mini-group approach allows you to obtain important and observable reactions to product stimuli and allow for more focused discussion leading to new ideas or refinements. In a focus group situation, the moderator poses questions and encourages the individuals to answer in their own words and to discuss the issues with each other. Often, the focus group sessions are watched by observers through one-way mirrors, and/or the sessions are videotaped. Of course, participants should be informed they are being observed and/or being taped.

Now it is even possible for the entrepreneur to conduct online FGs where participants and the entrepreneur interact in an online setting. The entrepreneur can present online participants with audio or video material for respondent evaluation and even present them with virtual product concepts to evaluate. Focus group sessions often provide the entrepreneur with valuable information for venture decision making or can uncover other issues that should be researched in a more quantitative fashion. For example, an entrepreneur who was trying to decide between three different ventures (a restaurant, a clothing store, and a sporting goods store) discovered participants were not interested in any of the proposed ventures but instead suggested that the entrepreneur consider an entirely new concept, a concept of great interest to the potential customers. They proposed that the entrepreneur open a gourmet bakery. He did, and it became an instant success.

Many entrepreneurs have to decide between the use of depth interviews versus focus groups. Like depth interviews, there are certain situations where the use of FGs can be a good choice when it comes to information gathering. For example, FGs can be effective used when (1) consensus or debate is required to explore possible disparate views of target customers and/or experts, (2) point-counterpoint among target customers can generate an opportunity to resolve differences, (3) broad, exploratory topics are covered and allow target customers to generate and share ideas, (4) when interaction between respondents can draw our latent issues not just obviously perceived ones, and (5) when group dynamics can aid in the discovery process.

When deciding between depth interviews and FGs, as an entrepreneur, you should keep in mind this mantra, "allow research objectives to drive your choice of method." In short, determine objectives first and pick the approach that will best achieve those objectives. For example, if your objective is to test usability of your product, service or process, than depth interviews make the best choice. On the other hand, if you objective to further explore your venture concept, than FGs might be the better option. Finally, of course, there are some experts you argue using both methods—combining the best of both worlds (i.e., depth interviews can allow you to probe individuals while FGs can help you better understand the social context of selecting and buying new concepts). Thus, it may not be an either-or decision between depth interviews and FGs but more of combining the methods in complementary ways.[2]

Fuzzy Front-End Methods

Successful entrepreneurs often use other creative methods to obtain marketing information and uncover marketing opportunities. For example, to unmask "the next big thing," some entrepreneurs use some unusual techniques sometimes referred to as **fuzzy front-end** or **FFE methods.** These techniques are designed to identify elusive consumer tastes or trends. In some cases, the entrepreneur uses motivational research or projective techniques to uncover what makes customers happy and/or what frustrates them. For example, an entrepreneur could use "sentence completion" to uncover a customer need (perceived or latent). The entrepreneur might ask the customer to complete the following sentence: "Thinking about shopping, wouldn't it be wonderful if. . . ." Or, the entrepreneur hoping to find a source of "market pain" might ask the customer, "What is your greatest source of frustration when you buy product X?"

The entrepreneur could even get customers to complete a drawing describing themselves as well as highlight what types of products and services are important to their self-concepts. The entrepreneur might even sit down and talk to **lead users** (e.g., innovative and early adopters, the cool kids, the trendsetters) to identify the next big thing. It is extremely important that you engage your "initial first customers" to find out what makes them tick as well as their reactions to your venture concept. If these customers are not excited by what you are doing, then it may be a signal about the viability of your venture concept.

Observation

Another basic marketing research method used to obtain primary data is **observation.** In general, observation involves watching, either mechanically or in person, how people behave. In some circumstances, the speed of events or the number of events being observed makes mechanical or electronic observation more appropriate than personal observation. Retailers, for example, can use electronic cameras to count the number of customers entering or leaving a store.

Watching consumers in person or by videotaping them can be insightful for the entrepreneur. For example, one toy company was given permission to observe children playing with toys at a nursery school and was able to come up with new toy concepts after these observations. Another company actually videotaped consumers brushing their teeth in their own bathrooms to find out how they really brush—not just how they say they brush. This resulted in the development of an entirely new type of toothbrush.

A specialized observational approach that is gaining popularity with entrepreneurs is **ethnographic research,** in which entrepreneurs and other trained observers seek to discover subtle emotional reactions as consumers encounter products in their "natural use environments," such as in homes, cars, or hotels. Some people consider ethnographic research as a fuzzy front-end method. Using ethnographic research can often reveal customer insights that cannot be obtained through other traditional research methods such as survey research.[3]

For example, before Moen, Inc. put its new massaging showerhead, the Revolution, on the market, it wanted to see what consumers thought about the new product design. But Moen did not want to just give consumers the showerhead and later ask them if they liked it or not. The company wanted to see the consumers actually using the product—in the shower. So, it hired a research firm to do some ethnographic research. The firm enlisted twenty nudists as their volunteers and paid them $250 each to answer questions about their lifestyles and to allow the research firm to install a tiny video camera in the shower of each volunteer to watch them use the new showerhead. As a result of the research, the product was redesigned and has become a major new product success for Moen.[4] The company behind this innovative research approach was Qualidata Research, Inc., and its founder, Hy Mariampolski, finds himself in the Entrepreneurial Marketing Spotlight!

Another novel approach to obtaining observational data is the entrepreneur as mystery shopper. The entrepreneur goes "undercover" posing as a real customer and goes through an exchange process with a provider (usually a possible competitor of the entrepreneur) and then interprets the encounter to determine how well the provider performed. The information provides the entrepreneur some unique insight into how competitors deal with customers that cannot be obtained any other way.

Entrepreneurial Marketing Spotlight

Dr. Hy Mariampolski is a professor turned entrepreneur. He is managing director of an innovative marketing research firm called QualiData Research, Inc. Hy is a pioneer in the application of ethnographic methods for marketing research. He believes that the best approach to marketing research is to use a variety of mixed methods, including depth interviews, focus groups, online research, and ethnographic observation. He calls this approach "triangulation," and according to Hy, it provides deeper, richer, and more valid insights into customer behavior and attitudes than any single method. His unique approaches to marketing research have helped many companies, large and small, in determining what products to create and how to brand and position those new products. He believes that delving deeper in understanding customers' everyday reality, at home, in their neighborhoods, at work, while shopping, or during leisure, can uncover customer needs, including unmet needs, which, in turn, means opportunities for entrepreneurs to meet those needs!

Hy is the author of two books: *Qualitative Market Research* and *Ethnography for Marketers*. As an entrepreneur, you will find that both of these books are excellent resources as you plan and carry out your marketing research that will help ensure the success of your venture. For his creative use of marketing research and his willingness to share his expertise, Hy finds himself in the Entrepreneurial Marketing Spotlight.

Personal observation is both useful and flexible, but it can be costly and unreliable, especially when different observers report different conclusions in watching the same activities. Also, although observation can reveal what people do, it cannot determine why they do it, such as why they are buying or not buying a product. To determine why consumers behave as they do, the entrepreneur must talk with consumers and record their responses. This is usually accomplished through the use of surveys.

Surveys

The most common research method of generating new or primary data or VOC is the use of **surveys.** A survey is a research technique used to generate data by asking people questions and recording their responses on a questionnaire. Surveys can be conducted by personal interview (face-to-face), mail, telephone, or online. In choosing these alternatives, the marketing researcher has to make important trade-offs (as shown in Figure 3.2) to balance, for instance, cost against the expected quality of information obtained. For example, personal interview (face-to-face) surveys have the major advantage of enabling the interviewer to be flexible in asking probing questions or getting reactions to visual materials but are very costly to conduct. Mail surveys are usually biased because those likely to respond have had especially positive or negative experiences with a given product, service, or brand. While telephone surveys allow flexibility, they are increasingly difficult to complete because respondents may hang up on the interviewer. Also, with many unlisted telephone numbers, it is becoming increasingly more difficult to obtain representative samples. Online surveys are restrictive in that they are limited to respondents having the technology.

Figure 3.2 Comparing Mail, Telephone, Personal, and Online Surveys

Basis of Comparison	Mail Surveys	Telephone Surveys	Personal Interview	Online Surveys
Cost of completed survey	Not very expensive	Moderately expensive	Most expensive	Very inexpensive
Ability to probe and ask complex questions	Little to none	Some; interviewer can probe and elaborate	Much; interviewer is face-to-face	Depends; can go back and ask respondent to clarify responses
Opportunity for interviewer to bias results	None	Some; because of voice and gender	Significant voice, appearance, and gender present	Little, if done correctly
Anonymity given to respondent	Complete, unless coded instrument is used	Some; because of telephone contact	Little, because of face-to-face contact	Some; e-mail/user name may be known
Response rate	Poor or fair	Fair; refusal rates are increasing	Good	Very good, if done correctly
Speed of data collection	Poor	Good	Good	Very good

The high cost of reaching respondents in their homes through personal interview surveys has led to an increase in the use of mall intercept interviews, which are personal interviews of consumers at shopping centers. These face-to-face interviews reduce the cost of personal visits to consumers in their homes while providing flexibility to show respondents product prototypes or to discuss business concepts. However, a critical disadvantage of mall intercept interviews is that the people selected for the interviews may not be representative of the consumers targeted for the interviews, causing possible bias in results.[5]

Sometimes, an entrepreneur will survey over time the same sample of people, commonly known as a *survey panel*. A panel can consist of a sample of consumers, stores, or experts, from which the entrepreneur can take a series of measurements. The use of panels is becoming more popular as entrepreneurs seek to obtain ongoing information about customers and markets. Now, ongoing panel data can even be obtained online.

Still, while surveys are a very popular marketing research method, the entrepreneur must be aware of the following important issues when using surveys:

1. You have to talk to the right potential customer.

2. You have to ask the right questions.

3. The respondent has to understand the questions.

4. The respondent must know the answers to the questions.

5. The respondent must actually answer the questions.

6. The respondent must answer the questions truthfully.

7. The entrepreneur must understand the answers provided.

Entrepreneurs must concern themselves with not only asking the right questions but also how to properly word those questions. Proper phrasing of a question is vital to uncovering useful marketing information. For example, suppose you were asked if you "dine out regularly." The word *regularly* is ambiguous. Two people might answer yes to the question, but one might mean "once a day" while the other means "once or twice a year." Both answers are yes, but the behavior of these prospective customers is quite different. Therefore, it is essential that marketing research questions be worded precisely so that all respondents interpret the same question similarly. Marketing researchers must also take great care not to use "leading" questions (wording questions in a way to ensure a particular response), which can lead to a very distorted picture of the respondents' actual feelings or opinions.

There are also a number of different formats that questions can take in a survey instrument. For example, an open-ended question is one in which the respondent can answer in his or her own words. In contrast, questions in which the respondent simply checks an answer are closed-ended or fixed alternative questions. The simplest fixed alternative question allows only a yes-or-no answer. A fixed alternative question with three or more choices often uses a scale such as a semantic differential scale (e.g., a 9-point scale in which the opposite ends have one- or two-word adjectives that have opposite meanings) or a Likert scale, in which the respondent is asked to indicate the extent to which he or she agrees or disagrees with a statement (e.g., a 5-point scale ranging from 1, which indicates *strongly disagree*, to 5, which indicates *strongly agree*).

You should remember that asking questions is always obtrusive. Some customers will not participate, and those who do might not provide truthful responses to your questions. Moreover, many customers want to preserve their privacy and/or may be uncomfortable answering certain questions. For example, personal questions relating to age, income, and so on may be an issue for the respondent. Therefore, any questions involving demographic information should always be asked at the end of the survey. Importantly, you should always use demographic information categories that are consistent with what is used in your industry sector or with the U.S. Bureau of the Census. In other words, if you want customers to report family income, age, education levels, and so on, use the established categories used by the Bureau. In this way, you can measure your categories against the benchmark categories already established to validate your research and/or make comparisons between your sample and the state or national population.

Experiments

Another research method that can be used to generate primary data is the **experiment.** Marketing experiments offer the potential for establishing cause-and-effect relationships (causal research). An experiment involves the manipulation of an independent variable (cause) and the measurement of its effect on the dependent variable (effect) under controlled conditions. In marketing experiments, the independent variables are often one or more of the marketing mix variables—sometimes called the "marketing drivers"—such as product features, price, or promotion used. An ideal dependent variable usually is a change in purchases by the customer. If actual purchases cannot be used as a dependent variable, factors that are believed to be highly related to purchases, such as preferences in a taste test or intentions to buy, are used. A potential difficulty with experiments is that an extraneous (or outside) variable can distort the results of an experiment and affect the dependent variables.

Experiments can be conducted in the field or in a laboratory. In field experiments, the research is conducted in the real world, such as in a store or bank or on the street, wherever the behavior being studied occurs naturally. Field experiments can be expensive but are a good way to determine people's reactions to changes in the elements of the marketing mix. Test marketing is probably the most common form of field experiments. Many entrepreneurs use test marketing to gauge customer response to their marketing offering.

However, because marketers cannot control all the conditions in the field, they sometimes turn to a laboratory setting. Laboratories are not the real world but do offer highly controlled environments. Unlike in the field, the entrepreneur has control over all the factors that may affect the behavior under investigation.

Today, the Internet has also opened up opportunities to do creative online market testing of products, packaging, advertising, and so on. For example, you can test customer responses to proposed new products or test out possible advertising campaigns.

Conjoint Studies

Conjoint studies can be a very useful marketing research method for the entrepreneur. Conjoint is a technique used to provide insight into customer preferences for particular brand or product features and their willingness to "trade off" one feature for more of another feature. Conjoint research uncovers the relative importance each customer attaches to different levels of each brand or potential product feature. Then, the entrepreneur can construct the correct brand/product with the appropriate features. Importantly, if different customers want different things, these customers might be grouped into particular market segments, and specific brands/products with specific features can be designed for such segments.

What the entrepreneur does is present the potential customer with a set of brands/products where the features of the brands/products vary. For example, a tool manufacturer presented descriptions of power tools where it varied the price, the motor power, warranty length, and so forth. It discovered that the household user wanted a cheaper power tool, while the professional contractor wanted a more powerful motor and was prepared to pay a higher price for that tool. The manufacturer then developed two lines of tools, one for the at-home do-it-yourselfer and one for the professional contractor. It was conjoint analysis that allowed this startup firm to develop the right brand/product with the right features and to serve two different market segments.

Other Research Issues

You should be mindful of several other important issues when considering the use of marketing research to ensure entrepreneurial success. These issues include research design, sampling, proper data collection and analysis, research conclusions, and taking action.

Research Design

In short, there is no optimal research design. As an entrepreneur, you may choose among a variety of alternative methods. A good entrepreneur understands that there is likely to be more than one way to tackle a problem. The ability to select the most appropriate research design develops with experience. Inexperienced entrepreneurs often embrace the survey method as the best design because they are most familiar with this method. More experienced entrepreneurs, on the other hand, recognize the value of other methods and can often put together creative research designs that can provide effective and accurate marketing information.

In my experience, entrepreneurs who want to uncover opportunities or test the viability of their venture concepts should probably use a combination of research methods, including exhausting all sources of secondary data, engaging in ethnographic research (observing customers in the marketplace and/or interfacing with products/services), following up with depth interviews to probe the customer and then deploy conjoint studies to properly configure the proposed offering, and engage in some field testing to refine, if necessary, any elements of the marketing mix. I believe this approach will increase your likelihood of venture success.

Sampling

Rarely can an entrepreneur research every possible customer. This is because of the time and cost involved in conducting research. Therefore, most entrepreneurs rely on **sampling** a portion of the total customer population.

If proper statistical procedures are followed, a researcher does not need to select every customer, because a properly selected sample should be representative of the customer population as a whole. However, errors can and do occur in sampling, and the reliability of the data obtained through sampling can sometimes become an issue. Thus, the first and most critical sampling question for entrepreneurs to ask is, "Who is to be sampled?"

Another key question concerns the sample size: How big should the sample be? As mentioned, it is usually unrealistic to expect a census of the entire customer population to be conducted. In general, larger samples are more precise than smaller ones, but proper sampling can allow a smaller subset of the total population to provide a reliable measure of the whole.

The final question in sampling concerns how to select the sampling units. There are two basic sampling techniques: probability and nonprobability sampling. *Probability sampling* involves precise rules to select the sample such that each element of the population has a specific known chance of being selected. For example, suppose you have a customer list with 1,000 names on it. You can randomly select 100 names of potential customers to contact, say by putting each individual name in a bowl and drawing out the names. The chance of being selected—100/1,000 or 0.10—is known in advance, and all customers have an equal chance of being contacted. This procedure helps select a sample (100 customers) that should be representative of the entire population (the 1,000 customers) and allows conclusions to be drawn about the entire population.

Nonprobability sampling involves the use of arbitrary judgment by the entrepreneur to select the sample so that the chance of selecting a particular element of the population is either unknown or zero. If you simply talked to 100 potential customers who lived closest to you, many other customers would be eliminated arbitrarily. This has introduced a bias, or possible lack of representativeness, which may make it dangerous to draw conclusions about the entire population of customers. Nonprobability samples are often used when time and budgets are limited and are most often used for exploratory research purposes. In general, you should use data from such samples with caution.

Proper Data Collection and Analysis

The process of gathering or collecting data is sometimes referred to as *fieldwork*. You are undertaking efforts to obtain data from the identified sources or respondents. Since several research methods could be used by the researcher, this means there may be multiple ways to collect the data. For example, with the survey method, data may be collected by telephone, mail, or personal interview.

However the data are collected, it is important to minimize errors in the process. Most research experts agree that the data collection stage of the research process is one of the major sources of error in marketing research. Some of the errors that occur are a result of a variety of problems ranging from failure to select the right respondents to incorrect recording of observations.

After your data are collected, the next step for the entrepreneur is to conduct data analysis. The level of analysis conducted on the data depends on the nature of the research and the information needed to provide insight into the marketing issue at hand. For survey data, frequency analysis is completed—calculating the responses question by question. The researcher may then wish to identify patterns in the data or examine how data pertaining to some questions may relate to data obtained from asking other questions. Probably the most widely used technique for organizing and analyzing marketing data is cross-tabulation. This method is particularly useful for market segmentation analysis

Research Conclusions and Taking Action

At this stage of the process, the entrepreneur must ask, "What does this information tell me?" A critical aspect of your job as an entrepreneur is to interpret the information and make conclusions with regard to what it means to your new venture. It is extremely important to make vital decisions about the opportunities you are investigating. In particular, it is fundamental that you arrive at a decision as to whether or not (1) you should proceed with the opportunity, (2) adjust or adapt the nature and scope of the opportunity based on the information you uncovered including customer input/feedback, or (3) kill the opportunity, walk away and move on and try to find something that has more potential for success. This is where the rubber meets the road—where research translates into action. Your research should provide valuable insight. But, you must also act on this insight. Do not be afraid to show that this learning has enabled you to make decisions and that you are prepared to act! Do not allow your ego to get in the way here. If the opportunity is not what it seems, accept this reality. If the customer insight gives you pause and makes you think you need to "flex" and adapt, then do it. If the results are positive and it seems like the opportunity is on target, then commit to move forward with it.

Designing a Marketing Information System

Once you launch your venture, it is important to stay close to the market, customers, and competitors. You can do this by putting in place a marketing information system inside your business. A marketing information system involves people, computers, and communication systems designed to satisfy your enterprise's need for information—information that will be used to make the right decisions about your business. The marketing information system will contain databases and statistical packages/models that can analyze data and present reports for interpretation. Your marketing information system should also allow you to engage in **data mining.**

Data mining is the extraction of information from the databases that can be used to determine the best strategies for growing and sustaining your enterprise. For example, mining the customer purchase data from my supermarket, I discovered that men buying diapers in the late evening often purchased a six-pack of beer as well. So, I placed diapers and beer near each other in an end-aisle display and increased sales.

I urge all aspiring entrepreneurs to make the investment in marketing research. And it need not be expensive or time consuming. The key is finding ways to get access to information that will help you uncover an opportunity, validate your opportunity, and/or help you reshape opportunity. I call this type of research *success insurance research*. While I am not going to guarantee this research will ensure venture success, it will go a long way in mitigating the chances of failure.

Key Takeaways

- Access to information and using it wisely is key to entrepreneurial success.
- Marketing research can help you uncover and/or test out your opportunities.

- Always exhaust secondary data before using more expensive and time-consuming primary data methods.
- Use *a* creative approach to obtaining information (e.g., secondary data, ethnographic research, depth interviews, focus groups, and conjoint studies).
- Look for market and customer insight and be prepared to act on this insight.

Entrepreneurial Exercise

You think, intuitively, that there is an opportunity to open an ice-cream shop in your town. What type of research would you conduct to help determine if this opportunity exists? Now, let's also assume that after using several research methods, you are still uncertain about the extent of the opportunity and you decide to do a survey to determine whether you should open the shop. What kind of questions will you ask? Whom do you ask?

Key Terms

Marketing research   44
Secondary data   44
Primary data   44
Depth interviews   45
Focus groups   47
Fuzzy front-end or FFE methods   49
Lead users   49

Observation   49
Ethnographic research   50
Survey   51
Experiment   54
Conjoint studies   55
Sampling   57
Data mining   59

Notes

1. Carey V. Azzara, "Qualitatively Speaking: The Focus Group vs. In-Depth Interview Debate," *Quirks*, June 10, 2010, p. 16.

2. Ibid.

3. Frederick G. Crane, "Using Ethnographic Research to Obtain Customer Insight in the New Product/Service Development Process," Working Paper, Northeastern University, 2008.

4. Hy Mariampolski, *Ethnography for Marketers: A Guide to Consumer Immersion* (Thousand Oaks, CA: Sage, 2006).

5. See Frederick G. Crane, Roger Kerin, Steve Hartley, and William Rudelius, *Marketing*, 7th Canadian ed. (Toronto: McGraw-Hill Ryerson, 2008).

Four

Understanding Customers and Competitors

A very important aspect of your venture planning process is to thoroughly understand the customers you wish to serve as well as the competition you will face in the marketplace. While customers are and should be a central concern of your venture, your competitors are also an important part of your external environment. In fact, it will not be possible to do a better job of meeting customer needs than the competition without a thorough understanding of the competitors. Thus, you must focus on both customers and competition if you wish to ensure the sustainability of your venture. We will discuss final consumers or customers in the consumer space first (business-to-consumer, B2C). Then, we will discuss "business customers" or consumers in the business-to-business (B2B) space. While there are some similarities between the two types of customers, there are also key differences that we will examine in this chapter. Finally, we will discuss the concept of competition and its relevance to your venture success.

Understanding the Customer

Behind every purchase is a customer. As an entrepreneur, you must know who the customers are, what they buy, how they buy, and why they buy. Customer behavior involves both the physical and mental behavior of individuals in the marketplace. It includes prepurchase behavior, purchase behavior, and postpurchase behavior. The stages a customer goes through in making choices about which products and services to buy is the called the **purchase decision process.** This process has five stages, as shown in Figure 4.1: (1) problem recognition, (2) information search, (3) alternative evaluation, (4) purchase decision, and (5) postpurchase behavior. The customer is also affected by psychological, sociocultural, situational, and marketing mix influences that you must also understand as an entrepreneur.[1]

Figure 4.1   Customer Behavior Model I

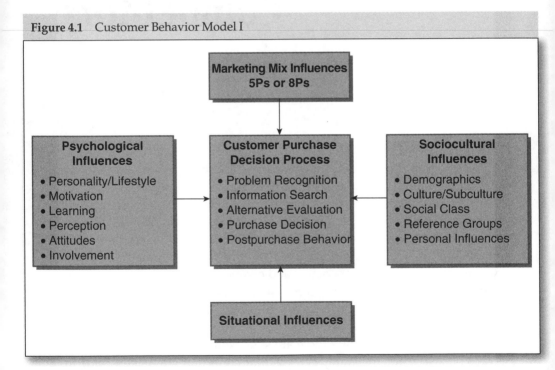

The first stage in the purchase decision process is problem recognition. The customer recognizes that he or she has a problem (need), which leads to a decision to make a purchase. For example, feeling hungry may lead to the decision to buy food at a grocery store or to go to a fast-food restaurant. Entrepreneurs should also understand that they can "trigger" customer recognition of a problem though advertising or other means. In this case, you are creating a need for the product.

After recognizing the problem, the customer undertakes an information search. In this case where the customer is hungry, the customer may need information concerning the types of food he or she might want to solve the hunger. The customer can scan his or her memory for previous experiences with particular foods. This is called an internal search. For frequently purchased products such as food, this search may be sufficient as the customer has past experiences with particular types or brands of food. If he or she does not, the customer can initiate an external search for information, learning from friends, advertising, or other sources.

The information search stage yields brand names and possible criteria that could be used to judge brands. The brands the customer becomes aware of constitute the **brand awareness set.** This is a very important concept for the entrepreneur to understand. If your brand is not part of the customer's brand awareness set, there is no possibility the customer will buy your brand. So, your first marketing task is to ensure your new entrepreneurial brand is part of the brand awareness set!

The customer then undertakes an alternative evaluation, assessing brands based on specific criteria he or she feels are important when making a purchase selection. The criteria can be objective criteria (such as nutritional content) or subjective criteria (such as the prestige of the brand). The brands that most closely meet the established criteria form the customer's **brand consideration set**—the brands from the brand awareness set that the customer would actually consider purchasing. Thus, it is possible for the entrepreneur's brand to be part of the brand awareness set but not part of the brand consideration set. So, brand awareness is required but is not sufficient. You must build an image of your new brand so that the customer will consider buying it.

Having examined the alternatives in the brand consideration set, the customer will make the purchase decision and complete the purchase. After the purchase, the customer will compare it with his or her expectations and can be satisfied or dissatisfied. The postpurchase stage may confirm or alter the customer's view of the brand purchased and dictate whether the customer buys the brand again. From a sustained growth perspective your venture needs repeat customers. Very importantly, from an investor's viewpoint, recurrent revenue is critical for a venture and without assurance of recurrent revenue investors are not likely to invest in your venture.

In addition to understanding the customer purchase decision process, entrepreneurs have also recognized and understood other factors that affect the customer purchase decision process. These include psychological, sociocultural, situational, and marketing mix influences.

Psychological Influences

Psychological influences affect why and how the customer behaves in terms of his or her purchase behavior. Psychological influences that the entrepreneur must be aware of include personality/lifestyle, motivation, learning, perception, attitudes, and involvement.

Personality/Lifestyle

Personality refers to a person's consistent behaviors or responses to recurring situations. Although numerous personality theories exist, most identify key traits—enduring characteristics within a person or in his or her relationships with others. For example, one model is the Big Five (sometimes called the Five Factor Model), which includes the traits of openness, conscientiousness, extraversion, agreeableness, and neuroticism. People are categorized into particular personality types depending on the extent to which they possess those particular traits.[2]

Lifestyle is a mode of living that is identified by how people spend their time and resources, what they consider important in their environment, and what they think of themselves and the world around them. The analysis of consumer lifestyles, called *psychographics,* has produced many insights into customer behavior. For example, lifestyle analysis has proven useful in segmenting and targeting consumers for new and existing products and services. As an entrepreneur, you must understand that a customer's personality/lifestyle affects the purchase decision process because people with different personalities or lifestyles will have different needs and different buying behaviors. For example, a budding wine entrepreneur discovered that some wine consumers are very introverted and unlike extroverts these introverts buy wine that they like and are not worried about the social reactions and consequences of others who may not like the wine purchased by such introverts. In short, the introverts will drink what they like and they do not care if others may not share their taste. Thus, this entrepreneur markets to this introverted group by reinforcing their view that it is fine to drink what you like and not to worry about others.

Motivation

Motivation is the force that causes us to act, including satisfying a need. Because customer needs are the focus of the marketing, entrepreneurs must understand customer motivation (e.g., why they are buying). Basically, a customer can have physiological needs (for basics such as water, food, and sex) and psychological needs, including the need for esteem and achievement. Most successful business ventures are built around satisfying customers' higher level psychological needs and not their basic physiological needs. Most customers have multiple motives at the same time, which can create motivational conflict (e.g., they cannot satisfy all motives). Such conflict, however, offers opportunities for the smart entrepreneur who can instill or activate customer motivation for the entrepreneur's product or service.

Learning

Learning is the process in which behavior capabilities are changed as a result of experience. For example, customers learn which sources to use for information about products and services, which criteria to use when assessing alternatives, and, more generally, how to make purchase decisions. *Behavioral learning* is the process of developing automatic responses to a situation built up through repeated exposure to it.

Consumers also learn through thinking, reasoning, and mental problem solving without direct experience. This type of learning, called *cognitive learning*, involves making connections between two or more ideas or simply observing the outcomes of others' behaviors and adjusting your own accordingly. Entrepreneurial firms can influence this type of learning through repetition in advertising.

Learning is also important because it relates to habit formation (routine problem solving). There is also a link between habits and *brand loyalty*—the favorable attitude toward and consistent purchase of a single brand over time. Brand loyalty results from the positive reinforcement of previous actions. In other words, if a customer buys your brand and is satisfied, he or she is likely to become loyal to your brand.[3] It is these loyal customers that allow your venture to survive and grow—and attract future funding from possible investors interested in your new venture.

Perception

The process of making sense of the world around you (external stimuli) is called *perception*. It is the process by which we select, organize, and interpret stimuli. All of us understand what we see, hear, feel, and smell through the filters of our experience, interests, and beliefs. As an entrepreneur, you will discover that some customers may not perceive stimuli in the way you intended them to be understood. For example, one person sees a Cadillac as a mark of achievement; another sees it as ostentatious. Customers use a filtering process called *selective perception*. The four stages of perception are selective exposure, selective attention, selective comprehension, and selective retention. In short, customers expose themselves only to selective information and attend to, comprehend, and retain only some information. Your job as an entrepreneur is to make sure the customer is exposed to your information (about your venture and brand), pays attention to the information, and understands and remembers it. Importantly, your goal is to have your potential customers to act on this information . . . buy your brand.

Attitudes

Attitudes are "learned predispositions to respond to an object or class of objects in a consistently favorable or unfavorable way."[4] This view of attitudes has important implications for entrepreneurs. First, if attitudes are learned responses, it is possible to change them over time by providing new information. Second, since attitudes are mental views, attitudes are not directly observable by the entrepreneur. Thus, attitudes are inferred by measuring what can be observed. Third, attitudes are related to behavior. It is this relationship that makes them most relevant to entrepreneurs. Entrepreneurs care about the customer developing a positive attitude toward their products/services because a positive attitude likely leads to positive behavior—buying the product/service.

As an entrepreneur, you may discover that you may have to engage in "attitude change strategies" to successfully execute your marketing program. For example, you may have to change the customer's beliefs about your product/brand so that it will be perceived more favorably. Or, you might have to change the customer's perceived importance of particular product/brand attributes. For example, 7UP stressed the importance of "no caffeine" in its soft drink and built market share.

Involvement

Involvement is the degree to which something is central to your sense of self as well as the personal, social, and economic significance of the purchase to the customer. Involvement, in fact, can result in the customer skipping or minimizing one or more steps in the purchase decision process. Thus, involvement can lead to three general variations in the purchase decision process. Extended problem solving (EPS) would be considered a high-involvement purchase, where each of the five stages of the purchase decision process is used, including considerable time and effort on external information search and in identifying and evaluating alternatives. Several brands are in the brand consideration set, and these are evaluated on many criteria (e.g., the purchase of a new automobile).

In limited problem solving (LPS), which would involve moderate involvement, customers typically seek some information or rely on a friend to help them evaluate alternatives. In general, several brands might be evaluated using a moderate number of different criteria. You might use limited problem solving in choosing a restaurant for lunch and other purchase situations in which you have little time or effort to spend.

Routine problem solving (RPS) would be low involvement, where the customer recognizes a problem, makes a decision, and spends little effort seeking external information and evaluating alternatives (e.g., buying toothpaste). The purchase process is virtually a habit and is typically the case for low-priced, frequently purchased products.

Low and high customer involvement has important implications for your venture. For example, if your new venture markets a low-involvement product, you must also break existing buying habits and encourage the customer to try your brand. If you are marketing a high-involvement product, you must be able to point out to the customer that your product is superior in some way to competing brands by making brand comparisons.

Sociocultural Influences

Sociocultural influences involve the customer's formal and informal relationships with others, which can affect the customer's purchase behavior. Sociocultural influences include demographics, culture/subculture, social class, reference groups, and personal influences.

Demographics

Demographics describe a population according to several chara-cteristics such as age, gender, income, education, occupation, marital status, population size, and population growth rate. Demographics affect consumption, and as an entrepreneur, you must understand the demographics of the market in which you intend to operate. You must not only study the existing demographics of your market but also, as we pointed out in Chapters 1 and 2, examine and evaluate demographic changes that will affect future consumption. For example, even something as simple as age can affect what a customer buys and uses. People in particular age categories have certain needs and preferences (e.g., youth market vs. baby boomers vs. the senior market). Customer income also affects what is purchased in the marketplace by particular customers. The same is true for other demographic variables such as gender and marital status. The size of different demographic groups is also important for you to know. For example, some entrepreneurs continue to focus on the baby-boomer market yet the Generation Y market is now larger in terms of population size and is eclipsing baby boomers as the primary spenders for many product categories.

Culture/Subculture

Culture incorporates the set of values, customs, traditions, ideas, and attitudes that a society possesses and transmits from one generation to the next. Subgroups within the larger, or national, culture with unique values, ideas, and attitudes are referred to as *subcultures*. For example, ethnic subcultures exist in America within the larger/national culture. An *ethnic subculture* is a segment of a larger society whose members are thought, by themselves and/or by others, to have a common origin and to participate in shared activities believed to be culturally significant.

Culture is the largest sphere of influence that affects individual customer behavior. It prescribes what is acceptable and unacceptable behavior, including consumption behavior. Thus, as an entrepreneur, you have to uncover how culture in a given society influences customer purchase behavior. For example, McDonald's sells mutton burgers in India because the cow is considered sacred in that country.

Cultural Rituals

Entrepreneurs must understand the notion of ritualistic behavior. Individuals in all societies across time and space have engaged in universal patterns of behavior—**rituals**—that you need to recognize. Some rituals are highly expressive, symbolic and episodic such as celebrating a marriage, death services, or special observances such as a birthday or

Christmas. Other rituals are common, daily, seemingly habitual behavior such as brushing one's teeth, taking a shower, getting or making a meal, or walking the dog. Either way, your job as an entrepreneur is to determine the rituals consumers engage in and to determine if there is an opportunity for you to capitalize on this ritual. In this case, you would attempt to cater to the existing ritual—the classic market fulfillment notion discussed in Chapter 1. Or, conversely, you could attempt to establish a new ritual—the classic market creation notion also discussed in Chapter 1. If you wish to focus in existing rituals, you need to think of opportunities that will help consumers with their existing ritualistic behavior. For example, you can offer to make such rituals better, faster, cheaper, more convenience, or more fun. For instance, most of us eat or dine outside your home (feasting) and it has become a ritual in many countries. Knowing this you could uncover ways to help customers with this ritual perhaps making it more fun, making it more economic, more convenient—including such things as late-night drive-throughs or delivery service. Let's consider another existing ritual—the buying and listening to music. The typical ritual for many consumers has been to go to a retail store and buy a CD containing 10–12 songs performed by a specific artist. However, Apple Inc. came along and offered consumers the opportunity to buy music online and to buy single songs. In doing so, they tweaked or changed an existing ritual and in doing so, iTunes achieved amazing success.

Now, let's think about the introduction of a new ritual. Yes, consumers in all societies, across time and space have engaged in some form of communication and have also sought out various forms of entertainment. Recently, however, new information technologies have come along that have radically changed consumer behavior and introduced an entirely new ritual—communicating and entertaining via social media. Whereas 10–15 years ago, individuals spent many hours a week talking on a landline telephone, watching television, and listening to radio, these rituals have been eclipsed by communicating online and being entertained online through social media. For example, millions of users spend countless hours on Facebook or on Pinterest. This is a case of introducing a new ritual and creating new markets that did not exist before. And, in some cases, this means displacing or replacing older markets. For example, how many of you pen a letter and mail it to a friend via the United States Post Office?

Again, as an entrepreneur you have to think about enabling customers with their existing rituals or introducing new rituals to these customers.

The latter may take more imagination and greater effort to shape consumers behavior to embrace the new rituals, but the payoff could be tremendous. Just think about what happened when Steve Jobs created and launched the first Apple computer. Could you now imagine a world without a computer?

Recently, BBDO Worldwide conducted a global study of the everyday routine of people across the globe—the commonplace rituals that consumers embrace on a daily basis in their lives. They discovered five rituals that are performed most often by most people throughout the world. As an entrepreneur, think about what these findings mean to you as possible opportunities for a new venture. The five rituals include the following:

1. *Preparing for battle: transforming us from the cocoon to "ready to face the day."* Preparing for battle includes an average of more than seven steps in less than one hour. These are functional, sequential steps that get people ready for the outside world. The most common task is brushing teeth, followed by taking a shower or bath, having something to eat/drink, and talking to a family member/partner. They found that most people relied on the same brands when preparing for battle. And, importantly, the company argues that the preparing for battle ritual is the biggest opportunity for products/services BUT the rituals is also the most entrenched and most jammed with existing brands.

2. *Feasting: the pleasure of eating that "reunites us with our tribes,"* transforming us from alone to connected. Sharing is at the core of this ritual. Everyone is expected to bring something to the table (literally or figuratively). Americans are most likely to meet in a restaurant, whereas the Spanish and French are most likely to meet at home. And, the car has now become a sizable dining venue. Still, the study found that convenience may have gone too far. It's important that people also feel a sense of involvement in the preparation of a meal. It's part of the emotional transformation.

3. *Sexing up: a highly pleasurable and indulgent ritual*, though not without stress (particularly for women), that transforms us from our everyday selves to our most fabulous selves. Globally, most people say that sex is spontaneous. Yet, many say they wait for the weekend for sex. Moreover, many say there is also preparation involved such as the use of outfits and special products.

4. *Returning to camp: that moment when we unwind and exhale,* transforming us from tense to relaxed. At the opposite end of the spectrum from "preparing for battle" is "returning to camp." This is the moment when people exhale. It lasts an average of four hours and includes fewer than five steps—quite a difference from the more than seven behaviors that are crammed into an hour at the start of the day. All over the world, people demonstrate they have ended their day by changing elements of their clothes—from kicking off shoes to changing into pajamas. Two out of three people let go with media, one out of five read a newspaper, more than one-third go online, and many bathe or shower. The study suggests there is an opportunity for those brands that can contribute to a sense of relaxation, calm, self-satisfaction, and at ease.

5. *Protecting yourself for the future: that last ritual of the day* that moves us from relaxed to feeling safe and secure before the next day comes around. The final ritual, and the shortest one, is protecting yourself for the future. This can take the form of leaving packed bags by the door, laying out clothes for the next day, turning off computers, pouring a glass of water, taking your medication, or setting the alarm. To husbands and fathers, the day is not complete until they've checked on kids and pets or locked doors and windows. The study suggests that brands play an important role in the ritual of helping someone feel safe and secure and protected for the future.[5]

You must also consider whether subcultural influences exist. Ethnic subcultures, for example, can influence not only what is purchased but also how and when. The growing ethnic diversity of America is presenting both opportunities and challenges to aspiring entrepreneurs. And, again, ritualistic behavior can vary by ethnic subcultures and you must recognize this variance and perhaps uncover opportunities to enable such rituals or create new ones in ethnic markets.

Social Class

Another sociocultural influence on customer behavior is social class. Social class is defined as the relatively permanent, homogeneous divisions in a society into which people sharing similar values, interests, and behavior can be grouped. A person's occupation, source of income (not level of income), and education determine his or her social class. Generally speaking, three major social class categories exist—upper, middle, and lower—with subcategories within each. Entrepreneurs should determine if and how social class may influence customer purchase behavior. For example, social class has been found to influence the type of clothing and automobiles people purchase. Social class has also been found to influence the media habits of customers.

Reference Groups

Reference groups are people to whom an individual looks as a basis for self-appraisal or as a source of personal standards. Reference groups affect customer purchases because they influence the information, attitudes, and aspiration levels that help set a customer's standards. For example, one of the first questions one asks others when planning to attend a social occasion is, "What are you going to wear?" Reference groups have an important influence on the purchase of luxury products but not of necessities. And reference groups exert a strong influence on the brand chosen when its use or consumption is highly visible to others.

Customers can have many reference groups, but four groups are important for the entrepreneur to understand. A *membership group* is one to which a person actually belongs, including fraternities, sororities, and social clubs. Such groups can be easily identifiable and easily targeted. An *aspiration group* is one that a person wishes to be a member of or wishes to be identified with, such as a professional society. A *dissociative group* is one that a person wishes to maintain a distance from because of differences in values or behaviors. Finally, we consider a customer's family as a special reference group. A family can influence how purchase decisions are made (e.g., joint decision making is common), the brands a customer buys, and even the media the customer selects to use. If you are an entrepreneur who is marketing a product for the "family," you must understand the dynamics of family purchase behavior.

Personal Influences

A customer's purchases are often influenced by the views, opinions, or behaviors of others. Two aspects of personal influence are important to entrepreneurial marketing: opinion leadership and word-of-mouth activity.

Individuals who exert direct or indirect social influence over others are called opinion leaders. Opinion leaders are considered to be knowledgeable about or users of particular products and services, and so their opinions influence others' choices. Opinion leadership is widespread in the purchase of cars and trucks, clothing and accessories, club membership, consumer electronics, vacation locations, and financial investments. Entrepreneurs should recognize, however, that only about 10 percent of customers are considered opinion leaders.

Thus, identifying, reaching, and influencing opinion leaders are major challenges for entrepreneurs. Some entrepreneurs use sports figures or celebrities as spokespersons to represent their products/services. Others promote their products/services in media believed to reach opinion leaders. Still others use more direct approaches such as actually inviting people deemed opinion leaders to try their products/services or providing such products/services for free to the opinion leaders in the hope that they will influence others to purchase.

The influencing of people during conversations is called word of mouth (WOM). WOM is often the most powerful and authentic information source for customers because it typically involves friends viewed as trustworthy. Increasingly, entrepreneurs who often have limited financial resources work hard to stimulate positive word of mouth about their products or services. This is called **buzz marketing.** The entrepreneur works with "influentials" to create buzz about the entrepreneur's brand or company. Like opinion leaders, these influentials represent a small portion of the population (estimated at 10–15 percent). Some entrepreneurs who have difficulty locating and engaging influentials simply hire outside firms to generate buzz.

More recently, many entrepreneurs have turned to an electronic or online version of word of mouth called **viral marketing.** This involves messages "infectious" enough that customers will pass them along to others through social media, online forums, social networks, chat rooms, bulletin boards, blogs, message board threads, instant messages, and e-mails. Some experts suggest that entrepreneurs should consider the use of viral marketing as an inexpensive way to get the message out about their companies and products.[6]

Situational Influences

Situational influences include the purchase task, social surroundings, physical surroundings, temporal affects, and antecedent states. The purchase task is the reason for engaging in the purchase decision in the first place (e.g., are customers buying for themselves or buying gifts for others?). For example, information searching and evaluating alternatives may differ, depending on whether the purchase is a gift, which often involves social visibility, or for the buyer's own use. Social surroundings, including the other people present when a purchase decision is made, may also affect what is purchased. For example, research shows that when women shop together, they spend more money than when a woman shops by herself. Physical surroundings, such as decor, music, and crowding in retail stores, may alter how purchase decisions are made. Temporal effects, such as time of day or the amount of time available, will influence where consumers have breakfast and lunch and what is ordered. Finally, antecedent states, which include the customer's mood or the amount of cash on hand, can influence purchase behavior and choice.

Marketing Mix Influences

Last, **marketing mix influences** also affect customer purchase behavior. And the good news is that these marketing mix influences are entirely within the control of the entrepreneur. Marketing mix influences are either the 5Ps of a product-based venture (product, price, place, promotion, and people) or the 8Ps of a service-based venture (product, price, place, promotion, people, physical evidence, process, and productivity). It is your task as the entrepreneur to construct an effective marketing mix to properly influence customer purchase behavior and achieve venture success.

Business Customers

As an entrepreneur, you may decide not to compete in the B2C space (business-to-consumer) but instead compete in the B2B space (business-to-business). Therefore, you must understand **business customers.** Business customers include all the buyers in a nation, except the ultimate (final) customers (previously discussed). Business customers include manufacturers, retailers, and government agencies that buy goods and services for their own use or for resale. There are millions of business customers in the United States, and an entrepreneur may find success catering to some of these customers in this B2B space.

Key Differences and Key Similarities

There are both differences and similarities between customers in the B2C space and B2B space. First, the key differences fall into two distinct categories: the nature of the purchase and the nature of the market. Business customers generally use their purchases for further production, for maintaining their businesses, or for resale to other customers. Products are often raw or semifinished materials that a B2C customer rarely buys. Business customers also tend to have more specific buying or purchase criteria and often use technical specifications as a basis for purchase decision making. Joint decision making is more likely with business customers, as is the use of competitive bidding and negotiations.

A key difference in terms of market characteristics is the fact that the demand of business customers is derived from the demand of final/B2C customers. For example, demand for Alcoa aluminum products is based on final customer demand for products such as beer or soft drinks. Another difference is that business customers may be more geographically concentrated and are more likely (than final, or B2C customers) to be able to make their own goods and services as opposed to purchasing them.

While there are differences between business and final customers, there are also similarities. First, one significant similarity is the purchase decision process. The same five-stage process used by B2C customers is also used by business customers (i.e., problem recognition, information search, alternative evaluation, purchase decision, and postpurchase behavior). Also, just as the final customer can deviate from the five-stage purchase process, skipping one or more steps, so can the business customer. In fact, the extended problem solving (EPS), limited problem solving (LPS), and routine problem solving (RPS) variations parallel what researchers have defined as the three buy classes of business customers: the new buy (equivalent to EPS), modified rebuy (equivalent to LPS), and straight rebuy (equivalent to RPS).

With the new buy, the business customer moves through the five-stage purchase decision process. This type of buy might involve an important, first-time buy. But with the modified rebuy, the business customer has some experience and is making a change in the product purchased or a change in the supplier. Finally, with the straight rebuy, the business customer is simply reordering. If you are targeting a business customer who is making a straight rebuy, you have to get the customer to rethink his or her purchase and to consider your offering. This can be difficult; however, if the customer thinks he or she knows all that is needed to know about available products and suppliers. Unless you can get the customer to break out of the straight rebuy mode, you have little chance of winning this customer's business.[7]

Business Buying Criteria

In making a purchase, the business customer must weigh key buying criteria that apply to the potential supplier and what it wants to market. Business customers use specific buying criteria—the objective characteristics of the supplier's products and services and the capabilities of the supplier itself. Some of the most commonly used criteria are (1) price, (2) ability to meet quality specifications, (3) reliability of delivery, (4) technical capability, (5) warranties and guarantees, (6) past performance on previous contracts, and (7) after-sale service. Entrepreneurs wishing to supply products/services to business customers must meet or exceed these criteria and deliver customer value.

The Buying Center

The **buying center** is the group of people in a business organization who participate in the buying process. The number and type of people in the buying center will vary depending on the purchase decision being made, but researchers have identified five specific roles that an individual in a buying center can play. In some purchases, the same person may perform two or more of these roles.

- *Users* are the people in the organization who actually use the product or service.
- *Influencers* affect the buying decision, usually by helping define the specifications for what is bought.
- *Buyers* have formal authority and responsibility to select the supplier and negotiate the terms of the contract.
- *Deciders* have the formal or informal power to select or approve the supplier that receives the contract.
- *Gatekeepers* control the flow of information in the buying center.

As an entrepreneur, you must find out the answers to the following questions: Which individuals are in the buying center for the product or service? What is the relative influence of each member of the group? What are the buying criteria of each member? How does each member of the group perceive our firm, our products and services, and our salespeople? Answering these questions will go a long way in ensuring a successful marketing effort.

Finally, an entrepreneur who wishes to successfully compete in the B2B marketplace should heed the following four lessons: (1) Understand the business customer's needs, (2) get on the right bidders' lists, (3) find the right people in the buying center, and (4) provide unique value to the business customer.[8]

Understanding Competition

As you know, in Chapter 1, we defined **competition** as any alternative that could satisfy a specific customer's needs. Others suggest another definition for competition: rivalry among providers for a given set of targeted customers. When you are considering marketing opportunities, you must know your competitors, including their strengths, weaknesses, and competitive strategies. Remember, there is no such thing as "no competition." We say this because competition runs on a continuum ranging from indirect competition, such as "total budget competition" and "generic competition," to more direct competition, such as "product competition," and the most direct form of competition, "direct brand competition"—directly substitutable products (see Figure 4.2).

Let's illustrate an example of this **competition continuum.** Suppose you want to enter the beverage industry with an "all-natural bottled blueberry drink." From a "total budget competition" perspective, your competitors are not just other beverage providers but any provider looking to attract dollars from your potential customer. This might include potato chip companies or even candy bar companies. "Generic competition" is next on the continuum, and this might include the customer deciding to simply get a drink of water from his or her household tap. Next is "product competition" (beverage category competition), which could include bottled water, tea, or beer. Finally, your most direct form of competition is "brand competition," which offers products similar to yours, including V-8 and Very Fine.

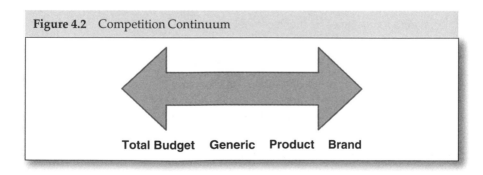

Figure 4.2   Competition Continuum

Total Budget   Generic   Product   Brand

You must identify and monitor all competitors who will compete for your intended customer base. This includes determining the number, size, strengths, weaknesses, and behaviors of the competitors. This also means determining how similar the competitor's product might be to your own.

In addition, you must "benchmark" your most direct competitors. This involves gathering competitive intelligence information, conducting a competitive analysis, and performing competitive benchmarking looking not only to assess your company/product compared to the competitor but also to discover an opportunity to "leapfrog" the competitors.

It is also extremely important to determine the "competitive advantage" held by each direct competitor (e.g., cost, quality, branding) and to use this information when planning your own competitive advantage. Also, if you are entering an existing market and intend to "steal share" from existing competitors, you must clearly identify from which competitors you will steal share. However, it is also important to realize that competitors are not likely to simply allow you to steal share ("to take their lunch"). Therefore, you must determine what the competitive response is likely to be to your entry into the market. Some of the key questions you should answer about your competition are shown in Figure 4.3.

Figure 4.3   Some Key Questions You Should Answer About Your Competitors

Who are the most direct competitors?

What is the sales volume of each of the direct competitors?

What market share does each of the competitors hold?

Which competitors are similar to your venture? And how are they similar?

What attracts customers to these competitors?

What are the key strengths and weaknesses of the competitors?

How are the competitors positioned in the market (checking out their advertising/promotion materials can help determine this)?

One of the other things to keep in mind regarding competition is the concept of "barriers to entry"—that is, competitive practices that might make it difficult for you to enter the market. The higher the entry barrier, the less likely it is that you can successfully enter. For example, a competitor might offer customers lower prices, thus deterring customers from trying your product. The competitor may also spend substantial money on marketing, which might significantly increase the cost of your entry into the market. Or, competitors might use their power with channel members and block distribution access (e.g., they may threaten a distributor by saying that carrying your product may cause them to withhold distributing their products through this channel member).

One of the problems many entrepreneurs often have is finding information on their competitors. Yet, there are plenty of quick and inexpensive ways to gather such information. For example, the following are some of your options:

1. Read your competitors' annual reports, newsletters, and so on.

2. Use competitive intelligence-gathering databases (e.g., Hoover's online at www.hoovers.com; Galileo Internet Resource; 10kwizard.com).

3. Talk to suppliers and ask about what the competition does well and what it does poorly.

4. Do a thorough Internet search.

5. Talk to some of your competitors' customers. Find out if they are happy or unhappy and if they might be happier doing business with you.

In the end, you must embrace the fact that it is only when you fully understand your competitors that you can do a better job of meeting intended customers' needs. One of the biggest mistakes the aspiring entrepreneur makes is underestimating the extent of competition he or she will face upon entry into a market and failing to plan for how exactly the venture can compete successfully. On the other hand, sometimes entrepreneurs are too quick to allow competitors to define the competitive landscape and to set the rules of engagement. But according to Margaret Heffernan, this can be a mistake. When it comes to the competition, she offers up some advice in the Entrepreneurial Marketing Spotlight.

Entrepreneurial Marketing Spotlight

Margaret Heffernan is an entrepreneur, author, and educator who has some interesting thoughts about the concept of competition. She says, rightly, that every venture capitalist and bank manager will ask you who your competitors are. If you say you have none, they'll think you don't know your market—or are proposing to enter a market no one else in their right mind wants. She further suggests that "most entrepreneurs identify a few competitors and construct self-vindicating scenarios that prove that they will triumph, leaving their competitor bloodied, bowed, and broke."

Heffernan suggests smart entrepreneurs resist such hackneyed, adversarial thinking and refuse to let the competitive landscape be defined by their competitors. She points to the example of Farrington's Farm Shop. Farrington's competes against food giant Tesco, which is located just down the road from Farrington's. Both offer much the same thing: meat, milk, bananas, carrots, cheese, jam, bread, easy parking, loyalty cards, and a café. If you ask Farrington's how their prices compare to Tesco's, they don't know. Moreover, Farrington's does not send in mystery shoppers and does not even subscribe to retail data that would tell them. They don't know Tesco's prices because they don't care. Are they out of their minds, Heffernan asks? No, far from it. The founders of Farrington's have beaten all their revenue projections and won awards because they don't compete on price. They compete on delivering a unique shopping experience. From the baby barn where customers see and touch calves, lambs, guinea pigs, and rabbits to the milking parlor where children can see where milk comes from, Farrington's is not about price—it is all about the "shopping experience." And Tesco cannot compete on this unique dimension.

Heffernan tells us that Farrington's knew that if they tried to compete with Tesco on price, they would be slaughtered. So, instead, they defined their own market and have gone after it with obsessive devotion. Instead of playing the competitor's game, they chose their own—one they could win on their own terms. Heffernan says what she loves about Farrington's isn't just the food and the service but the smart way that Farrington's competes: offering something different to the customer. When you do this, you can worry less about the competition and focus more on your customer! This type of competitive thinking keeps quality businesses such as Farrington's alive and well![9]

Key Takeaways

- Remember that behind every purchase is a customer whom you must understand fully.

- Take the time to examine the psychological, sociocultural, and situational influences that affect customer purchase behavior and plan accordingly.
- Remember that you can influence the customer with the marketing mix you offer.
- Knowing the customer will allow you to construct the proper marketing mix.
- There are opportunities in the market to cater to final customers (B2C marketing) and business customers (B2B marketing).
- Customers may be the essence of why your business might exist, but the competition is part of your atmosphere.
- Know your competitors and benchmark against them. But importantly, find a way to compete on your terms, not the competitors' terms.

Entrepreneurial Exercise

Map out how you think your potential customer goes about making his or her purchase decision for the product/service your venture will market. What are the key internal influences (e.g., motivation) and external influences (e.g., personal influences) that affect their decision to buy? Now pinpoint how you might be able to influence their decision with your marketing program.

Now, identify your two to three most direct competitors and list their key behaviors. What can you conclude about how you might best compete against these players?

Key Terms

Purchase decision process 62
Brand awareness set   63
Brand consideration set   63
Psychological influences   64
Sociocultural influences   67
Buzz marketing   73
Viral marketing   73

Situational influences   73
Marketing mix influences   74
Business customers   74
Buying center   76
Competition   77
Competition continuum   77
Rituals   68

Notes

1. This section is adapted from F. G. Crane and T. K. Clarke, *Consumer Behaviour in Canada*, 2nd ed. (Toronto: Dryden, 1994).

2. L. L. Thurstone, "The Vectors of the Mind," *Psychological Review* 41 (1934): 1–32.

3. Sharon Morrison and Frederick G. Crane, "Building the Service Brand by Creating and Managing an Emotional Brand Experience," *Journal of Brand Management* 14, no. 5 (2007): 410–421.

4. Gordon W. Allport, "Attitudes," in *A Handbook of Social Psychology*, ed. C. A. Murchinson, 798-844 (Worcester, MA: Clark University Press, 1935).

5. Global Study of Consumer Rituals: http://www.bizcommunity.com/Article/196/12/26341.html, Downloaded February 10, 2012.

6. This section is based on Frederick G. Crane, Roger Kerin, Steve Hartley, and William Rudelius, *Marketing*, 7th Canadian ed. (Toronto: McGraw-Hill Ryerson, 2008).

7. This section is adapted from F. G. Crane and T. K. Clarke, *Consumer Behaviour in Canada*, 2nd ed. (Toronto: Dryden, 1994).

8. Ibid.

9. Margaret Heffernan, "Country Competition," *Real Business Magazine*, March 2004.

Five

Segmentation, Targeting, and Positioning

The concept of segmentation is based on one unassailable premise: Customers are different because they have different needs and behave in different ways. Clearly, the fact that customers are different is not necessarily comforting for the entrepreneur. Indeed, it would be easier for entrepreneurs if all customers were the same. This would allow you to deploy a "one size fits all" marketing approach. But unfortunately, you cannot, and you must understand that proper market segmentation, targeting, and positioning will be the cornerstones of a successful venture.

As an entrepreneur, you must determine the segments of the market you wish to seek, why you are seeking those segments, how you will seek them, what the cost will be to do so, and what your return on investment will be. The entrepreneur must segment markets to enable him or her to respond more effectively to the specific "needs" of prospective customers and thus increase the sales and profitability of the venture. Remember, in earlier chapters, we pointed out that you cannot be all things to all people and that your venture needs focus. Once you segment markets, you must then determine which segments will be your targets. Finally, you must then effectively position your offer in the hearts/minds of the customer in a way that clearly differentiates you from your competitors. We call this process **STP** (segment, target, position).

Market Segmentation

Market segmentation involves aggregating prospective customers into groups that (1) have common needs and (2) will respond similarly to a specific marketing offer or marketing mix. From these groups (market segments), you will pick target segments (target market)—segments toward which you will direct your marketing efforts. Segmentation is, in fact, a means to a clear end: Segmentation is a way to link customer needs to the venture's marketing actions.[1] In fact, the ultimate test of the segmentation process is whether it leads to effective marketing. If it does not pass the test, then it is likely you have a segmentation problem.

Questions Any Segmentation Analysis Must Answer

I have always said that segmenting markets is not a pure science and that, perhaps, there is no single best way to segment a given market. However, while there may be several different approaches to segment markets, each approach should answer the following questions:

1. What is purchased?
2. Who is purchasing?
3. Where is it purchased?
4. How is the product/service purchased?
5. How much is purchased?
6. When is it purchased?
7. Why is the product/service purchased?

A good segmentation analysis provides answers to all of these questions. But something important must be pointed out. Question 7 is perhaps the most important question to answer. Answering the other questions is certainly required, but it is not sufficient for effective segmentation. "Why" products/services are purchased by prospective customers is a critical question for you to answer since it relates directly to the notion of customer "needs" that we have stressed throughout this book.

Additional Requirements for Effective Segmentation

In addition to answering the above-mentioned questions, market segments must meet several criteria to be considered bona fide segments: (1) The customers within the segments must have similar needs, (2) there must be differences in needs across the segments, (3) the segments must be measurable (size, location, profile), (4) the segments must be big enough to serve economically, and (5) there must be a way to reach the segments.[2] Reaching customers, again, has two dimensions, communicating with customers (promotion) and delivering products to them (distribution, or place).

Ways to Segment Markets

Segmenting markets effectively is not an easy task. In fact, it can be quite difficult. As an entrepreneur, you need to have a good working knowledge of the market as well as use your common sense and good judgment. Since there is no single way to segment markets, you have to become familiar with the various approaches to segmentation. These approaches include geographic segmentation, demographic segmentation, psychographic segmentation, and behavioral segmentation.

Geographic Segmentation

Some entrepreneurs segment markets based on where customers live or work. This is **geographic segmentation** and can include geographic units such as countries, regions, states, counties, cities, or even neighborhoods. The entrepreneur might also consider a number of other variables when using geographic segmentation such as population density, population growth, and climate. An entrepreneur might decide to operate his or her venture in one or two geographic areas or operate in all areas but pay attention to geographic differences that might lead to different customer needs or buying preferences in specific geographic markets.

Demographic Segmentation

One of the most common ways to segment markets is to use **demographic segmentation,** or segmenting a market based on population characteristics. This approach will segment customers according to demographic variables such as age, gender, income, education, and marital status. If you are segmenting business markets, you could use size of firm, revenue of firm, and so on as possible segmentation variables. Demographic segmentation is popular among entrepreneurs for two reasons. First, customer needs are often tied to demographic characteristics (e.g., age, gender, size of firm). Second, demographic information on markets is often easier to locate and measure than other variables used in other segmentation approaches.

An entrepreneur can consider single or multiple demographic variables when segmenting markets. Age, for example, can affect what a customer buys and uses since customers in particular age cohorts have different needs. For example, an aging senior is more likely to have a need for an adult disposable diaper than a Generation Y consumer.

An entrepreneur could also use gender as a way to segment markets. Clearly, men and women are different physiologically and anatomically, and this may explain differences in needs. However, a single demographic variable such as gender is rarely sufficient for understanding and segmenting a given market and can, in fact, be very misleading. For example, even though condoms are a gender-based product (used by men), condom manufacturers have mistakenly focused on males when marketing their product only to find out that it was, in many cases, the female who purchased the condom!

Thus, entrepreneurs often combine several demographic variables that might clearly distinguish one segment from another. For example, when age and gender are combined, the resultant information is often more useful in segmenting certain markets. For instance, the face soap market is more effectively segmented when using both age and gender than either variable alone. Still, I urge entrepreneurs not to fall into what is commonly called the "demographic trap" of segmentation. Trying to segment markets based on several demographic variables in multiple combinations such as age, gender, income, and education can get pretty complicated very quickly and often results in so many possible market segments that they cannot be operationalized by the entrepreneur.

Psychographic Segmentation

Sometimes an entrepreneur will use **psychographic segmentation** when segmenting markets. This means using the "lifestyle" of the individual. Researchers have found that people with very similar demographic characteristics can be very different from a psychographic or lifestyle perspective.

A person's psychographic or lifestyle profile is based on his or her activities, interests, and opinions, and this often affects the types of product and the particular brands a person buys. For example, a small cereal company used psychographic segmentation and discovered a very serious "health-conscious" segment. It then launched its all-natural and fortified cereal to cater to this segment. Another startup identified a psychographic segment it labeled "night owls" (young, affluent, urban, liberal singles who partied late at night very frequently). It targeted this group with its premium alcohol drink.

Behavioral Segmentation

The major shortfall of the other approaches to segmenting markets (geographic, demographic, and psychographic) is that they all fail to answer the critical question: Why do customers buy? To answer this critical question, entrepreneurs turn to **behavioral segmentation.** In short, behavioral segmentation uncovers the "why" behind customer behavior (benefits sought) and reveals product/service usage (heavy, moderate, and light usage).

It has long been known that customers do not buy products/services but instead buy the "benefits" that particular products/services deliver. In other words, customers desire certain products/services to satisfy their needs and translate those needs into the desired benefits sought from particular products/services. For the entrepreneur, customer needs or benefits sought mean the same thing. Stated differently, the customer may say, "I want product X because it satisfies my particular needs," or "I want this product to deliver this particular benefit."

I believe a behavioral approach to segmentation is the best basis for explaining customer behavior in the marketplace and really gets to the "why" behind customer behavior. This is why I prefer to use behavioral segmentation—specifically, a "benefits sought" or "needs-based" approach to segmentation when I conduct segmentation analysis. I believe that customer needs (benefits sought) "define" segments, and variables such as geographics, demographics, and psychographics help "describe" segments. Once you group customers into segments based on needs (benefits sought), you can then determine if your product/service can meet those needs or deliver those benefits.

Of course, in addition to defining segments based on needs, you have to be able to describe ("identify") and locate these segments in concrete terms. In other words, while your starting point "should be" to focus on the given needs of segments (the benefits sought), you must determine the geographic, demographic, psychographic, and usage characteristics of the customers who make up those segments. In doing so, you answer why customers buy (needs/benefits), who the customers are (demographics, psychographics), and where they are (geographics). Let's look at a simple example of this approach.

The clothes detergent market is a multibillion-dollar industry in the United States. There are numerous competitors offering an array of products intended to cater to specific customer needs (benefits sought) in this market. Let's assume we did some basic marketing research to determine basic segment needs. What we discovered was that there were four distinctive market segments based on customer needs or benefits sought:

- Needs (benefit) group 1: wants/seeks cleaner, brighter clothes and soil removal (brand—Tide)
- Needs (benefit) group 2: wants/seeks clean clothes but at the lowest price (brand—ABC)
- Needs (benefit) group 3: wants/seeks a cold-water wash to save money on hot water (brand—Cheer)
- Needs (benefit) group 4: wants/seeks an all-natural, ecofriendly product to save the planet (brand—Seventh Generation)

The major players in this product category then follow up on this needs-based approach to segmentation by locating where the customers live (geographics) and who they are (demographic/psychographic profiling). In this way, most questions required for effective segmentation are answered.

I say, "most questions" because one important question should also be answered. This is "how much" the customer buys. Thus, in addition to needs/benefits, an important aspect of behavioral-based segmentation is the product/service "usage rate." In reality, while customers have particular needs, some customers simply consume more products or services than other customers. This is an important concept for you, as an entrepreneur, to recognize. Not all customers are of "equal" value; some customers are more valuable than others based on their usage rate or consumption level. For example, in the fast-food business, a "heavy" user is worth five times the revenue as a "light" user. That is why many venture startups wish to focus on what is called the "heavy half" of the market.

In other words, the entrepreneur often elects to focus on the group of customers who represent a disportionate amount of overall consumption. There are, in fact, many markets where a small percentage of customers represent the bulk of consumption for a given product/service category. Take pizza, for example, where less than 25 percent of customers account for more than 75 percent of total pizzas consumed. Or the fluid milk market, where less than 20 percent of households consume more than 60 percent of all fluid milk. As an entrepreneur, you have to know the usage rates of given customers in the market you intend to serve because the actual value of a given segment is largely determined by its usage rate.

A Composite Approach

Using a composite approach, an entrepreneur combines geographic, demographic, psychographic, and behavioral segmentation. One might start with geographic and demographic segmentation to gain insight into the location and sizes of market segments for broad product categories. Or, one might start with behavioral segmentation (e.g., benefits sought) to uncover details behind brand purchase behavior (i.e., why people buy a specific brand within a product category). Then, working backward, the entrepreneur can relate the behavioral-based segments to various psychographic, demographic, and geographic variables to determine the size and locations of the market segments.

The composite approach to segmentation is a difficult but necessary task for you to complete if you wish to have a meaningful basis for segmentation as well as to engage in effective marketing. And, while difficult, it is not impossible to do. Let's look at a good example of a composite approach to segmentation that offered a new startup company keen insight into market segments for wine consumers.

In Figure 5.1, you will see the results of segmentation efforts that led to a successful wine retail specialty shop. Note that the geographic aspect of segmentation is unstated in Figure 5.1. But the company used its segmentation research to pick its trade area and specific site location that would be near the core segment it was seeking: the experiential connoisseur.[3] The segment, while representing only 25 percent of total customers, is, in fact, the most lucrative segment of the market given that its average expenditure is two to three times higher per bottle than the other segments. Moreover, this segment prefers to shop specialty and not supermarket, and thus the new wine store was perfectly aligned with the needs of this segment.

Figure 5.1 Example of Composite Approach to Segmentation—Wine Specialty Store

Segments and Percentage of Market	Demographics	Psychographics	Behavioral
Experiential connoisseurs, 25 percent	Affluent, educated, very knowledgeable wine consumer, $150K+ household income, male/female, ages 35 to 54	Adventurous; quality oriented; has affinity for finer things; seeks or lives a luxury lifestyle; inner and not other directed	Core needs: premium products; extensive variety; knowledgeable salesperson Usage: shops one to two times weekly Other: rarely shops supermarket; influenced by recommendations of salespeople; shopping is social experience; will spend more than planned; spends two to three times more per bottle than other segments
Mainstreeters, 60 percent	Middle income, moderately educated, not very knowledgeable, under $100K household income, male/female, ages 25 to 64	Low-risk shopper; very social; entertains at home; seeks validation from others; a conformer	Core needs: good taste, good value, requires only limited choice Usage: shops one to two times weekly Other: supermarket is first choice, will shop specialty for special occasion buying
Price seekers, 15 percent	Lower income, less educated, least knowledgeable but a frequent drinker, under $75K household income, male/female, ages 25 to 64	Present-day orientation; driven by habit; stick to what they know and like	Core needs: best price Usage: shops one time per week Other: supermarket and club shopper, will bargain hunt at specialty but only on rare occasions

One expert tells us that the segmentation process is extremely important for the aspiring entrepreneur, and it is a process that must be done with great care. Performed correctly, segmentation can provide vital insights as to which segments to initially focus on and which ones might offer opportunities for venture growth in the future. Check out the Entrepreneurial Marketing Spotlight.

Selecting Target Segments

There is an old axiom in entrepreneurship that suggests that those who properly select target segments (target markets) are more likely to be successful than those who do not. In fact, there is also an old saying in entrepreneurship that says, "You cannot chase too many rabbits—focus on catching one." Thus, you must take great care in choosing your target segments (targer markets). If you pick too narrow a target segment, you may fail to reach the volume of sales and profit needed to support your venture. If you select too broadly, you may spread your marketing efforts too thin and incur greater expenses, which may offset the increased sales and profits. Therefore, successful entrepreneurs use several criteria to select their target segments (target markets):[4]

- *Size of segment:* The estimated size of a segment is important in determining whether it is worth pursuing.
- *Expected growth:* Although the size of a segment may be small now, perhaps it is growing significantly or expected to grow in the future.
- *Competitive position:* Is there a lot of competition in the segment now, or is there likely to be in the future? The less the competition, the more attractive a segment might be.
- *Cost of reaching a segment:* If a segment cannot be reached cost-effectively, it probably should not be pursued.
- *Compatibility with your venture's objectives and resources:* Is the segment compatible with your venture's objectives and resources? Do you want to serve this particular segment? If so, can you achieve your venture's objectives by doing so?

After evaluating the different segments, you must make a selection decision. You could decide to choose to market to all target segments, some of the target segments, or just one segment. This is referred to as undifferentiated marketing, differentiated marketing, and concentrated marketing, respectively.

Entrepreneurial Marketing Spotlight

Marc Meyer, founder of the Institute for Enterprise Growth, argues that segmentation is fundamentally important for entrepreneurs. With finite resources, a new venture cannot be all things to all people. Done correctly, segmentation succinctly unveils different types of potential customers for a new venture's products or services. Moreover, it uncovers the segments the venture should focus on given the unique needs of specific segments and the venture's abilities to meet the needs of those segments.

Meyer suggests that it is very important for entrepreneurs to think expansively at first but to then focus their efforts for their initial products and services. Imagine an initial market segmentation framework for a new social networking company, for example, that has for its segmentation dimensions age arrayed across the top of a grid and uses for social networking along the side of the grid. The top axis includes kids, teens, millennials, Gen Ys, Gen Xs, baby boomers, and so on. The side axis might include social networking uses for nondirected chat, school work, finding a job, sports activities, or political discussion. Seeing the entire landscape helps the entrepreneur think through his or her market possibilities. However, then the entrepreneur must decide where to focus first, the intersection between age, and the social networking application in which to succeed first. Segmentation becomes the driver of focus—perhaps the most important characteristic of any new firm. All entrepreneurial effort becomes focused on understanding a specific segment and providing world-class solutions for customers in that segment. Then, once the entrepreneur has achieved success in the target market segment, he or she can expand to adjacent applications. In this way, segmentation transforms itself from an instrument for initially establishing the startup focus to one of planning the next stage of venture growth.

Importantly, Meyer argues that segmentation is not a onetime exercise for the entrepreneur. Market segments are always changing. New customer groups emerge over time, and existing customer groups can change their buying and usage behaviors. Accordingly, the entrepreneur must continue to revisit his or her initial segmentation schema and continue to look for new opportunities for growth.[5]

You may decide not to distinguish between any segments and go after the market as a whole using one marketing mix targeted to all segments. This is **undifferentiated marketing.** You assume that there are more commonalities among the segments than there are differences, and thus you assume the same marketing mix will appeal to all segments.

Certainly, undifferentiated marketing can, in theory, keep your marketing costs down. But many successful entrepreneurs question the wisdom of undifferentiated marketing, sometimes called *mass marketing*. Remember, segmentation is done because we believe customers are "different," and distinctive differences between customers lead to different needs and behaviors. Thus, developing one product or service for all customers actually runs counter to the notion of segmentation. Moreover, you may leave yourself vulnerable to competitors who may seek to better serve certain customers who might feel ignored or overlooked by your undifferentiated approach.

A **differentiated marketing** approach means the entrepreneur will target more than one segment and will design specific marketing mixes for each segment. In some cases, you might develop unique products or services for each segment. In other cases, a common product or service might be used, but you will use different distribution or marketing communications strategies. With differentiated marketing, you are accounting for the differences between segments and are attempting to cater to those differences.

A **concentrated marketing** approach is perhaps the most common strategy used by venture startups. In this case, you decide to select just one segment and specifically tailor the elements of your marketing mix to this segment. This strategy is sometimes called a niche strategy. With a niche strategy, the entrepreneur is seeking a smaller (but still profitable) segment and will serve this segment creatively and innovatively to gain a large share of the segment. In fact, some entrepreneurs speak of "owning" a niche segment. A concentrated or niche strategy is very appropriate for a startup with limited resources, and it allows the business to get a foothold in the market. Moreover, by providing special attention to a niche segment, the entrepreneur can often achieve a strong market position by gaining the loyalty of customers in the segment. However, this strategy has a risk in that a change in demand by the segment can cause the venture's sales to plummet.

Rapid advances in technology are now enabling entrepreneurial firms that are not really concentrated marketers to appear as concentrated marketers. The Internet and flexible manufacturing and marketing processes have made "mass customization" possible, that is, tailoring products or services to the needs and tastes of individual customers on a high-volume scale. On the other hand, the same technology is also enabling entrepreneurs who want to be concentrated marketers to become "ultracustomizers." In this case, the entrepreneur can cater to each individual customer as a segment of one. Ultracustomizers can offer customers very personalized vacations, highly individualized clothing designs, and even individualized news information. One example of an ultracustomizer is By Terry, a boutique that uses the DNA of customers to create personalized lipstick for each customer. But this will cost the customer about $1,200![6]

Several factors influence the type of market segmentation strategy you should select.[7] One is market sensitivity. If customers are not particularly sensitive to product or service differences, then an undifferentiated approach would be appropriate. But if there are several segments with distinctive differences between them, a differentiated or concentrated approach is a better choice. Product variability is another factor to consider. Undifferentiated marketing may be more appropriate for commodity-based products (e.g., cement, oranges). But products that can be modified, such as electronics, automobiles, or clothes, lend themselves to differentiated or concentrated approaches.

Product life cycle is another factor to consider. If the product or service is new, a concentrated approach might be best. In the later stages of the product life cycle, differentiated marketing becomes more appropriate. Venture size and venture resources are also a consideration. A small startup with limited resources should probably use concentrated marketing. Finally, the competitors' strategies are also a consideration. If competitors are using undifferentiated marketing, your best bet is to use differentiated or concentrated marketing. If there are many competitors, then concentrated marketing is appropriate.

Positioning

The final step in the STP process is **positioning.** After segments have been analyzed and target segments (target markets) selected, you must now determine how to position your offering to the target segments. Positioning is the place the product or service will occupy in the hearts or minds of the customers in relation to your competitors.

Some consider positioning as creating your "value proposition" or as your "marketing promise" to the customer. It is critical to link the "benefits sought" by the target segment to your positioning strategy. In other words, you must connect your intended position to the unique desired benefits of the customer.

You must also distinguish your product or service from competitive offerings so the customer sees the value in purchasing it over others available. If your product or service is perceived to be the same as another on the market, the customer has no real reason to buy it. It is also critical that your entire marketing effort (including all elements of the marketing mix) be built to support the chosen positioning. For example, if you are positioning your product as a high-quality offering, your price should be premium and distributed in an exclusive manner.

There are two basic approaches to positioning: head-to-head in direct competition with other products/services or avoiding direct competition through differentiation. With head-to-head positioning, you will be competing directly with competitors offering similar products/services to the same target market. With differentiation positioning, you are avoiding direct competition and stressing the "uniqueness" of your product/ service. This typically involves positioning your product or services on a special or unique feature or benefit. For example, Tom's of Maine entered the toothpaste category, stressing its unique "all-natural" toothpaste.

There are numerous options you can consider with regard to differentiation, depending on the benefits your target segment is seeking. For example, if "lowest price" is the benefit sought, then you can decide to compete on price. Other options could include "best quality," "most convenient," or "best customer service." More and more often, however, entrepreneurial startups are using a "hybrid positioning" strategy. That is, they are not competing on a single dimension but rather on multiple dimensions (e.g., best quality and most convenient). This is becoming popular since many competitors come along and attempt to take over your position (called repositioning by the competition) by matching the one benefit you offer. Having a hybrid positioning strategy makes it more difficult for the competitors to dislodge you and to take your space.

Perceptual Mapping

The key to effective positioning is understanding the perceptions customers have of product categories and brands within those categories. To determine the right position for your product/service (brand), you must have the following information:

1. The purchase criteria deemed important by the customers (or segments of customers) when selecting products/services

2. Customer ratings of existing brands on those criteria

3. What an "ideal" brand would offer

From this information, you can construct a **perceptual map,** a means of displaying customer perceptions of alternative products/brands. The maps display the relative ratings/performance of competing products on key criteria. The maps provide a "visual awakening" of the space occupied by the various brands and if there is any particular valuable space available for you to occupy. For example, a young entrepreneur developed a "new health bar" as a result of perceptual mapping (see Figure 5.2).[8]

Figure 5.2   Perceptual Map: Health Bar Market

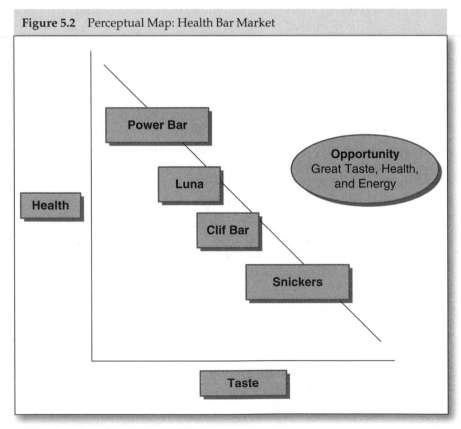

SOURCE: Used with permission of Marc Meyer.

He found the customers wanted health and taste and could place existing brands on a perceptual map depending on how well the brands measured on these important criteria. For example, PowerBar scored well on health but not on taste. Snickers scored well on taste but not so well on health. However, he also asked what an "ideal" brand would offer and discovered that some customers wanted something more in a health bar besides health and taste. Specifically, he found that one segment also wanted "an energy boost" as well. His opportunity was to provide a great tasting, healthy, and energy-boosting bar!

It is also important for you to remember these fundamentally important caveats about positioning. First, your positioning should be distinctive and consistent. Second, your positioning must set off your product/brand from the competitors. Third, positioning is not a onetime exercise. Customer needs change, and this changes how products are perceived and valued. Plus, competitors also change and evolve. Both of these changes necessitate a monitoring of your positioning to determine its meaningfulness to the customers and its sustainability compared to competitors.

Finally, it is extremely important to recognize that positioning can involve "real" differences or "perceived" differences between products/brands. In fact, your product may not have any real differences compared to competitors, but you can still create a perception of difference. For example, most beer customers cannot objectively perceive differences between the tastes of various beers. In fact, in blind taste tests, many brand-loyal beer drinkers could not pick out their own beer brand based on taste. So, many entrepreneurial microbrews go to great lengths to create a perception of difference between their brands and their competitors. So, while it would be nice to have a product or service that is objectively evaluated by the customer as being better than the competitors, it is possible to build a venture based on how well you can get the customer to subjectively perceive your product as being better. We will discuss this notion more completely when we discuss branding in Chapter 7.

Key Takeaways

- The proper application of the STP process (segmenting, targeting, positioning) can mean the difference between venture success and failure.

- The true test of the segmentation process is whether it leads to effective marketing.
- The most important question you must answer during the segmentation process is "why" customers buy. This is what creates differences between segments.
- A composite approach to segmentation is optimal. It combines geographics, demographics, psychographics, and behavioral dimensions of the market.
- It is unlikely that you will be able to serve every segment in a given market, so you must pick your target segment(s)—target markets carefully.
- Effectively positioning is the final step in the STP process. You can do this effectively through the use of perceptual mapping.
- Positioning can be based on competing on real or perceived differences between brands.

Entrepreneurial Exercise

Using the composite approach to segmentation discussed in this chapter (also see Figure 5.1), map out a segmentation scheme for the market in which you intend to compete. What insight does it provide? Is there a segment (or segments) that provides an opportunity upon which to build your venture? Why?

Key Terms

STP   84
Market segmentation   84
Geographic segmentation   85
Demographic segmentation   85
Psychographic segmentation   86
Behavioral segmentation   87

Undifferentiated marketing   92
Differentiated marketing   93
Concentrated marketing   93
Positioning   94
Perceptual map   96

Notes

1. This section is based on Frederick G. Crane, Roger Kerin, Steve Hartley, and William Rudelius, *Marketing*, 7th Canadian ed. (Toronto: McGraw-Hill Ryerson, 2008).

2. Frederick G. Crane, E. Stephen Grant, and Steven W. Hartley, *Marketing: Canadian Insights and Applications* (Toronto: McGraw-Hill Ryerson, 1997).

3. Based on proprietary research conducted by QMA Group. Used with permission.

4. Crane et al., *Marketing: Canadian Insights and Applications.*

5. Based on an interview with Marc H. Meyer, April 16, 2009.

6. Liz Torlee, "Not My News," *Marketing,* November 28, 2005, 29–32.

7. Crane et al., *Marketing: Canadian Insights and Applications.*

8. Modified from an example provided by Marc H. Meyer, with permission. Also see Marc H. Meyer, *Fast Path to Corporate Growth* (New York: Oxford University Press, 2007).

Six

Developing New Products and Services

A s we discussed in Chapter 2, there is often a debate about what an entrepreneurial startup needs to be successful: a superior product or service or a better business model. Frankly, I believe that a new venture needs both. A superior product or service housed within a venture with a poor business model is not likely to be successful. Conversely, a venture with a good business model but lacking a valuable product or service (as perceived by the customer) is also just as likely to fail. While we have already discussed the central elements of what constitutes a successful business model, we must now focus on the process of developing viable new products and services. It is not an easy process, and in most cases, entrepreneurs are more likely to experience new product or service failure than they are success. The goal of this chapter is to outline a process that is likely to improve your chances of success. One of the key aspects of the process discussed in this chapter is a reliance on a customer-centered approach to new product or service development.

Types of New Products

There are numerous ways to define and categorize **new products.** For example, you could compare the new product with existing products to

101

determine if it is functionally different from what is currently available. In many cases, most so-called new products are modifications or enhancements of existing products. Or, some existing ventures might simply add new products to its current offerings and would consider these offerings as "new." But I argue that the best way to view new products is from the customer's perspective. In other words, examine how "disruptive" the new product is with regard to existing customer consumption patterns. Using this perspective, there are really only three types of new products:[1]

1. **Continuous innovations.** These are new products that will have little, if any, disruptive influence on existing consumption patterns. These new products generally involve minor product modifications (e.g., a new flavor, a new package) or simple product line extensions (e.g., light beer). Customers are already familiar with the basic product category and require little education regarding the new offering. In other words, there is an existing ritual and your goal is to have customers embrace your solution to that ritual.

2. **Dynamically continuous innovations.** These new products will have some disruptive effect but still do not alter existing buying patterns completely. They may be new products but do not involve major technological break-throughs or advances. For example, a new electric (or battery-powered) toothbrush that replaced a regular toothbrush did not necessarily completely change the teeth-brushing behavior of the customer but may have altered the way teeth are brushed. In other words, teeth-brushing is a well-established ritual but the general solution to complete the ritual was a regular toothbrush. The introduction of electric or battery-powered tooth-brushes requires a tweak in the ritual and new learning.

3. **Discontinuous innovations.** These are new products that involve major technological breakthroughs that create fundamental changes in consumer consumption patterns. And, in effect, they can create new markets. When the automobile was first introduced, it changed how we traveled. When the personal computer was introduced, it changed how we lived and worked. With discontinuous innovations, the customers have to be educated about the product in terms of how they will benefit from it and how to use it. This is a classic case of introducing a new ritual unknown to the customer and encouraging them to incorporate this new ritual into their lives.

The reality is that most new ventures are built around new products that are either continuous innovations or dynamically continuous innovations. Very few ventures are built upon discontinuous innovations or new-to-world breakthroughs. In fact, some research indicates that about 80 percent of new products are simple continuous innovations, about 20 percent are minor innovations (dynamically continuous), and less than 1 percent of new products are truly discontinuous innovations.

So, as we pointed out in earlier chapters, while "new market creation" can be the path to long-term sustainable growth for your venture, the truth is that most entrepreneurs build their ventures around continuous or dynamically continuously innovations and thus have to compete against existing alternatives that customers are well aware of. Therefore, you must really focus on how to convince the customer to embrace your new offering in light of the fact that the customer has an established consumption pattern (or current rituals as we discussed in Chapter 4). This is not the case with discontinuous innovation, where your task is to convince the customer to create an entire new consumption pattern with a completely unknown product—a new ritual altogether. Later in this chapter, you will see how the "newness" of a product affects the adoption and diffusion of products.

Types of New Services

I have argued for many years that creating and delivering **new services** is much more difficult than creating new tangible products. Furthermore, new services differ from product innovations in several important ways. First, for labor-intensive, interactive services, the actual providers (the service delivery staff) are part of the customer experience and thus are part of the innovation. Second, many services require the physical presence of the customer, which demands local decentralized production of the service. Third, new services usually do not have a tangible product to carry a brand name. The new service development process is also difficult to map out for the service venture and is often difficult for the service customer to observe.

Services marketing experts generally agree that there is a hierarchy of new service categories that is somewhat similar to the continuous, dynamically continuous, and discontinuous innovation continuum discussed previously for physical products. Several categories of new services in this hierarchy range from major service innovations to basic service improvements:[2]

1. Major service innovations are entirely new concepts (discontinuous innovations) for markets that have not been defined previously. In other words, these new services create "new markets." For example, FedEx's overnight

express delivery, CNN's 24/7 global news service, and eBay's online auction services would be examples of major service innovations.

2. Major "process" innovations consist of new processes (new ways) to deliver existing services so that the customer receives new value. An example would be a new "virtual" university that offers a totally new online MBA program where you never have to visit the campus to complete your degree and can complete it cheaper and in a shorter length of time.

3. Service-line extensions are additions to existing lines of services. For example, one of my former students came up with the idea to offer "pet health insurance," which he added to his existing insurance business.

4. Supplementary service innovations take the form of adding new elements to the core service or improving existing supplementary services that accompany the core service. For example, one smart entrepreneur saw an opportunity to work with his local hospital to provide valet parking for patients and their families. He entered into a contract with the hospital to provide this service and created a successful venture.

5. Basic service improvements (continuous innovations) are the most common type of new service innovation. This involves modest changes in the performance of an existing service. For example, you might observe and talk with customers eating at a fast-food restaurant and discover they would like to get in and out of the restaurant quicker. Thus, you decide that your new fast-food restaurant will really focus on "fast," where serving your customers more quickly than the competitors will be your value proposition.

Most new service-based ventures, like their counterpart product-based ventures, focus on creating only incremental improvements (continuous innovation) as the cornerstone of their business. But the few new service ventures that focus on breakthrough or truly discontinuous innovations can create entirely new markets or dramatically reshape existing markets so that they can enjoy the benefits of unforeseen profits for a considerable length of time. Can you say Google?

Characteristics of Successful New Products and Services

In Chapter 2, we outlined some essential criteria that should be used to assess the "marketing opportunity" for your venture. Some of those criteria deal directly with the product or service your venture will be marketing. For example, does the product or service offer significant value to the customer? Is the product or service well differentiated from competitors' offerings? Does the customer have a need for the product or service? And, importantly, does consumer feedback confirm there is demand for the product or service? But in addition to these criteria, you should also consider the following characteristics that are inherently part of successful new products or services:[3]

1. *Superior advantage.* The customer should "perceive" the product or service to be superior to the existing alternatives. This superiority can be real or perceived. This advantage can be based on a better price or outstanding performance (nonprice) that the customer is prepared to pay for. Without this clear superiority, the product or service is not likely to be successful.

2. *Compatibility.* A product or service that is aligned with the values, attitudes, and norms of customers is more likely to succeed than one that is incompatible.

3. *Simplicity.* If the product or service is difficult to understand and use, it is likely to fail. Products or services with complex instructions or requiring skill to use tend to be rejected more than those with simple instructions or those needing little skill to operate.

4. *Observability.* If the product or service's innovative characteristics can be easily observed by the customer and/or easily communicated to the customer, the product or service is more likely to be successful.

5. *Trialability.* A new product or service that can be purchased on a trial basis (in small amounts or for a limited time) is more likely to be successful than one that cannot be tried before actual purchase. Most consumers want to try before they buy so free-sampling or offering small trial package sizes or low introductory pricing can encourage trialability.

6. *Low perceived risk.* A new product or service that is perceived as being a low-risk purchase is more likely to succeed than a product or service with high perceived risk. Warranties and guarantees are good ways to reduce perceived risk.

7. *Intellectual-property protection.* While this characteristic may not be important from a customer perspective, good products or services usually have an intellectual-property component (patent, trademark, copyright) that offers you a possible competitive advantage or protection from encroachment by competitors.

Seth Godin, author, speaker, and founder of several successful companies, believes a successful new product must also possess another characteristic: it must be a "purple cow." He explains this in the Entrepreneurial Marketing Spotlight.

Entrepreneurial Marketing Spotlight

Seth Godin is an entrepreneur and the author of a book called *Purple Cow.* He suggests that the checklist of tired Ps (promotion, pricing, etc.) marketers have used for decades to create successful products is not working anymore. He argues that an exceptionally important P that has to be put in place is the purple cow.

Seth says, "Cows, after you've seen one or two or ten, are boring. A purple cow, though . . . now that would be something." A purple cow is something phenomenal, something counterintuitive, exciting, and flat-out unbelievable. Every day, he suggests, consumers come face-to-face with a lot of boring products—a lot of brown cows—but if they saw a purple cow, they would not soon forget it.

He argues that all too often, we build boring products and hope that marketing can make them exciting. But a purple cow has that excitement inherently built into the product. And it is something truly noticeable to the customer. A purple cow is actually worth marketing in the first place.

He advocates that entrepreneurs should focus on creating "remarkable" purple cows. Furthermore, Seth suggests that purple cows are rare because people are afraid to stand out. This actually makes your job easier. If everyone else is petrified to build a "purple cow," you can be remarkable with even less effort. His simple logic rings true: If successful new products are the ones that stand out, and most people desire not to stand out, therein lies your opportunity. In a crowded marketplace, if you try to fit in, you are likely to fail. That is why building a purple cow is not as risky as playing it safe; in fact, being boring can be the most risky strategy of all.[4]

The New Product/Service Process

Research reveals that more than 90 percent of new products introduced in America annually do not succeed in the long run. Experts suggest that preventing new product/service failure is embarrassingly simple. First, find out what customers need and want. Second, produce what they need and want, and do not produce what they do not need or want.[5] This sounds simple but is much more difficult to do in reality. But if you embrace a rigorous, customer-centered **new product/service process,** you can improve your chances of success. The process consists of six stages: idea generation, screening and evaluation, business analysis, development, market testing, and launch.

Idea Generation

Idea generation is typically the most difficult stage of the new product/service process. At this stage, you develop a pool of ideas/ concepts as possible candidates for new products or services. One of the most frequent questions asked about this stage is, "Where do good ideas come from?" Well, there are a variety of sources for new ideas. But first, let me point out the myth of serendipity or the flash of brilliance. While it can happen that a great idea can be generated in this manner, it is actually a rarity. Therefore, you must be mindful that the best ideas are generated in an "information-rich" environment, and typically this means immersing yourself in the marketplace.

In earlier chapters, we pointed out the importance of environmental scanning and the use of secondary data as ways to uncover possible venture opportunities. This holds true at the new product or new service level. With environmental scanning, for example, an important idea or concept can emerge. This is called *pattern recognition.* In this case, you recognize a situation that is recurrent, and from this recurrence, a novel idea may emerge. For example, the founders of Crate & Barrel developed their business concept as a result of their travels in Europe, where they noticed that upscale household kitchen products were being sold in unique designs and colors in multiple fine shops. They felt that housing all these offerings under one roof would work in America, and it clearly did.

In addition to pattern recognition, some experts suggest that one of your best sources of new ideas may come from potential customers. Observing and talking with customers can often lead to ideas that will be deemed valuable to the customer. Remember the caveat earlier in this chapter: Find out what customers need and want. And while many aspiring entrepreneurs use "voice of the customer" to validate their intended venture concept and/or new products/services, the smart entrepreneur actually uses customers' input from the onset to generate possible ideas that can be converted into products or services that would be deemed valuable by the customer.

There is one group of customers that you should focus on during the idea generation stage. These customers are called "lead users"—a small group of potential product or service users who desire new products or services before the general market recognizes this need. These lead users can provide valuable information and assistance very early in the process, helping you better shape the nature and scope of what should be created for the market. These lead users can collaborate or coparticipate with you to ensure you develop new products or services that will really meet customer needs and wants. These lead users are innovators or early adopters of new products or services, and we will discuss them later in the chapter when we cover the adoption and diffusion process for new products/services.

Another excellent source of ideas is uncovering customer frustration or complaints about existing products or services. Remember, if customers are ideally happy with the products and services they currently consume, if is unlikely you will be able to attract them to your business. Fortunately for you, it is highly likely there will be customers out there who are currently unhappy with available products or services. What you need to do is unveil the reasons for such dissatisfaction and determine exactly what you have to do to create and keep a happy customer. Customer complaints may simply reveal that they want something a little cheaper, a little better, a little faster, or a little healthier. For example, customer research revealed that some fast-food customers wanted a healthier offering, and from that research, Panera was born.

Another major source of new product or services ideas is research and development (R&D). Sadly, in many cases, the "development" component often trumps the "research" component of R&D. In other words, many entrepreneurs get caught up in the excitement of developing products or services without really doing a good job researching what should be developed. To be successful, the R&D has to be fueled with "information" from the market and from the consumer. However, the one exception to this is new-to-world breakthroughs, where customer input or "voice of consumer" is rarely able to inform and instruct the new product/service process. Still, since more than 90 percent of all new products and services are not new to the world, the R&D process must be customer centered.

Other sources of ideas can come from suppliers and channel members working in the business arena in which you wish to compete. The competition also represents a source of ideas. Finally, brainstorming can also be used to generate ideas. You can generate your own ideas through this process or work with others presenting and reacting to new product/ service suggestions. Information technology also now allows for brainstorming (electronic brainstorming) to occur very easily by breaking down time and space barriers.

Screening and Evaluation

The objective of **screening and evaluation** of the new product/service process is to effectively "kill" bad ideas quickly and eliminate them from further consideration. This can be done through internal and/or external approaches. Internally, some form of "checklist" procedure is developed to screen and evaluate the ideas. Ideas not meeting the criteria on the checklist are screened out. Typically, the checklist criteria include the characteristics inherent in successful new products/services discussed previously in this chapter. It might also include some of the criteria used in evaluating the venture opportunity discussed in Chapter 2. Fundamentally, the checklist should include whether the product/service has a superior advantage over competing alternatives, delivers value to the customer, has consumer demand, and can be profitable.

Using an external approach, the entrepreneur goes into the market to solicit feedback from target customers. A common external approach is the use of a concept test where customers will respond to the product/service idea presented to them. Sometimes the customer is given a written description of the idea (what it is and what it does), or the test may include a mockup to accompany the written description. The customers are asked a series of questions about the idea/concept, including their perception of the product/service, their level of interest in the product/service, and the likelihood they would buy it. Smart entrepreneurs would also ask the customers how they might improve the idea/concept. Moreover, the entrepreneur might also use a conjoint approach to present the concept, where the product/service would have varying levels of product attributes and the customer is asked to pick the "ideal" product/service concept.

Business Analysis

Ideas/concepts that survive the screening and evaluation stage of the process then proceed to the **business analysis** stage. Here the finalized concept undergoes detailed product, marketing, and financial scrutiny. With the product/service features now defined, you must examine the costs to develop and market the product/service, forecast demand and revenue, and determine the product/service's profitability. Having customers' feedback, including their likelihood of purchase, is really beneficial at this stage because it provides critical input for developing your financial projections, particularly your revenue potential for the product/service.

Development

New product/service concepts that survive the business analysis stage of the process can now proceed to actual **development.** In other words, the idea/concept comes to life and typically is turned into a prototype. If you have followed a customer-centered approach to the new product/service process, it should be relatively easy to generate the proper design for the new product/service. If you are creating a physical product, you will test it to determine if it meets the standards set for it. You may even have the customer test the prototype to see how it works in a real-life situation. If it is a service concept, you will map out the process of creating and delivering the service, including allowing the customer to "beta test" the service to ensure it works. Also at this stage, the product/service name, branding, and marketing mix elements are developed.

Market Testing

At this stage, the entrepreneur takes the product/service to market to expose the target customer to the concept under realistic purchase conditions to determine if the product/service will be bought. **Market testing** often provides a good surrogate indication of how the product will be received in the overall marketplace when fully launched. At the market testing stage, the entrepreneur still has an opportunity to further refine and retest the concept again.

Typically, market testing involves offering the product/service for purchase on a limited basis in a well-defined area. In the test market, the entrepreneur can gain an indication of potential sales as well as check elements of the marketing mix such as price, promotion, and channel approaches. However, market testing can be time consuming and expensive. So, many entrepreneurs opt to engage in *simulated market testing*. This approach simulates a full-scale market test but in a very limited way. In general, the simulations are run in shopping malls, where target customers are exposed to the new product/service and are often given money to buy either the new product/service or the competitors' offering in a real or simulated purchase environment. This helps the entrepreneur gauge the customer response to the new product/service.

With new information technology, many entrepreneurs also turn to virtual reality market testing. The entrepreneurs create virtual markets on the Internet and ask target customers to participate in these markets. The goal is to determine how well the new products/services perform in those markets. Virtual reality market testing is less expensive and very flexible, and it can radically reduce time to market compared to the real thing.

However, some entrepreneurs elect not to do market testing at all. First, some are concerned about "unveiling" what they are doing to their competitors. Second, entrepreneurs who are marketing intangible services often find it difficult to use market testing. Third, entrepreneurs who market expensive, physical products (e.g., automobiles or personal jet aircraft) would find market testing impractical.

Launch

If all goes well in the preceding stages of the new product/service process, the entrepreneur is ready to **launch** his or her new product/service. This means rolling out the new product/service to the market on a full commercial scale. New products/services launched using a customer-centered process will have a higher likelihood of success than those that have not followed such a process. Still, this is the most costly stage of the new product/service process. Therefore, some entrepreneurs will choose to launch using regional rollouts, introducing the new product/service sequentially into particular geographic areas to minimize costs and to allow proper ramp up in production and marketing.

An important concept to keep in mind is the imperative of moving quickly from idea generation to launch. In fact, time to market has been found to be highly correlated with new product/service success. But while speed is important, so is the quality of execution of the launch, including a good product/service, product/service availability, channel support, and quality of promotion. And while some entrepreneurs wish to obtain first-mover advantage (being the first to launch), others elect to engain later entry. The costs to obtain first-mover advantage, including informing the market about the new product/service, can sometimes be high. Thus, some entrepreneurs elect for later entry after a competitor has incurred such costs.

Adoption and Diffusion of New Products and Services

New products and services cannot be successful unless enough customers are prepared to purchase them. The acceptance and continued use of a new product/service by an individual is called **adoption.** The five basic stages of the adoption process are (1) awareness, (2) interest, (3) evaluation, (4) trial, and (5) adoption or rejection.

As we have discussed in previous chapters, awareness of a new product/service is critical; without it, no adoption can occur. At this stage, the potential customer becomes aware of the new product/service but generally will lack information about the value or benefits it can offer. At this stage of the process, it is vital that the entrepreneur emphasize brand awareness and get the product into distribution channels. Repetition of messages, focusing on brand name, packaging, and where the product can be obtained, is fundamental.

If the customer becomes interested in the new product/service, he or she will gather information about the product. The entrepreneur's job at this stage is to relate the new product/service to the needs of the customer through proper brand positioning.

The customer will then commence a mental trial or examination of the new product/service. During the evaluation stage, the customer will compare the new product/service with available alternatives. Thus, at this stage, the entrepreneur must focus on building the most appropriate brand image for the new product/service and stress why it is different from the alternatives.

The customer may try or experiment with the new product/service before buying it. The entrepreneur must make it easy for the customer to try the product/service. In this case, sampling, trial packages, and product demonstrations are appropriate strategies for the entrepreneur to deploy.

Finally, a decision is made by the customer to adopt or reject the new product/service. The continued use of the new product/service will depend largely on the postpurchase evaluation of the product/service. If the new product/service has satisfied the customer's needs, then acceptance of the product/service is likely. The entrepreneur can help make this happen by making the right promise to the customer and making sure to deliver on that promise. The entrepreneur can also communicate with customers to reassure them that they have made the correct choice.

Entrepreneurs should also recognize that research reveals that the type of information used by the customer in the adoption process may vary as he or she moves through the different stages. For example, in the early stages of the adoption process, mass media are often more effective in generating broad awareness quickly, whereas in the later stages, personal sources of information appear to be more important in the adoption process.

It is also important to point out that customers do not go through the adoption process at the same speed. Some customers will adopt a new product/service more quickly than will others. Thus, there will be various adopter categories since some customers accept new products/services earlier or later than do others. As an entrepreneur, you must become aware of the concept of new product/service **diffusion.** This refers to the manner in which customers accept new products/services and the speed of new product/service adoption by various customer groups. In other words, diffusion is all about how new products/services diffuse (spread) over time across or among particular adopter groups. Entrepreneurs must understand who will be the first and who will be the last to adopt the new product/service.

Experts have classified five categories of adopters based on time of adoption: innovators, early adopters, early majority, late majority, and laggards (see Figure 6.1).[6] *Innovators* (representing less than 3 percent of the total market) are the first to try new products/services. They are risk takers and tend to have higher incomes and education than noninnovators. Innovators tend not to rely on group norms when making purchases. The *early adopters* (about 14 percent of the total market) are next to purchase the new product/service. Early adopters are socially integrated and are likely to be "opinion leaders." The early adopters tend to be used by later adopters as sources of information and advice about the new product/service.

As an entrepreneur, you must be aware that adoption by innovators and early adopters is critical if your new product/service is to be successful. But diffusion of new products/services can often "stall" out at the innovator and/or early adopter categories and not proceed to later adopter categories. Sometimes this is referred to as a failure to "cross the chasm."[7] In other words, there is a chasm between the innovators/early adopters (who represent a small part of the market) and later adopters, which might prevent the wider diffusion of a new product/service. It is suggested that this occurs because innovators/early adopters are

Figure 6.1   Adopter Categories

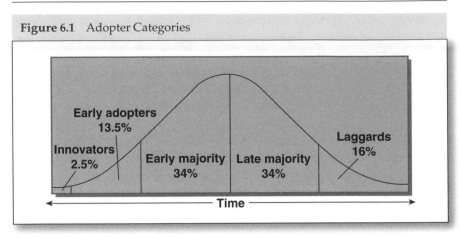

SOURCE: Based on Everett M. Rogers, *Diffusion of Innovations* (New York: Free Press, 1962).

"different" and have different needs and expectations compared to later adopters. If your new product/service does not cross the chasm, it is likely the new product/service will fail since the later adopters represent the bulk of the total market, and without their adoption of the product/ service, your venture is unlikely to generate the revenue required to remain profitable. Some suggest that the "crossing the chasm" notion is only relevant to discontinuous innovations and does not apply to continuous or dynamically continuous innovations.[8] But in my experience, this chasm can be relevant for all categories of innovation. I will suggest strategies for crossing the chasm later in this chapter.

If the product is adopted by the early adopters, the next group to purchase is the *early majority* (about 34 percent of the total market). This group tends to be risk averse compared to innovators and early adopters. Members of this group take more time to consider the new product/ service and tend to use more information and evaluate the innovation more cautiously. However, they tend to enjoy the status of being the first in their peer group to purchase the new product/service and can "legitimize" the new product/service for later adopters.

The *late majority* (about 34 percent of the total market) are individuals who tend to be skeptics and will adopt the new product/service after the early majority has done so and only when the product/service is widely popular and the risk associated with purchasing is considered minimal. This group tends to adopt based on social pressure (e.g., keep up with the

Joneses) but has limited means so they will buy only when the product/service has become more affordable.

Finally, *laggards* (about 16 percent of the total market) are the last group to adopt a new product/service. They embrace the new product/service only reluctantly since they are often suspicious of new products/services. Typically, they are forced to make a purchase because the new product/service supersedes or replaces existing products or services. Laggards also tend to have the lowest socioeconomic background of the adopter groups.

However, as an entrepreneur, you should recognize one caveat about the categories of adopters. In theory, it is suggested that everyone will, sooner or later, become an adopter of a new product/service. But in practice, this is not always the case. In fact, it is possible that a sizable segment of the market may never adopt a particular new product/service. Thus, when it comes to forecasting demand, many entrepreneurs assume a 100 percent diffusion rate of their new product/service (meaning everyone will adopt). This can be very problematic, especially if revenue projections are based on complete diffusion. Many ventures have missed their target projections based on this assumption. In fact, many entrepreneurs now use a simpler three-part classification of adopters: innovators (innovators and early adopters), later adopters (early majority, late majority, and laggards), and nonadopters. For example, while you might have an ATM bank card, more than 20 percent of Americans do not! This is a significant percentage of nonadopters, which means complete diffusion has not occurred.[9]

By definition, diffusion involves the adoption process (where the individual moves from awareness of a new product/service to adopting/rejecting it), but diffusion has more to do with how new products/services "spread" across or among groups of customers over time. In general, an entrepreneur wants the largest adoption rate in the shortest period of time (fast diffusion). But a variety of factors also affect how well a new product/service will diffuse and the speed of its diffusion. Some of these factors are product/service based. For example, a new product/service with a clear superior advantage over existing alternatives tends to diffuse faster. But in addition to product/service-based factors, some other variables affect the speed and how well a new product/service diffuses. For example, competitive intensity plays a role. Aggressive pricing, extensive distribution, and heavy investment in promotion common in competitive environments will tend to lead to rapid diffusion. Product/service standardization is another factor to consider. If products/services are standardized, customers perceive lower risk, and diffusion is encouraged. Also, the greater the amount of information disseminated to the customer about the product/service, the more likely there is to be rapid and extensive diffusion. For example, heavy spending on advertising can create broad awareness as well as encourage word of mouth, which can enhance diffusion. A high degree of vertical integration will also help diffusion of new products/services. For example, close relationships between channel members encourage product/service coordination and information flow, thus assisting the diffusion process. Finally, a greater commitment to R&D (getting the product/service right in the first place) will encourage diffusion, as will a company's commitment to promotion and distribution support.

Another strategy to enhance diffusion and to "overcome" the chasm is to focus on one group of adopters at one time. In other words, target very specifically one user group as a base and use this base for marketing to the next group. For example, zero in on innovators first and use the innovators to help you diffuse the new product/service. Making the product "popular" with this one group will create a bandwagon effect and induce diffusion among adopter groups.

Leveraging "opinion leadership" is also an effective strategy. Opinion leaders influence others through word of mouth and can accelerate the diffusion of new products/services. Members of the early adopter category are most likely to be opinion leaders, so as an entrepreneur, you may have to identify these opinion leaders and target them specifically in the hope of speeding up and extending the diffusion process. Another strategy is to actually "create" an opinion leader. It is often difficult to identify and target "known" opinion leaders, and thus many entrepreneurs simply create their own opinion leaders. You simply offer an inducement to a group of individuals in the early adopter group (e.g., a free product) in return for them promoting the product to friends and family. Finally, as you now know, social media can play a very important role in helping your products/services diffuse. Reaching the influential on social media that will talk about your products/services is very important and can speed up the diffusion process.

Managing Your Products/Services Over Their Life Cycles

After you launch your new product/service, you will discover that you must manage it well as it moves through the product/service life cycle—the stages a new product/service goes through in the marketplace: introduction, growth, maturity, and decline. Specifically, you will need to make adjustments to your product and your overall marketing mix as the product/service moves through this life cycle (see Figure 6.2).

Figure 6.2   Managing Products/Services Over Their Life Cycles

	Introduction	Growth	Maturity	Decline
Industry sales	Low	Increasing	High/stable	Decreasing
Industry profit	Low	Increasing	Decreasing	Decreasing
Marketing objective	Awareness	Differentiation	Brand loyalty	Harvest/ delete
Target market	Innovators	Early adopters/early majority	Early/late majority	Late majority/ laggards
Product	One	More versions	Full line	Best sellers only
Price	High[a]	Decreasing	Lower	Low
Promotion	High	High	Decreasing	Low
Distribution	Limited	Expanded	Maximum	Fewer
Competition	Little	Growing	Many	Reduced

a. While you could price high (skim) or low (penetration), my personal bias is to price high.

At the *introduction stage*, the product/service is available for sale for the first time to the target market. During this period, sales grow slowly and profit is minimal. Your marketing objective is to gain awareness, and an investment in promotion is probably high and highly targeted to innovators. Pricing can be high or low, although my bias, in most cases, is to price high. However, while there may be little competition initially, high prices tend to attract competitors. Gaining distribution is also important at this stage, but it can be challenging.

At the *growth stage*, there should be an increase in sales and profitability. The marketing objective here is to stress differentiation (why your product or service is different from the competitors). The target is early adopters/early majority, and more versions of the product are perhaps introduced to appeal to this group and to stay ahead of competitors. Promotion expenditure is probably high, while price is decreasing as a way to gain or hold share. Distribution is also now expanded, and competition is growing.

At the *maturity stage,* sales are probably high or stable, but profits are decreasing. The marketing objective here is to maintain brand loyalty. The target market is now the early/late majority, and a full line of products is developed to appeal to these groups. Both prices are dropping, as is the investment in promotion. Also, distribution has now maxed out at this point, while the market is highly competitive and crowded.

Finally, at the *decline stage,* sales and profit are decreasing. At this point, the marketing objective is to harvest (keep the products but reduce marketing support) or delete the product and replace it with entirely new ones. The target market is now the late majority/laggards, and only the best-selling products are available. Price and promotion are both low, and distribution is being reduced. At the same time, competition is dropping out of the market, leaving behind only the strongest players.

As an entrepreneur, effective management of your product/service over the life cycle will involve at least three key strategies: (1) modifying the product/service, (2) finding new customers, and (3) finding new uses for your product/service. For example, product/service modification will be necessary to appeal to new target markets and to stay ahead of the competitors. This modification can include altering the product/service characteristics (performance, appearance, packaging improvements, etc.) to try to increase and extend sales. A key product modification strategy is "value migration"—making *good, better, and best versions* of the product/service geared to specific target markets (e.g., innovators to late majority). Smart entrepreneurs plan for this eventuality from the onset, knowing that a "full line" will be necessary over the life cycle. This involves the construction of a "platform" strategy in the beginning of the new product/service stage that will allow for future value migration.

Finding new customers is also going to be a necessary strategy. For example, a women's clinic chain decided to target males by offering new men's health clinics, thus effectively reaching new customers they had not sought before. Finally, finding new uses for your product/service can also be an effective strategy when managing your product/service over the life cycle. For instance, when demand for Arm & Hammer baking soda slowed because home baking was declining, the company encouraged customers to use the product in new ways such as a deodorizer for the refrigerators or as a deodorizer for cat litter. These new uses enabled the company to sustain its growth over the product life cycle.

Consider a Different Approach to New Product/Service Development

The six-stage new product/service process is often criticized by many in the new venture field. The arguments about the process is that it takes too much time, costs too much money, treats all products/services as the same, and is a linear, sequential and handing-off approach much like a relay race. In my experience, this model does not work well in the entrepreneurial space where fast companies beat slow companies and where flexible companies beat rigid companies. Instead I argue for an *iterative/spiral approach* to new product/service development that is more likely to produce successful outcomes, at least for entrepreneurial firms. This approach means you incorporate the concepts of speed, agility, parallelism, adaptability, flexibility and scalability into the process. In other words, you follow a rapid build, test, feedback, adapt and reload approach—but with each of these being overlapping phases. Moreover, work can be done out of the so-called sequencing inherent in the six-stage process. In short, you can spiral (overlap) up and down within each task and across all tasks in the process to ensure you are creating fully-featured and customer-delighting concepts. For example, based on fuzzy-front end customer insight you might quickly build a crude prototype and take it to customers for their reactions. Customers might green light the prototype, ask for changes or suggest you kill it! You then use the feedback to adapt and test again. Next, you might find the customers are unwilling to pay a particular price for the concept and this will then affect your financials. Thus, you may decide to reengineer to strip costs out of the concept, which may also mean reconfiguring or removing certain features from the concept. Then, you retest the new concept at the new price point. And, you are open to iteration and reloading throughout the entire process.

This iterative/spiral approach also allows you to think about scalability, including the notion of product/service platforms—building out multiple products/services from essentially the same core which might also involve what we call value migration—good, better, best product options. In other words, it takes you away from a single product/service focus often inherent in the traditional six-stage approach. And, I can tell you, investors simply do not like venture that are wedded to single products/services. They want to see a portfolio of products/services as part of the sustainability aspect of the venture. The iterative/spiral approach compared to the more rigid six-stage approach to product/service development allows you to accomplish this goal. In any event, while the six-stage new produt/service process is the most commonly used framework in the United States, it has not proven to actually enhance new product/service success rates. Therefore, as an entrepreneur you should be open to new approaches and methods. This iterative/spiral approach is one that I have used successfully for many years and perhaps it might work for you.

Key Takeaways

- You must understand the type of new product/service you will be introducing (e.g., continuous, dynamically continuous, discontinuous) since it will affect how you must market it.
- New product/service failure is the norm, but you can increase your chances of success by evaluating your concept against the characteristics inherently part of successful products/services.
- Using a customer-centered new product/service process will also increase your chances of new product/service success. Ultimately, this process always begins with "the customer."
- It is important for you to understand how individual customers adopt new products/services as well as the strategies you can use to ensure successful adoption.
- Diffusion is how new products/services spread across or among a group of customers (adopters) over time. You must be aware of numerous strategies to ensure successful diffusion.
- You must also be capable of managing your product/service over its life cycle, including modifying your product, finding new customers, and finding new uses for the product/service.
- You may wish to consider an iterative/spiral approach to new product/service development as opposed to the traditional six-stage process discussed in this chapter. The former method has proven to be successful in the new venture space.

Entrepreneurial Exercise

Take your top two to three best new product/service ideas/concepts. Now, evaluate them using the characteristics found in successful new products/services—for example, superior advantage, compatibility, simplicity, observability, trialability, low perceived risk (to the customer), and intellectual-property protection. And perhaps include the "purple cow" characteristic. Score them on a rating scale of 1 to 5 (1 = *characteristic is completely absent, 5 = characteristic is completely present).* Now, take the highest scoring concept to the market and solicit feedback from the target customer. Determine the customer's interest in the concept and likelihood of purchase (talk to 10 to 15 customers). Ask for their help to refine the concept. Now, do a more robust concept test. Prepare a written description and visual depiction of the concept and present it to 10 to 15 potential customers. What did you discover?

Key Terms

New products   101
Continuous innovations   102
Dynamically continuous
   innovations   102
Discontinuous innovations   102
New services   103
New product/service process   106
Idea generation   107

Iterative/spiral approach   000
Screening and evaluation   109
Business analysis   109
Development   110
Market testing   110
Launch   111
Adoption   112
Diffusion   113

Notes

1. This section is based on Frederick G. Crane, Roger Kerin, Steve Hartley, and William Rudelius, *Marketing,* 7th Canadian ed. (Toronto: McGraw-Hill Ryerson, 2008).

2. Christopher Lovelock and Jochen Wirtz, *Services Marketing,* 5th ed. (Upper Saddle River, NJ: Pearson, 2004).

3. This section is adapted from F. G. Crane and T. K. Clarke, *Consumer Behaviour in Canada,* 2nd ed. (Toronto: Dryden, 1994).

4. Seth Godin, *Purple Cow* (New York: Portfolio, 2002).

5. Robert M. McMath and Thom Forbes, *What Were They Thinking?* (New York: NY Times Business, 1998).

6. Based on Everett M. Rogers, *Diffusion of Innovations* (New York: Free Press, 1962).

7. Geoffrey A. Moore, *Crossing the Chasm* (New York: Harper Business, 1991).

8. Ibid.

9. This section is adapted from Crane and Clarke, *Consumer Behaviour in Canada.*

Seven

Building and Sustaining the Entrepreneurial Brand

I have argued for more than 20 years that building and sustaining a powerful entrepreneurial brand is critical if a venture is to survive, grow, and endure in a complex and competitive marketplace. Moreover, a new venture has a relatively short time frame to establish its brand. If it misses this critical window of opportunity, it is very likely to fail. Unfortunately, however, many people have suggested and continue to believe that "branding" is the sole province of large corporate firms. Of course, my response to those who adhere to this belief is "Where did these large corporate firms come from?" Well, in fact, in many cases, they started out as small, entrepreneurial firms and grew into large corporations, and much of that growth can be directly attributed to successful branding!

Despite the importance of branding and its contribution to entrepreneurial success, most entrepreneurship textbooks provide little, if any, guidance as to how to build and sustain an entrepreneurial brand. But make no mistake about it: Entrepreneurs must focus on creating brands that clearly communicate the value desired by the customer as well as reinforce the intended position the entrepreneurial firm wishes to occupy in the market.

Importantly, the brand must be consistent and sustained over time. And in fact, there is a process that you can use to build and sustain a brand that will attract and retain customers for your venture. In this chapter, we will discuss what a brand is, why branding is important, the characteristics of a good brand, picking a good brand name, the branding process, branding strategies, and the concept of brand equity.

What Is a Brand?

As you recall from Chapter 2, a brand is a name, sign, symbol, design, or combination of these elements intended to identify the products or services of one marketer and to differentiate them from those of the competition.[1] One of the most basic definitions of a brand is that it is something of "value" for both the customer and the company.[2] At a practical level, a brand embodies your offer of value—your promise—to the customer. Ultimately, a brand is a blend of what you say it is, what others say it is, and how well you deliver on your promise—from the customer's perspective. Finally, a brand is a powerful asset that must be carefully developed and managed.[3] You should also realize that some brands can be spoken, while other brands contain certain symbols that cannot be spoken, such as the rainbow-colored apple logo that Apple, Inc. puts on its products and in its ads. The name of your brand and the visual aspect of your brand are important considerations as you begin to think about the branding process.

Why Is Entrepreneurial Branding Important?

As I stated in the chapter opener, most people believe that branding is the sole domain of large corporate firms. And in fact, it seems many entrepreneurs also believe this assertion. Yet, I have argued strongly for many years that branding is important not only to your entrepreneurial firm but also to the customer you intend to serve. For you and your venture, the brand you select is important because it can set you apart and truly differentiate your venture (and its products/services) from your competitors. But branding brings other benefits to your venture.[4] First, branding can be an integrative tool for the entire venture. For example, the branding process, even the simple naming of your business, forces you to consider very carefully the core "value" you will create and deliver to your key customers. In addition, branding also helps you sharpen your business model (how you will make money and from whom you will make it). Second, branding increases the chances of acquiring your initial set of customers in the early stages of your venture. And, of course, branding will help solidify customer loyalty to your venture in the later stages. Third, branding can increase your access to suppliers and improve your chances of channel support. Fourth, branding can increase access to new venture capital. And in fact, through personal experience, I have seen how a strong brand increases the likelihood of obtaining financial support for the venture.

While a brand is extremely important to you and your venture, it might be argued that customers, in fact, may benefit most from branding. Recognizing competing products by distinctive branding allows customers to be more efficient shoppers. Consumers can recognize and avoid products with which they are dissatisfied while becoming loyal to other, more satisfying brands. In fact, brand loyalty often eases customer decision making by eliminating the need for an external search.

Strong brands reduce customers' perceived risk when purchasing and can increase their trust with the brand. In fact, one branding expert suggests that a strong brand is a "safe place for customers."[5]

Finally, strong brands also help the customer visualize and better understand the product or service.

Characteristics of a Good Brand

A good brand will possess a number of important characteristics.[6] You should keep these characteristics in mind as you begin the branding process. For example, a good brand has the following qualities:

1. Effectively communicates the distinctive value you wish to offer the customer

2. Is "relevant" to the customer

3. "Resonates" with the customer

4. Reinforces the company's intended positioning in the marketplace

5. Is consistent and unifying

6. Serves as an umbrella for current/future brands in the company's portfolio

7. Allows for the building of strong brand equity (to be discussed later)

8. Enables you to command premium pricing

9. Is easily understood by your customers and your employees

10. Can be sustained over time

You should consider these characteristics as you begin to ponder your possible brand(s) for your venture. It is clear that brands lacking the above characteristics are likely to be weaker brands that may not survive in a crowded and competitive marketing environment.

The Entrepreneurial Branding Process

As mentioned earlier, entrepreneurial brands have to be crafted and managed with care. In effect, branding will follow a particular process. I suggest there are five basic stages in this branding process:

1. *Conduct a brand analysis.* At this stage of the process, you will examine your customers, competitors, and your venture (and its products/services) to determine what the possible branding opportunities are available for you. You are looking for the "right fit" in terms of your core strengths, customer needs, and competitive opportunity.

2. *Determine your brand positioning.* Your brand analysis conducted in the first stage of the branding process is designed to help you to select your proper **brand positioning.** In Chapter 5, you read about STP (segment, target, and position). As you learned, positioning is the place the product or service will occupy in the hearts or minds of the customers in relation to your competitors. It is with strong branding that your positioning comes to life!

It is critical to link the "benefits sought" by the target segment to your positioning strategy. In other words, you must connect your intended position to the unique desired benefits of the customer. But I have also argued that with strong branding, you must go even further. That is, in addition to connecting your brand with the benefits the customer is seeking from the product/service, you can also connect with the customer emotionally. In this way, your brand positioning goes beyond mere product/service benefits and engages the customers on a much deeper level. In fact, emotional branding is often the best way to position your new brand, especially if it is a "service brand." For example, you can position your brand as the "best product" but also as one that offers a very meaningful experience to the customer. This emotional branding is a higher-level step from the benefit approach. It is designed to forge a deep, lasting, and intimate emotional connection to the brand so that the customer develops a special bond with and unique trust in the brand. If you can achieve this, you will have a tremendously strong brand positioning.[7]

3. *Select a brand name and identity.* After establishing your brand positioning you will now craft your **brand name and identity** (your identity would include logos, color language, etc. used in conjunction with your brand name). One recommendation I have for you is to engage your intended customers and ask them to help you coconstruct the brand name and identity. This will provide valuable feedback in terms of the appropriateness of your brand name and identity. In terms of your brand name and identity, you have several options to consider. You can build the brand name and identity around yourself as "founder" if you believe you have important attributes/characteristics that would be valued by the customer. Or, you could focus on the strengths of your products/services or even leverage your people working for your venture.

When you are thinking about brand names, you should consider the following important criteria when actually selecting a good "brand name."[8]

- The name should suggest key product benefits. For example, "Bug-Be-Gone" clearly describes the benefits of purchasing this product.
- The name should be distinctive and convey a positive meaning.
- The name should fit the company or product image.
- The name should have no legal or regulatory restrictions. (Increasingly, brand names need a corresponding address on the Internet. This further complicates name selection because millions of domain names are already registered.)
- The name should be easy to pronounce and remember (e.g., Bic pens).
- The name should have an emotional appeal.
- The name should translate easily into foreign languages.
- The name should have enough "flex" so as not to constrain the growth and expansion of the venture.

4. *Select a branding strategy.* Now you must determine the appropriate branding strategy for your venture. For example, corporate branding (the "branded house"), individual product/service branding (the "house of brands"), and hybrid branding (subbranding) are three specific options for you to consider. These branding strategies are discussed in more detail in the next section of this chapter, including conditions under which you would use these strategies.

5. *Construct a brand communications strategy.* The final stage of the process is for you to prepare a brand communications strategy that will result in a consistent and unified message about your brand. We will discuss communications strategy in Chapter 10.

Entrepreneurial Branding Strategies

In a highly competitive environment, your choice of branding strategy will be pivotal if your venture is to survive and grow. To help you determine the appropriate branding strategy for your venture, some experts have developed a discipline called "brand architecture"—an approach to the design and management of a venture's brand portfolio. Using brand architecture can help you make the right branding strategy decisions.[9]

As mentioned earlier, an entrepreneurial firm can consider several different branding strategies: corporate branding (the "branded house"), individual product/service branding (the "house of brands"), or a hybrid strategy (subbranding).[10] These options are part of the brand architecture discipline and appear as part of a spectrum or continuum. We will now discuss these branding options and the conditions under which they are appropriate for use by your venture (see Figure 7.1).

Corporate Branding—Branded House

On one end of the branding continuum is **corporate branding,** sometimes called the **branded house.** In this case, a single brand (corporate) covering all products and services is used. In short, with a corporate or branded house strategy, the venture is using an "umbrella" under which to manage its offerings. Virgin, for example, uses a corporate or branded house strategy. There is Virgin Airlines, Virgin Rail, Virgin Cola, and Virgin Music. Also, one of the firms I founded was called the

Figure 7.1   Branding Continuum

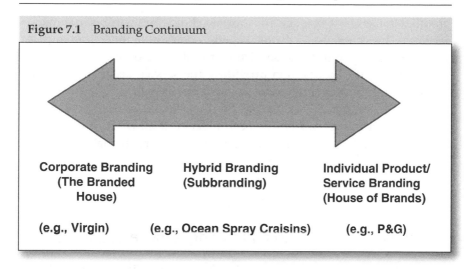

Corporate Branding (The Branded House)	Hybrid Branding (Subbranding)	Individual Product/ Service Branding (House of Brands)
(e.g., Virgin)	(e.g., Ocean Spray Craisins)	(e.g., P&G)

QMA Group. Under the branded house, we offered a variety of services, including a strategic turnaround service for troubled businesses, research services, communications services, and innovation and design services.

A corporate branding or branded house strategy maximizes brand clarity because the customer knows exactly what is being offered. Virgin, for example, stands for innovation, service quality, and fun, and the descriptors indicate a specific business (e.g., Virgin Rail). This approach is simple, and a single brand can be communicated across products and services over time. Plus, it is easier for the customer to understand and recall versus a dozen individual brands. Moreover, employees, suppliers, and channel members also benefit from the brand clarity.

In addition, a branded house can maximize synergy as participation in one market creates associations and visibility that can help in another. Also, every exposure of the brand in one context provides visibility that enhances brand awareness in all contexts. It also makes it easier to move into new markets or offer new products and services. Finally, the brand house provides leverage—it works harder in more contexts and can do so at lower costs.

Since the role of a branding strategy is to create and leverage assets, the brand house is a logical choice for new ventures. In fact, experts argue strongly that a corporate or branded house strategy should be the "default brand architecture option" unless there are compelling reasons not to pursue it![11] In addition, experts suggest that a corporate brand or branded house strategy is the appropriate choice for ventures that market services. This is because in the packaged-goods sector, there is a tangible/ physical product, but in the service sector, there is only an "intangible" service. Thus, the corporation providing the service becomes the focus. Thus, strongly branding the corporation becomes critical.[12]

However, the branded house option does put all the venture's eggs in one basket, so the brand has to be protected at all costs. But it can be difficult to manage the image of the brand when participating in many markets. It can also limit the venture's ability to target very specific customers. Finally, too many uses for one brand name can dilute the meaning of the brand for consumers.

Individual Product/Service Branding—House of Brands

Alternatively, on the other end of the branding continuum is **individual product/service branding**—the **house of brands** strategy. This branding strategy involves creating and managing an independent set of stand-alone brands to maximize the impact on a market segment. As Virgin is a branded house, Procter & Gamble (P&G) is a classic example of a house of brands. P&G manages more than 80 major brands with little link to the corporation or to each other. The house of brands strategy allows a company to clearly position brands on functional benefits and to dominate particular market segments. The individual brand is used to connect directly to the customer with a very targeted value proposition.[13]

A house of brands strategy also helps the company to avoid a brand association that would be incompatible with a particular product/service offering. It can also help signal a breakthrough advantage of a new offering and minimize channel conflicts (e.g., by placing different brands in different types of channel outlets).[14]

However, with a house of brands strategy, the company sacrifices the economies of scale and synergies that can be derived by leveraging a single brand across multiple markets.[15]

Hybrid Branding—Subbranding

In between the two extremes on the brand continuum is a **hybrid branding** option, specifically, **subbranding.** With subbranding, the corporate brand or branded house is the primary frame of reference, but it is augmented or modified by additional naming. For example, Microsoft

Office and Dell Dimension are subbrands. In short, the branding strategy is to combine the corporate brand with a new subbrand component to add attribute or application associations or to signal a breakthrough. One common role of subbranding is to extend the corporate or branded house into a new segment. For example, Ocean Spray Craisins takes Ocean Spray from juice to snack foods.[16]

In some cases, the corporate brand will play the major driver or purchase role for the customer. In other words, buying the corporate brand will dominate the customer decision. But in other cases, the subbrand can play a codriver role. That is, the customer is buying both the company and the product. In a codriver situation, the two brands should be compatible and reinforce one another. If not, this might cause customer confusion or even harm the corporate brand. Therefore, having a subbrand closely linked to the corporate brand can be both a risk and an opportunity.[17]

Other Branding Options

Other branding options that are available to your venture are private branding or mixed branding. With **private branding,** instead of creating your own brands, you will be producing brands for resellers (particularly retailers) who, in turn, sell the brands under the brand name selected by the wholesaler or retailer.

Another branding possibility is **mixed branding.** With mixed branding, you would market products under your own brand name but also under that of a reseller. This type of branding is undertaken because you can reach customers attracted to the reseller who are different from those attracted to your brand. Michelin Tire, for example, sells tires under its own brand name but also manufactures tires for Sears that are sold under the Sears name.

The Importance of Brand Equity

There are many definitions of **brand equity.** The simplest one is that brand equity is the value added by the brand to the product. Another definition of brand equity is the positive differential effect of brand awareness and brand meaning on customer response to the brand. Another definition of brand equity is the added value a given brand name provides to a product beyond the functional benefits it offers.

Finally, another definition of brand equity is when more people line up to pay more for a branded versus a nonbranded or other branded offering![18] Ultimately, you must remember that while your marketing efforts will attempt to influence the customer's perception of a product's brand equity, it will be the customer who will actually determine whether your brand has such "equity." In short, the customer must perceive there is brand equity and must have the desire to seek out and pay for that equity.

In fact, for many entrepreneurs, the most important measure of a brand's equity is the extent to which customers are willing to pay more for a particular brand. For example, one study found that more than 70 percent of customers would pay a 20 percent premium for their brand of choice relative to the closest competing brand; 40 percent said they would pay a 50 percent premium. Moreover, Heinz Ketchup lovers are willing to pay a 100 percent price premium![19] Thus, it is easy to realize why building and maintaining brand equity should be a priority for your venture. Brand equity not only provides you with a competitive advantage (strong customer loyalty) but also allows you to command a premium price.

Creating Brand Equity

Brand equity does not just happen. It is carefully crafted and nurtured by communications strategies that forge strong, favorable, and unique consumer associations and experiences with a brand. Brand equity resides in the hearts and minds of consumers and results from what they have learned, felt, seen, and heard about a brand over time. Thus, brand equity is not easily or quickly achieved. Rather, it arises from a sequential building process consisting of four steps: [20]

1. The first step is to develop positive brand awareness and an association of the brand in the customers' minds. Virgin has done this at the corporate or branded house level, while P&G has done so at the house of brands level (e.g., Tide, Pantene).

2. Next, you must establish a brand's meaning in the minds of customers. Meaning arises from what a brand stands for and has two dimensions—a functional, performance-related dimension and an abstract, imagery-related dimension. Gatorade has achieved both dimensions by combining the promise of increased athletic performance with the image of champions consuming its product.

3. The third step is to elicit the proper customer response to the brand. Here, attention is placed on how customers think and feel about a brand. Thinking focuses on a brand's perceived quality, credibility, and superiority relative to other brands. Feeling relates to the consumer's emotional reaction to a brand. Michelin elicits both responses for its tires. The Michelin brand is thought of as a superior-quality brand, but customers also acknowledge a secure feeling of safety and self-assurance without worry or concern about the brand.

4. The final and most difficult step is to create a customer brand resonance— an intense, active loyalty relationship between customers and the brand. A deep psychological bond characterizes customer brand resonance and the personal identification customers have with the brand. Examples of brands that have achieved this status include Harley-Davidson and Apple.

Forging a strong emotional connection between the brand and the consumer can lead to brand differentiation, strong customer loyalty, and evangelical promotion of the brand. Moreover, research on business startups also suggests that building the brand and creating brand equity based on emotional branding are key imperatives for new venture success. This is especially true in crowded and competitive markets.[21]

Valuing Brand Equity

As mentioned, brand equity provides a financial advantage for the brand owner. Successful, established brand names, such as Google, Nike, Gatorade, and Virgin, have an economic value in the sense that they are intangible assets. Unlike physical assets that depreciate with time and use, brands can actually appreciate in value when effectively marketed. However, brands can also lose value when they are not managed properly. Attaching monetary value to brands can often be complicated, and there is little agreement among experts concerning the optimal way to calculate brand equity. Therefore, marketers often use a variety of direct and indirect measures to determine the equity of a brand, including communication investment in the brand and customer loyalty to the brand. But one thing is for certain: If you build and maintain a strong entrepreneurial brand, you increase the value of your brand as well as your business. One successful entrepreneur who has learned this lesson is Tony Hawk. And, he has some advice for you when it comes to building and sustaining a powerful brand that has good brand equity. He provides three key pieces of advice to you and this is why he finds himself in the Entrepreneurial Marketing Spotlight!

Entrepreneurial Marketing Spotlight

Tony Hawk—super skateboarder—is also a successful entrepreneur. Hawk has built a billion-dollar enterprise consisting of video games and clothing lines. Much of this success is tied to his ability to building and sustaining a powerful entrepreneurial brand. Hawk offers some good advice for aspiring entrepreneurs when it comes to branding. First, be authentic. He insists that consumers want to connect with real people and can spot a fake in an instant. So, he tells people to "stick to your core values and beliefs and base your brand off of them." Second, be unique. Hawk believes in Tom Peters' mantra "distinct or extinct." He argues if you cannot differentiate your brand no one will pay attention to your brand. Hawk suggests entrepreneurs need to determine what makes their brand different and then take that distinctive brand story to the market in a convincing way. He also stresses the need to innovate and renovate the brand to stay ahead of the competition. If you are standing still, you are dying. He also urges entrepreneurs to use social media to stay connected to their customers. Third, Hawk tells entrepreneurs to network with the right people. He suggests that entrepreneurs "need a good support system of family, friends, mentors, and business contacts." Additionally, he cautions entrepreneurs to not surround themselves with yes-men. The right people will help you make the right choices when it comes to building and sustaining your brand. For his insight, Tony Hawk deserves to be featured in the entrepreneurial spotlight![22]

Finally, today, especially with a fully networked younger generation, it is critical for your brand to stand for honesty, relevance, and as Tony Hawk tells us, authenticity. And, as discussed in earlier chapters, remember that social media will play a huge role in helping to build or crush your brand. So, you must recognize that your customer is likely to play a major role in your brand-building process. Thus, the customer must feel part of the brand. To accomplish this, your brand must be, as Hawk says, authentic and unique as well as fresh and capable of reinvention and renovation in order to keep abreast with consumers' evolving needs, tastes, and trends. Importantly, make sure your brand stands for something much bigger than the product or service your venture offers. You must work hard to make sure it stands for trust because it is trusted brands that create brand equity and enduring value.

Key Takeaways

- A brand embodies your offer of value—your promise—to the customer. A brand is a powerful asset that must be carefully developed and managed.
- A strong entrepreneurial brand differentiates your venture and sets you apart from your competitors.
- A strong entrepreneurial brand delivers other benefits, including a greater chance of acquiring your first set of customers and a greater likelihood of securing financial support for your venture.
- There are numerous characteristics of a good brand, and you must screen your potential brand against these characteristics.
- Before settling on a brand, you should go through the five-stage branding process outlined in the chapter.
- Be sure to screen your specific "brand name" against the criteria for judging a "good brand name."
- You must select the right branding strategy given your venture and the conditions under which you will compete. The default strategy for a new venture is corporate branding (the branded house) unless you have compelling reasons not to use this strategy.
- One of your most important tasks is to create and sustain brand equity. Brand equity provides you with a competitive advantage and allows you to command a premium price. It also increases the value of your business.
- An authentic brand, a trusted brand, and one that evolves to meet the needs of the market will be one that endures.

Entrepreneurial Exercise

Determine your brand positioning option (the space your brand will occupy in the hearts and minds of the customer, e.g., best product with best customer service). Next come up with some possible brands that will reinforce your positioning. Use the characteristics of a good brand to assess the possible brands. Also, use the criteria for "picking a good brand name." Now, take the best two to three options to the marketplace. Be sure to test your intended brand positioning and also your brand name options with 10 to 15 potential customers. Is your brand positioning correct? What about your brand name options? What specific feedback did the customers provide?

Key Terms

Brand   124
Brand positioning   126
Brand name and identity   127
Corporate branding (branded house)   128
Individual product/service branding
    (house of brands)   130

Hybrid branding
    (subbranding)   130
Private branding   131
Mixed branding   131
Brand equity   131

Notes

1. For an in-depth discussion, see K. L. Keller, *Strategic Brand Management* (Mahwah, NJ: Prentice Hall, 1998).

2. Leslie de Chernatory and Malcolm McDonald, *Creating Powerful Brands* (London: Buttersworth Heinemann, 1992).

3. Philip Kotler and Gary Armstrong, *Principles of Marketing,* 10th ed. (Upper Saddle River, NJ: Pearson, 2004).

4. Bill Merrilees, "A Theory of Brand-Led SME New Venture Development," *Qualitative Market Research: An International Journal* 10, no. 4 (2007): 403–415.

5. Stan Richards, "Building a Brand." Speech presented at Texas A&M University's Center for Retailing Studies Fall Symposium, Dallas, October 8, 1998.

6. K. L. Keller, 'The Brand Report Card," *Harvard Business Review* 78, no. 1 (2000): 147–56.

7. Sharon Morrison and Frederick G. Crane, "Building the Service Brand by Creating and Managing an Emotional Brand Experience," *Journal of Brand Management* 14, no. 5 (2007): 410–421.

8. Daniel L. Doden, "Selecting a Brand Name That Aids Marketing Objectives," *Advertising Age,* November 5, 1990, p. 34; Kotler and Armstrong, *Principles of Marketing.*

9. David A. Aaker and Erich Joachimsthaler, "The Brand Relationship Spectrum: The Key to the Brand Architecture Challenge," *California Management Review* 42, no. 4 (2000): 8-23; James Devlin, "Brand Architecture in Services: The Example of the Retail Financial Services," *Journal of Marketing Management* 19 (2003): 1043–1065.

10. Ibid.

11. Ibid.

12. Leonard L. Berry, "Cultivating Service Brand Equity," *Journal of the Academy of Marketing Science* 28, no. 1 (2000): 128–137.

13. See Aaker and Joachimsthaler, "The Brand Relationship Spectrum."

14. Ibid.

15. Ibid.

16. Ibid.

17. Ibid.

18. See F. H. Farquhar, "Managing Brand Equity," *Marketing Research* 1 (1989): 24–33; K. L. Ailawadi, D. R. Lehmann, and S. A. Neslin, "Revenue Premium as an Outcome Measure of Brand Equity," *Journal of Marketing* 67 (2003): 1–17; Keller, *Strategic Brand Management.*

19. Kotler and Armstrong, *Principles of Marketing.*

20. This section is based on K. L. Keller, "Building Customer-Based Brand Equity," *Marketing Management,* July–August, 2001, 15–19.

21. Morrison and Crane, "Building the Service Brand."

22. See, Dan Schawbel, "Three Steps to Establishing an Entrepreneur Brand," *Businessweek*, December 10, 2010, http://www.businessweek.com/managing/content/dec2010/ca2010128_942112.htm, downloaded February 14, 2012.

Eight

Entrepreneurial Pricing

O ne of my students in my Creating Enterprise for Women Program had developed a business based on beautiful Aboriginal art that she created. However, she could not determine what price to charge for her art. One of the accountants teaching in the program helped her to determine her costs and then recommended a price that would cover her costs and provide a small profit margin (cost-plus pricing). But I was not convinced this was the correct strategy. I told her that while cost-based pricing is a simple approach to set prices, it might not be the best approach. Price too high (because of high cost structure) and customers might walk away. Price too low and customers may not buy because they might perceive the art as poor quality.

I recommended that we test her pricing in the real world. At one art show, we priced her art using the accountant's recommended cost-based pricing (cost plus). At another art show, we priced her art using **competition-based pricing** (pricing her art in line with competitors selling comparable-quality art being sold at the show). The results? She actually sold more art at the higher price! And that higher price was more than 100 percent greater than the cost-plus pricing recommended by the accountant. However, I intuitively believed she was still underpricing her art, so we did a follow-up survey with customers who purchased her art. Guess what? They told us they would have paid more for her art. In fact, in most cases, customers said they would have paid 50 percent more!

So, as you can see, pricing is not as simple as you might think. In fact, many entrepreneurs are simply in the dark when it comes to effective price setting. Some guess, some pray, and some simply hope the price is right. And as my Aboriginal artist found out, price is not always simply about cost. A variety of factors affect the prices entrepreneurs set for the products/services. In this chapter, we will discuss these factors as well as provide some real-world advice for setting effective prices.

The Pricing Parameters

Essentially, there are three basic **pricing parameters** for your venture: the price floor, the price range, and the price ceiling. Your price floor is set by your business costs. You need to generate enough money to cover your costs, or you are simply going to go out of business. Your competitors set the price range for comparable products that are available to customers. If you price your products or services above or below this range, it can be problematic. We will discuss why this is so a little later in this chapter. Finally, the price ceiling is set by the customer's ability and willingness to pay for your products or services (see Figure 8.1). Successful entrepreneurs carefully consider all three basic pricing parameters before selecting an effective price point for their products/services. In fact, these three basic pricing parameters form the basis for the three most common approaches to price setting: cost-based pricing, competition-based pricing, and customer-based pricing.

Figure 8.1   The Pricing Parameters

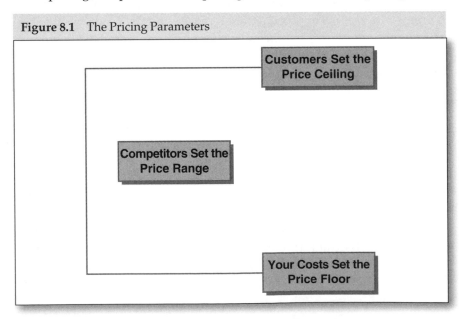

Cost-Based Pricing

When an entrepreneur uses **cost-based pricing,** he or she is focusing on the "cost" side of the business and not the demand side of the business. Price is set by determing the costs of doing business and adding enough to cover costs and provide some profit. The most common cost-based approach to pricing is **cost-plus pricing.** With cost-plus pricing, the entrepreneur simply adds an amount—called a markup—to costs. Entrepreneurs who run retail outlets often use a cost-plus approach known as **standard markup pricing.** This involves adding a fixed percentage to the cost of items in particular product categories. Thus, the percentage markup will vary depending on the type of retail store (supermarket, furniture, etc.) and the type of product. For example, typically, high-volume products will have smaller markups than low-volume products.

There are two ways to look at standard markups: markup on selling price and markup on cost. For example, suppose you run a retail shoe store and buy a pair of shoes from a manufacturer at $20 and sell them at $40. Your markup on the selling price is 50 percent ($20/$40). This markup is equated with gross margin percentage and is the method most retailers use. Your markup on cost, on the other hand, is 100 percent ($20/$20).

Another type of cost-based pricing is target profit pricing. In this case, the entrepreneur begins with a specific profit objective in mind and then determines the product's price based on the number of units he or she expects to sell. A target profit price can be determined using the following equation:

$$\text{Target profit price} = \frac{\text{Fixed costs} + \text{Target profit}}{\text{Sales volume in units}} + \text{Variable costs per unit}$$

However, cost-based pricing can be seriously flawed in that it ignores the customer (his or her willingness and ability to pay) and what the competitors are charging for comparable products/services. Furthermore, this approach tends to take a narrow view as to what constitutes cost (or price) in the minds of the customer. In fact, cost/price is not just the mere "financial outlay" for the product or service. Price also includes the customers' time (time cost), physical effort required to buy, and psychic costs involved in the buying process. So, the customers do not simply consider the actual "price tag" on the product; they also consider the other costs to them that are not generally captured in cost-based pricing.

Also, as an entrepreneur, you must remember that price is not just a pure cost signal; it can also serve as a surrogate indicator of "quality" to the customer. For example, one physician I know almost went out of business when he set the price of his Lasik surgery well below the going market rate. He discovered that patients were inferring poor-quality Lasik because of the low price he had set for his service.

However, knowing your costs of being in business (the price floor) is an important consideration and can be a useful starting point to determine what revenue you may require to sustain the business. In particular, one of the things that can be accomplished by knowing the costs of being in business is a break-even analysis.

With a **break-even analysis,** you can determine the relationship between your venture's costs and the revenue required for the venture to break even; the **break-even point** is the quantity at which total revenue and total costs are equal. You can also analyze the relationship between total costs and total revenue to determine profitability at various levels of output.

Your break-even point (BEP) is determined using the following equation:

$$BEP_{Quantity} = \frac{Fixed\ cost}{Unit\ selling\ price - Unit\ variable\ cost}$$

Fixed costs (FCs) are the expenses of the venture that are stable and do not change with the quantity of the product that is produced and sold. Examples of FC are rent, executive salaries, and so on. **Variable costs** (VCs) are the expenses of the venture that vary directly with the quantity of product that is produced and sold. For example, as the quantity sold doubles, the variable cost doubles. Examples of VC are direct labor and direct materials used in production. Total cost (TC) is the total expense incurred by the venture in producing and marketing a product/service. Thus, TC is the sum of fixed cost and variable cost.

Let's look at an example of calculating a BEP using my Aboriginal art friend's business. Her FCs were $25,000; her VCs were $10. If she had taken the accountant's advice and used a cost-plus approach to pricing, her unit selling price would have been $20, and thus her break-even would have looked like the following:

$$BEP_{Quantity} = \frac{\$25,000}{\$20 - \$10} = 2,500\ units$$

That is a lot of art to sell in one year! But using the competition-based approach to pricing her FC remains at $25,000, her VC remains at $10, but her unit price moves to $50 and thus her breakeven could be achieved at only 625 units:

$$\text{BEP}_{\text{Quantity}} = \frac{\$25,000}{\$50 - \$10} = 625 \text{ units}$$

In fact, she achieved unit sales, annually, well beyond the 625 units and had a nice profitable lifestyle business for herself for many years. And, if you recall from the chapter opener, she actually raised her prices based on the fact that customers were willing to pay more for her art! Thus, her break-even point was actually lower than the 625 units. Her case also illustrates the weakness of a cost-based approach to pricing, including ignoring the competitive context for pricing and the customer's willingness to pay a price beyond what a cost-based approach might indicate.

Competition-Based Pricing

Another option to set prices is for the entrepreneur to consider what the competition is doing—what they are charging customers. And remember, it is the *competition* that establishes the price range for given product/service categories. If you perform your competitive analysis properly, you will know the prices charged by your competitors. In other words, you will be able to establish the current "going rates."

What you must decide as an entrepreneur is how you will price your products/services given this range. For example, do you wish to be at the high end of the range? Do you wish to be at the low end of the range? Or, do you wish to be at the middle of the range? Now, of course, the key question is how do you know whether to price at the high end, low end, or middle of the range? Well, here is some guidance. For example, if you have a high-quality and highly differentiated product/service, you should probably charge a price at the high end of the price range. If, on the other hand, you are marketing a product/service designed to appeal to the price-sensitive customer, then you will price it at the low end of the price range. If your product/service is similar to your key direct competitors, you will charge basically the same price.

Customer-Based Pricing

As you know, it is the customer who establishes the "price ceiling." Therefore, it is important for you to determine the customer's willingness and ability to pay. Unlike cost-based pricing that emphasizes the cost side of the business, **customer-based pricing** focuses on the demand side of the business. The price ceiling is the maximum amount that customers are willing to pay for a product/service. This ceiling is contingent on the elasticity of demand. And elasticity of demand is generally driven by availability of substitutes and the urgency of need for the product (or strong desire for it). So, one thing you need to determine is whether there will be elastic demand (demand that increases as price decreases or demand that decreases as price increases) or inelastic demand (demand does not change if prices increase or decrease) for your product/service.

In general, when you consider customer-based pricing, there are two key pricing options to consider: skimming pricing or penetration pricing. If customers have a strong desire for the product and are willing and able to pay a high price, then **skimming pricing** (charging a high initial price) is an appropriate pricing option. In this situation, customers are not price sensitive but instead are benefit sensitive (e.g., are seeking a high-quality, better performing product/service). If you find that enough customers are willing and able to buy at this initial high price, then skimming pricing makes sense. If customers interpret the high price as connoting high quality, then skimming pricing is also an appropriate pricing strategy. Finally, if your product/service has an intellectual property component (e.g., patent, copyright) or its uniqueness is understood and appreciated by the customer, then skimming pricing is probably your best pricing option.

On the other hand, **penetration pricing** (charging a low initial price) is appropriate if you have a market with price-sensitive customers; you want to use the low initial price to discourage competitors from entering the market and when production and marketing costs fall dramatically as demand (volume) increases.

There is also something else to consider when deciding on skimming versus penetration pricing. If you start with a skimming price strategy, you can, over time, lower your price to attract more price-sensitive customers. However, if you enter the market with a penetration price strategy, it is often very difficult to raise your prices. In other words, while you can move down the going price range with a skimming price strategy, you may not be able to move up the going price range if you initially used a penetration price strategy.

In previous chapters, we discussed the growing trend toward value consciousness. In other words, some customers are demanding better value (increased benefits at the same price). Therefore, many new ventures appeal to this type of customer using value-based pricing. For example, they might offer customers "better value" by offering a greater quantity of product at the same price as competitors. A startup yogurt company, for example, offers 20 percent more product per package at the same price as a competitor that offers the standard amount. Another value-based pricing strategy is "bundling" two or more products/ services in a single package deal, thus lowering the total cost compared to if the customer purchased each item separately.

One of the good things about using a customer-based pricing approach is that you should be able to determine the "target price" based on the customer's perspective. Knowing this target price, you can then "back into that price." In other words, you can "design to price." For example, I know of an upstart commercial furniture manufacturer that used customer input to establish the optimal price point that customers were willing to pay for particular furniture pieces. The company then went back and pulled costs out of its production system, stripped away costly features the customers do not value, and designed and produced the product to meet the customers' target price.

Another advantage of using a customer-based pricing approach is the possibility of uncovering the opportunity to "price by segment" and to offer "good, better, best" product options. In other words, you might be able to develop a line of products with specific price points designed to appeal to very specific segments.

For example, one of my former entrepreneurship students, who started a casual clothing store for women, determined she could sell three different lines of casual dresses priced at $39, $59, and $79, and this appealed very well to the customers shopping at her store.

If you are running an Internet-based venture, you might also consider the concept of *dynamic* or flexible pricing depending on the behavior of individual customers you serve. In fact, it is possible for you to customize your prices to fit the customers' purchasing patterns, product preferences, and tolerances/sensitivity to given prices. By offering price customization, you might continue to win the customers' business and block out your competitors from ever acquiring them.

Ultimately, you need to consider cost, competitors, and customers when setting prices. You must know your price floor (your cost), know what your competitors are charging (the price range), and know your customers' willingness and ability to pay (the price ceiling). Smart entrepreneurs take all these variables into consideration, and some very smart entrepreneurs actually test their prices with the customer and act accordingly. Stan Joffe and Steve Batzofin, cofounders of Earthwise Bag Co., Inc. did exactly this and, in doing so, ensured that the price was right!

Entrepreneurial Marketing Spotlight

Stan Joffe and Steve Batzofin, cofounders of Earthwise Bag Co., Inc. in Commerce, California, know something about the importance of entrepreneurial marketing and, in particular, entrepreneurial pricing. Through creative test marketing, these entrepreneurs determined the best price for their reusable shopping bag (99 cents). Joe Kennedy, author of *The Small Business Owner's Manual*, suggests 99 cents is a really attractive price for an earth-friendly product that is simple to buy and use. Within the first year, the company sold more than 2 million bags! The key to this success, according to Joffe, was doing the market research and determining, from the customer's perspective, the perceived value of the product and then using this information to make the right pricing decision. Originally, Stan and Steve thought they should charge $7, but customers told them this price was far too high. Good thing they talked to the customers. And because they did, Joffe and Batzofin deserve to be in the Entrepreneurial Marketing Spotlight.[1]

Some Entrepreneurial Pricing Advice

Pricing can often make the difference between venture success and failure. You cannot guess, pray, or hope you have set the right price. In this section, we provide some guidance and direction regarding your pricing decisions.

1. Make your pricing just one small part of your overall revenue-generating strategy. In other words, try to be as independent of price as possible. It is better to look at other ways to make money such as adding new products, expanding distribution, and improving your marketing rather than trying to pull the price lever all the time.[2]

2. If your venture is selling a high-quality product or service, do not under-price that offering. Often, this underpricing is rationalized as a require-ment to gain market share. But this may cause two problems: (1) the customer perceiving the product as not being a high-quality offering and (2) increasing your break-even point.[3]

3. Your final price does not have to be tied to your cost! Yes, you need to know your costs to understand the profitability implications of price, but do not overrely on your costs as a way to set prices![4]

4. If you enter a competitive environment and find competitors are beginning to drop prices, you do not have to necessarily follow suit. Yes, there is a nat-ural tendency to price match, but this may be a foolish move, especially if you offer a better product, a superior service, or a memorable experience.[5]

5. Your price strategy should always be connected to the customer segment you are seeking. There is no such thing as an average price because there is no such thing as an average customer. If you wish to seek a price-sensitive customer, then you may have to be the low-cost provider. But remember, contrary to popular belief, not every customer is price sensitive. Some cus-tomers are, in fact, "benefit" sensitive, which means they are willing to pay more money for greater benefits.[6]

6. If you can build your entrepreneurial brand and develop high brand equity, you can command premium prices for your products/services. And this illustrates the importance of branding we pointed out in Chapter 7.

7. Leverage the principle of just noticeable difference (JND). JND is the point at which a customer notices a change in your pricing. If you wish to dis-guise an increase in your prices, change your price but do so below the JND point. If you want to drop your price and show the customers you are pro-viding greater value, then make the price change beyond the JND point.

8. Add value instead of price discounting. Frankly, discounting can kill your business. Just a 10 percent discount on prices may require you to sell 50 percent more units to keep the same bottom-line profit. So, instead, focus on giving the customer more value, such as a more satisfying experience.[7]

9. Do not use the same price margin for all your products/services. There is no rule that says all products/services need to be priced the same. You can afford a smaller margin for products/services with a high sales volume, but slower moving items might need higher margins.[8]

10. You will know you have pricing problems if (1) there is poor customer response, (2) your channel members complain, (3) intense price bargaining is the norm, (4) there is high elastic demand, and/or (5) you are forced into chronic markdowns. When this occurs, you must take corrective action.

In addition to this advice, the Entrepreneurial Marketing Spotlight features two experts and what they have to say about pricing in a new venture. Mark Stiving is a pricing expert from California and Brad Sugars is the Founder of ActionCoach. Both provide some good insight you should heed as you map out your pricing strategy for your new venture.

Entrepreneurial Marketing Spotlight

Mark Stiving is a pricing expert based out of California. Brad Sugars is the Founder of ActionCoach and both know something about pricing in new ventures. Mark Stiving warns entrepreneurs to not use a cost-based approach to pricing. He also suggests you avoid using a competition-based approach to pricing. Instead he suggests that a new venture determine its price based on customers willingness to pay. And, he suggests you do not need to hire a marketing research firm to do this for you. Stiving says take the time yourself and talk with potential customers. Find out how much value they attach to the products/services you are marketing. At the same time, ask them who they currently buy from and how they value your competitors' products/services. This provides some keen insight into where you stand and your possible latitude for setting prices. And, remember don't constrain yourself by thinking you should charge what the competitors charge! Offer something that the customer is willing to pay extra for. Finally, what you charge for your products/ services is really all about what type of customer you want to attract, so set prices for a specific target customer—and not all customers.

Brad Sugars says if he had to give just one piece of advice to an entrepreneur just starting out he would tell that entrepreneur—*never discount*—no matter how much you may be tempted to—always look instead to add value. He also says it is extremely important for the entrepreneur to know his/her costs and margins and to protect margins at all costs! It is important to keep your costs low—run a lean business—because most new ventures cannot achieve significant scaling up that reduces costs. Sugars says instead of discounting always look to add value to your products/services, both real and perceived. This could be bundling offerings or providing a better customer experience. Since most new ventures are not able to cost-cut their way to success, growth is your only option. So focus on ways to grow such as a private label at a higher price point. Finally, do not fall for the notion that if you do not give discounts, you'll lose sales. The discount trap could truncate your business's future. Good advice from Mark and Brad and that is why they find themselves in the entrepreneurial marketing spotlight![9]

Key Takeaways

- You must know and understand the three pricing parameters for your venture: the price floor (set by your cost), the price range (set by your competitors), and the price ceiling (set by your customers).
- There are three basic approaches to set prices: cost based, competition based, and customer based. You need to examine and consider all three of these parameters.
- Using a cost-based approach will help you to, if nothing else, determine your break-even point.
- You must identify your competitors and understand their pricing practices. However, do not follow them into the ditch!
- Researching your customers is imperative to determine the price ceiling.
- Understand when to use skimming pricing and penetration pricing and the implications of their use.
- Be careful not to underprice your offerings. It can affect how the customer perceives your products/services and drive your break-even point higher than necessary.

Entrepreneurial Exercise

Identify your most direct competitors and record the prices they charge. Plot those prices on paper to establish a "price range." Now, given your costs and the established price range, where could you price your offerings along that range? Record your price on the range. Set this aside. Now, take a copy of the competitive price range (without your product/service on it) and go talk to some customers. Present to them the exact nature of the value you will be offering them and ask them to pinpoint where on the price range your offerings should be. Now, compare where the customers say your price should be located on the range with the one you established knowing only your costs and the competitors' prices. Is there a difference? If the customer located your price higher on the range than you did, then that is probably the price you should use. If they located your price lower on the range, ask them why they did so. Perhaps you might need to rethink your proposed value proposition.

Key Terms

Notes

1. Adapted from Nichole L. Torres, "Biz 101," *Entrepreneur,* June 2007, 90.

2. Allan MaGrath, "Ten Timeless Truths About Pricing," *Journal of Business and Industrial Marketing* 6, no. 3/4 (1991): 15–23.

3. Jeffry Timmons and Stephen Spinelli, *New Venture Creation,* 8th ed. (Burr Ridge, IL: McGraw-Hill, 2009).

4. Charles Fishman, "Which Price Is Right," *Fast Company,* March 2003, 92–99.

5. Ibid.

6. MaGrath, "Ten Timeless Truths."

7. Brad Sugars, "7 Biggest Mistakes in Setting Prices," *Entrepreneur.com,* August 26, 2008.

8. Ibid.

9. Mark Stiving, "Four Rules for Pricing Products," Entrepreneur.com, November 15, 2011; http://www.entrepreneur.com/article/220746?cm_sp=nextarticle-_-220746-_-222519. Retrieved February 15, 2012. Brad Sugars, "How to Compete and Win, When Rivals Cut Prices," Entrepreneur.com, December 22, 2011; http://www.entrepreneur.com/article/222519. Retrieved February 15, 2012.

Nine

Entrepreneurial Channel Development and Supply Chain Management

I was sitting in my office one day when my assistant came in and told me someone wished to speak to me. A young, well-dressed woman walked in with a frozen pie in her hand! She told me she baked the best pies in the world. She began selling fresh pies at church fairs and farmers' markets but decided she wanted to grow her business. She determined that getting into the frozen pie segment would be the best way to extend her market reach. After she researched the market, she put together a business plan and began producing the product. Her business plan called for reaching her customers through supermarkets. But when she approached a large supermarket chain to take on her line, she was shocked. It wasn't that they were not interested in her product; they were. The problem was that in order for the supermarket to carry her line, she would have to pay a "slotting fee"—a payment many retailers require from manufacturers or producers to place a new item on a retailer's shelf—or in this case, the refrigerator.

She had worked out her pricing without the knowledge of such slotting fees, and now this fee would either eliminate much of the profitably of her new venture or she would be forced to raise her price significantly and thus risk losing the retail shopper's business. Now she did not know what to do.

I told her that slotting fees were very common because retailers have limited space and have too many companies who want that space. But, I told her, not all supermarkets require slotting fees. Then, when she told me her production capacity, I told her I knew of a specialty food store that would be perfect for her. It sold upscale premium products (consistent with her offering) and did not charge slotting fees. I made a phone call to the owner, a friend of mine, and arranged a meeting; within two weeks, her product was in the refrigerators of this store—slot-fee free!

The previous story illustrates an example of an entrepreneur who felt she had planned well for her venture, including various business contingencies. But gaining access to her customers was obviously something she had overlooked or had taken for granted. She simply assumed she could get her pies in the "pipeline"—the channel—and reach her target customer. She was correct in choosing a retail channel, but unfortunately, she had not planned for the cost of obtaining this access.

In this chapter, you will see that channel development—reaching your target customers with your products/services, either directly or indirectly (or both)—is a critical prerequisite for venture success. Any channel system you design should be effective in reaching your target customer, with the right product/service, at the right place, at the right time, and at the right price. Importantly, your channel system must achieve these goals while still being profitable. Profitable, including the possibility of paying slotting fees!

When it comes to determining your channel strategy, you may have to make important trade-offs between channel effectiveness, market coverage, and cost/profitability. But in the end, you must ensure that your channel system will drive sales growth and deliver customer value. Therefore, your job is to determine the best way to get your products/services to your customers while achieving profitable sales levels. And remember, if you intend to move your products through retail channels, do not forget to find out if slotting fees will be required!

Understanding Channels

One of the 5Ps and 8Ps you learned about that make up the marketing mix of product/service-based ventures is place—or distribution. Distribution is the means of getting your product/service to your target customer. A **distribution channel** consists of the organizations and individuals involved in the process of getting the products/services that you produce to your customers. These organizations or individuals in the distribution channel are generally known as intermediaries or channel members. Simply put, think of the distribution channel as the pipeline through which your product/service flows.

Channel Options

Basically, you have three channel options: direct, indirect, or multichannel. You must consider numerous factors when making a channel decision. Optimally, with most new ventures, the preference would be to distribute directly (you will not use an intermediary or channel member) to your target customer because it offers you the most control.

Moreover, I have often argued that as an entrepreneur, you should not think about adding channel members until you've actually learned everything you need to know about selling directly to the customer. Even if in the end you decide to use channel members, having sold directly to customers is a valuable learning experience that can be passed along to channel members.

In some cases, you may simply not have the expertise and/or resources necessary to build and support a direct channel, and thus you might decide to reach your target customer through an indirect channel—using an intermediary or channel member. Or, the venture may use a combination of direct and indirect channels, a "multichannel" option (see Figure 9.1).

Direct Channel

If you elect for a **direct channel,** you will not be using an intermediary or channel member. In short, you will sell directly to your target customer. Three Dog Bakery, for example, runs its retail stores where it sells its high-end, natural, and healthy dog treats. But a direct channel may not involve selling via a retail location. In fact, you can sell directly through a direct

Figure 9.1   Channel Options

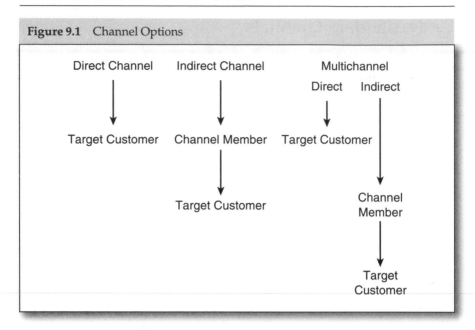

sales force, via telemarketing, mail/catalog, or online. With a direct channel, you retain ownership of your products/services and are responsible for sales, distribution, customer service, and collection of payment from the customer.

The use of a direct sales force offers you a large degree of control over customer interaction, but it can also be expensive to reach your customers with a direct sales force strategy. In fact, the costs of a direct sales force have been increasing. Thus, many new ventures have turned to other types of direct channels such as telemarketing, direct mail, catalogs, infomercials, and televised home shopping, which are less expensive direct channel alternatives. Now, electronic or online marketing channels are growing in popularity, and many new ventures operate only in "virtual markets" and thus save money by not having physical locations as well as achieving lower sales and distribution costs. One small startup that I know that used to have a retail outlet recently shifted entirely to an online store format and reduced its operating costs significantly while improving sales/revenue. Before making the shift, the owners discussed the possible move with their customers, who supported the change and remained loyal to the company.

A major trend when it comes to direct channels is the concept of **disintermediation.** This means the removal or bypassing of intermediaries so the venture can deal directly with the customer. Disintermediation has been fueled by the desire of the entrepreneur to reduce channel cost and maintain greater control, as well as because of technology, specifically the Internet. Dell is a classic example of disintermediation, selling computers directly to customers online and bypassing traditional retail channels. Zappos, the online upstart fashion merchandiser, has also achieved tremendous success as a disintermediated business. In some cases, disintermediation is initiated by the customer who wishes to avoid intermediaries and to buy direct with the hope of achieving better prices and/or improved customer service. Disintermediation is popular for many companies selling a variety of products/services such as computer hardware and software, books and music, and even stock trades (e.g., E-trade). Many alcoholic beverage companies are also seeking disintermediation but will have to overcome legal obstacles to achieve it.

Indirect Channel

An **indirect channel** involves one or more intermediaries or channel members positioned between you and your target customer. If you have more than one channel member, you have a multitiered channel. While your first channel option, a direct channel, may be optimal in terms of control and customer interaction, a direct channel can be expensive. Therefore, many new ventures turn to an indirect channel option.

An indirect channel can include agents, brokers, dealers, distributors, wholesalers, retailers, or other channel members. Indirect channels are more complex than a direct channel, and the channel member(s) can take both ownership of the product/service and can control both the sales and distribution function. See Figure 9.2 for descriptions of key intermediaries or channel members.[1]

Multichannel

Multichannel distribution is growing in popularity. Multichannel distribution reaches your customers by employing two or more different types of marketing channels. Multichannel distribution can be used to reach similar customers with the same basic product, different customers with the same basic product, or different customers with different products. For example, Avon sells its products through independent representatives, while its website, kiosks, and some outlet and department stores reach similar customers with the same products. Hallmark sells its Hallmark

Figure 9.2   Key Intermediaries or Channel Members

Agent	• Intermediary or channel member who markets a product/service for a fee. Sometimes called manufacturer's agents or selling agents depending on the industry.
Broker	• Intermediary or channel member who brings buyers and sellers together to negotiate purchases. Does not take title to or possession of products and has limited authority regarding prices and terms of sale. Often used on a onetime or as-needed basis.
Dealer	• Not a precise term; can mean the same as distributor, wholesaler, or retailer.
Distributor	• Not a precise term, usually used to describe an intermediary or channel member who performs a variety of distribution functions, including maintaining inventory, marketing, and so on.
Wholesaler	• Intermediary or channel member who sells to other intermediaries or channel members, usually retailers. Takes possession of products and then markets them. Common in consumer markets.
Retailer	• An intermediary or channel member that sells directly to customers, ultimate consumers, and business customers.

SOURCE: Adapted from F. Webster Jr., *Marketing for Managers* (New York: Harper & Row, 1974).

greeting cards through Hallmark stores and select department stores and sells its Ambassador brand of cards through discount and drugstore chains, thus reaching different customers with different brands.

I also know of a startup company that sells its bikes through retail bike specialty stores but also sells directly (through its online website) to high-end bike buyers who want to make customized bikes not available through the retail stores. And remember Three Dog Bakery? It sells through its retail stores and online, and it distributes to major retailers across America. Finally, I know two enterprising young brothers who have built two separate businesses leveraging two types of channels. While both their businesses involve seafood (specifically lobster), one of their businesses is wholesale based. In this case, instead of cutting out the middleman, the brothers became the middleman! Their other business is an innovative online retail concept with a twist. Read the Entrepreneurial Marketing Spotlight for some details.

Channel Drivers

As an entrepreneur, you must recognize the key drivers that will affect your channel alternatives. There are several drivers, including the customer, the product, the environment, and the venture itself.

Of course, your customer will have a direct bearing on your channel choice. Determining which channel is most appropriate is based on answers to some fundamental questions, such as the following: Who are potential customers? Where do they buy? When do they buy? How do they buy? What do they buy? The answers also indicate, if necessary, the type of intermediary or channel member best suited to reaching your target customer. In general, fewer customers would indicate a direct channel as your best alternative, while many customers buying your products might indicate that the indirect channel might be best.

Entrepreneurial Marketing Spotlight

As undergrads, John and Brendan Ready spent their weekends catching lobsters in Maine. At Northeastern University, John won the $60K Business Plan Competition, which led to the birth of Ready Seafood, a wholesale seafood company specializing in lobster. The company catches its own lobsters and also buys lobsters from other fishermen throughout Maine. The lobsters are then packed live in moist newspaper and with fresh picked seafood and shipped to five-star restaurants, hotels, and supermarkets all over the United States. Ready Seafood has grown into a $10 million lobster wholesale business. But the brothers have also started another innovative venture, called Catch a Piece of Maine. It is a lobster trap timeshare of sorts. For $2,995, customers take ownership of a trap for a year and receive a credit every time their traps catch one of Maine's favorite crustaceans. They can then redeem the credits for the real thing, for themselves or to give as gifts. This business is operated online, where the customer can order directly and receive the product right from the source. This business model allows John and Brendan to earn substantial profit margin. Catch a Piece of Maine already projects $1.2 million in revenue for 2008—its first full year in operation—and employs a staff of five. For their entrepreneurial efforts, the Ready brothers received the Small Business Administration's 2008 National Young Entrepreneur Award and find themselves in the Entrepreneurial Marketing Spotlight![2]

The products/services you are marketing will also help drive your channel alternatives. For example, highly sophisticated products, unstandardized products, and products of high unit value will generally be distributed directly to customers. Unsophisticated, standardized products and products with low unit value, on the other hand, will tend to be distributed through indirect channels. A product's stage in the life cycle will also drive channel options. For example, early in the life cycle, you might use direct channels, but as the product matures, you might expand distribution through the use of channel members.

The changing environment will also help drive your channel choice. For example, advances in the technology of growing, transporting, and storing perishable cut flowers have allowed 1-800-FLOWERS to use a direct channel to get its flowers to its customers, eliminating or bypassing traditional channels. The Internet has also been a major technological innovation that has created a new channel opportunity for many entrepreneurs who sell a range of products/services, including consumer electronics, books, music, and video products.

Finally, your venture itself is also a driver of channel alternatives. In particular, your financial, human, or technological capabilities will ultimately affect channel choice. For example, if your venture does not have the financial means to employ a sales force, you might use manufacturers' agents or selling agents to reach other channel members (e.g., wholesalers) or your customers.

Choosing a Channel Strategy

Recognizing that numerous routes to your target customers exist, the entrepreneur must consider the following when choosing a channel strategy:[3]

1. Effectiveness—How well does the channel strategy meet customers' needs/requirements?

2. Market coverage—Can the customer find and appreciate the value of your venture's offerings?

3. Cost-efficiency/profitability—Can the venture gain access to customers in a cost-efficient way and achieve profitability?

4. Adaptability—Can the channel handle new products/services and incorporate emergent channel forms?

A major consideration in choosing a channel strategy is determining which channel(s) will be most effective in satisfying the buying needs/requirements of the target customer. In fact, one of the most critical questions you need to answer is, "How do the customers like to buy?" Would they prefer to buy from you directly? Or, do they mind buying through a channel member? Some of the target customer buying requirements to consider are the desire for information, the demand for convenience, the need for variety, and level of customer service expected.

Information is an important requirement when customers have limited knowledge or desire specific information about a product or service. Properly chosen channel members communicate with customers through in-store displays, demonstrations, and personal selling.

Convenience has multiple meanings for customers, such as close proximity or little driving time to get access to the product/service. For example, 7-Eleven stores with outlets nationwide offer customers nearby convenience. For other customers, convenience means a minimum of time and hassle. Jiffy Lube, for example, promises to change engine oil and filters quickly, which appeals to this aspect of convenience. For those who shop on the Internet, convenience means that websites must be easy to locate and navigate, and image downloads will be fast.

Variety reflects customers' interest in having numerous competing and complementary items from which to choose. Variety is evident in both the breadth and depth of products and brands carried by channel members, which enhances their attraction to buyers. Thus, manufacturers of pet food seek distribution through pet superstores, such as PETCO and PetSmart, which offer a wide array of pet products.

Customer service provided by channel members is an important buying requirement for such products as large household appliances that require delivery, installation, and credit. Therefore, some appliance manufacturers will seek and select channel members (dealers) who will provide good and consistent customer service, including both before and after the sale.

The second consideration when choosing a channel strategy is the notion of market coverage. Appropriate market coverage requires that you understand distribution density and the role channel members play in this distribution density. Three degrees of distribution density exist: intensive, selective, and exclusive. If an entrepreneur selects an **intensive distribution** strategy, it means he or she is attempting to achieve broad access to customers and full physical market coverage, making the product/service widely available to all target customers when and where they want it. Convenience products and staples such as milk, snacks, fast food, and soft drinks are generally distributed using intensive distribution. While a high level of total sales can be achieved with this strategy, the entrepreneur gives up a degree of channel control (needs channel members) as well as reduces per unit profit due to increased channel expenses.

Using **selective distribution,** the entrepreneur will limit distribution to a select group of channel members in specific market areas. The entrepreneur will achieve less access and coverage but can achieve a little more channel control (fewer channel members) as well as reasonable sales volume and profits. Selective distribution is the most common form of distribution intensity and is usually associated with shopping goods or services, such as Rolex watches and Ping golf clubs.

Exclusive distribution is the extreme opposite of intensive distribution. The objective is to achieve a high degree of control of the channel and to limit the number of channel members and outlets. This strategy is intended to create prestige for the venture's products/services, gain strong channel member support, and gain high per unit profit. Designer clothing, expensive fragrances, and luxury electronics tend to use exclusive distribution.

The third consideration when considering channel strategy is cost-efficiency and profitability. Channel cost is the critical dimension of profitability. These costs include distribution, advertising, and selling expenses associated with different types of marketing channels. The extent to which channel members share these costs determines the margins received by each member and by the channel as a whole. As an entrepreneur, you have to determine if you will be better off, profit-wise, using channel members versus going it alone and using direct channels only. Moreover, you have to ask if the venture can justify a trade-off in cost-efficiency to gain greater effectiveness and market coverage because of the multiplier effect that distribution has on increasing the impact of the other marketing variables.

For example, one of my former clients sold products through wholesalers who, in turn, sold to retailers. The company understood the current costs of this channel arrangement as well as its profitability, but it decided to reexamine this strategy and to determine if an alternative strategy would be better. It found that if it bypassed the wholesalers, it would increase slightly its costs of doing business but would also increase its overall profitability. Accordingly, it changed its channel strategy.

The final aspect of channel strategy is to consider its adaptability. In essence, given fast-changing market conditions, you have to consider if the strategy is flexible enough to respond to such changes. For example, can the existing channel strategy be modified to take advantage of new channel opportunities (e.g., electronic channels)? Or, can the channel strategy adapt to handle new products/services your venture may roll out in the future?

Three Channel Design Imperatives

If I am pressed to give advice to young entrepreneurs starting new ventures regarding channel design, I prescribe three imperatives:

1. Design your channel from "the market back." In other words, focus on the needs and requirements of your target customer first and then allow this to dictate your channel design.

2. Try to leverage your channel strategy as a competitive advantage either in the form of creating and delivering superior customer value or as a way to "lock out" potential competitors.

3. Use channel innovation strategies. In essence, this means constantly thinking about the best ways to reach customers—knowing where you need to be given where the customers actually are. For example, in addition to traditional channels you may have to include a direct-to-consumer (D2C) channel. You also need to think about how to reach both existing core customers and your future customers who may not currently be core customers. For instance, the Gen Y cohort is now the largest group of consumers in the United States, estimated at more than 82 million people and outnumbering Boomers by almost 6 million. While the Boomers are often the core customer group for many ventures, consideration has to be given to the Gen Y group. To be effective in reaching this group you have to innovative and enhance your existing channels to meet the "anything, anytime, anyplace" demands of Gen Y. This means making investments in technology to meet Gen Y's high standards of e-commerce/mobile technology performance. In other words, think electronic channels. Channel innovation also involves social media channel innovation. For example, 15 years ago, 70 percent of grocery purchasing decisions were made at a store. Now, it is fewer than 50 percent. More and more often consumers research products online and

decide what they will buy before going to a store, or they forgo a trip to the store altogether and make purchases via the Internet. Thus, you have to innovate and leverage social media channels. Finally, true channel innovation means constructing integrated multichannel formatting and providing seamless cross-channel coverage to extend your reach.

Formalized Channel Arrangements

In many cases, channels are simply a loose-knit network of independent producers and intermediaries brought together to distribute products/ services. However, there are more formalized channel arrangements. For example, **vertical marketing systems** are professionally managed and centrally coordinated channels designed to achieve channel economies and marketing impact. There are two basic types of vertical marketing systems: corporate and contractual.

With a *corporate vertical marketing system*, successive stages of production and distribution are controlled by one single owner. For example, a producer might own the intermediary at the next level in the channel. This is called *forward integration* (e.g., a manufacturer also runs retail shops, like Polo). Alternatively, a retailer might own a manufacturing operation, which is called *backward integration* (e.g., Safeway operating its own bakeries).

Under a *contractual vertical marketing system*, independent production and distribution companies integrate their efforts on a contractual basis to obtain greater functional economies and increased marketing impact than they could achieve alone. There are three variations of contractual systems. *Wholesale-sponsored systems* involve a wholesaler that develops a contractual relationship with retailers (often small retailers) to standardize and coordinate buying practices, merchandising, and inventory. *Retail-sponsored systems* exist when small, independent retailers form an organization that operates a wholesale facility, cooperatively. Finally, the most visible variation of contractual systems is *franchising*, a contractual arrangement between a parent company (a franchisor) and an individual or a firm (a franchisee) that allows a certain type of business to be operated under an established name and according to specific rules, terms, and conditions. For many entrepreneurs, growing through franchising is a major consideration and may, in fact, be an excellent path to achieve high-growth venture status (e.g., McDonald's started with one single outlet). More recently, College Hunks Hauling Junk (1–800-JunkUSA.com), an upstart junk removal business, has grown dramatically through franchising.

Supply Chain Management

Supply chain management (SCM) encompasses the planning and management of all activities involved in sourcing and procurement, conversion, and all logistics management activities.[4] It also includes coordination and collaboration with channel partners, which can be suppliers, intermediaries, third-party service providers, and customers. In short, SCM integrates supply and demand management within and across companies. The entrepreneur should view SCM as an integrating concept that links major business functions and business processes within the company and across companies, supporting the venture to achieve a cohesive and profitable business model. SCM also includes manufacturing processes and all logistics management activities.

As part of SCM, logistics management is the planning, implementation, and control of the efficient, effective forward and reverse flow and storage of goods, services, and related information between the point of origin and the point of consumption to meet customer needs and requirements. Logistics management activities include inbound and outbound transportation management, fleet management, warehousing, materials handling, order fulfillment, logistics network design, inventory management, supply/demand planning, and management of third-party logistics providers. To varying degrees, the logistics function also includes sourcing, procurement, production planning and scheduling, packaging and assembly, and customer service.

Many entrepreneurs assume that SCM is the bastion of large companies because of its cost and complexity. But to successfully compete in a highly competitive global marketplace, your venture must create and implement an SCM program. In fact, a study comparing high-performing ventures to low-performing ventures revealed that the high-performing ventures performed better on every SCM performance dimension.[5] For example, high-performing ventures with SCM programs did better in terms of customer-facing performance (delivery, responsiveness, flexibility), internal-facing performance (cost reduction, asset utilization, and quality), market performance (customer value perceptions, new customer gains, market share, customer retention, and product availability), and financial performance (cash flow, return on investment, return on assets and net profit). In fact, new ventures that place an initial high priority on SCM can simply achieve "best in class" performance (e.g., Zara, upstart Spanish fashion manufacturer and merchandiser).

As an entrepreneur, you should know there are a variety of SCM program configurations. To construct the appropriate program, you must do the following:[6]

- Understand your customer. Identifying the needs/requirements of the customer is a key step in the process. For example, you must know whether the customer places a higher value on price, convenience, or customer service. Once this is known, you will configure your SCM program to meet that customer's highest priority.
- Understand your supply chain. You must understand that different supply chains are designed to do different things. For example, some supply chains emphasize responsiveness to customer needs/requirements, while others focus on efficiency—supplying products at the lowest-delivered price. You need to select the one that will best meet your customers' needs.
- Align the supply chain with your marketing strategy. Your goal is to align the supply chain's capabilities to the customers' needs/requirements as well as with your marketing strategy. A misalignment will require either a change in the supply chain or a change in the marketing strategy. Remember, a poorly configured SCM program can ruin an otherwise effective marketing strategy.

One of the major problems with many new ventures when it comes to SCM is the inability or unwillingness to invest in information technology (IT), yet such technology is a fundamental requirement for a good SCM program. Costs for IT have dropped dramatically over the past few years, so there is really no reason why you cannot make the investment in IT, which will enable you to create and execute a sound SCM program. It is an investment that will pay off.

Key Takeaways

- Channels are an often overlooked element of your ventures marketing mix. But if you do so, you do it at your peril.
- You have three basic channel options: direct, indirect, and multichannel. While many factors will affect your channel choice, your target customer should be a key driver.

- The multichannel option is a popular choice for entrepreneurs since it can balance effectiveness, market coverage, and cost-efficiency/profitability.
- It is extremely important to design your channel from "the market back" and to leverage your channel strategy as a possible competitive advantage. You also have to be innovative with both channel selection and channel execution including multichannel formats.
- Supply chain management (SCM) is not just a large company concept. SCM can help your venture achieve high performance in terms of customer-facing performance, internal-facing performance, and financial performance.
- An investment in information technology (IT) will be critical for your venture to create and execute an effective/efficient SCM program.

Entrepreneurial Exercise

Do an assessment of your possible channel options. Complete the following template. What conclusions can you draw from the exercise? What might be your best channel strategy? Why?

	Direct Channel	Indirect Channel	Multichannel
1. Ability to reach desired customer?			
2. Ability to meet customer requirements?			
3. Market coverage achieved?			
4. Time to market?			
5. Time to scale up distribution?			
6. Cost of each channel?			
7. Potential sales levels?			
8. Profitability of each channel?			
9. Ability to use channel as a competitive advantage?			
10. Ability to adapt to market changes?			

Key Terms

Distribution channel   153
Direct channel   153
Disintermediation   154
Indirect channel   155
Multichannel distribution   155

Intensive distribution   159
Selective distribution   160
Exclusive distribution   160
Vertical marketing systems   162
Supply chain management   163

Notes

1. F. Webster Jr., *Marketing for Managers* (New York: Harper & Row, 1974).

2. See the Ready brothers' websites at www.readyseafood.com and www.catchapieceofmaine.com.

3. Erin Anderson, George Day, and V. Rangan, "Strategic Channel Design," *Sloan Management Review,* Summer 1997, 59–69.

4. This section is based on Council of Supply Chain Management Professionals, "Definitions," Lombard, Illinois, 2009.

5. D. Kim, T. Ow, and M. Junc, "SME Strategies: An Assessment of High vs. Low Performers," *Communications of the ACM* 51, no. 11 (2008): 113–117.

6. Sunil Chopra and Peter Meindl, *Supply Chain Management: Strategy, Planning, and Operations,* 2nd ed. (Upper Saddle River, NJ: Prentice Hall, 2004).

Ten

Entrepreneurial Promotion

Doing More With Less!

Whenever I opened up a new food store location, I used a particular promotion strategy that was always effective, and effective on a shoestring budget! I would send, by mail, personally addressed invitations for the grand opening to all families in my trade area, asking them to come and see the new store. To encourage them to show up, I also offered a gift to each family who came to visit the store during the first week of the opening. This was typically a flower for the female head of household and a fresh baked cookie for each child accompanying a parent. I also held a ribbon-cutting ceremony, usually with a local celebrity (athlete, musician) who I knew well and would help me out at no cost. I would also ask the media to cover the opening and gained plenty of free publicity. I would also place a "grand opening" ad in the local newspaper that typically contained a coupon that the customer could redeem when purchasing a particular product. The coupon redemption rate also gave me some indication of the success of the newspaper ad. I would also set up a series of demonstrations throughout the store where customers could try our products. I have always found that in-store demos/samples were very effective in driving sales and did so very cheaply. Then, when the customers finished shopping and checked out, they received a coupon to be used during their next visit. The type of coupon given to the customer was based on what the customer purchased during his or her first visit. And, of course, I continued to promote the business throughout the year, including regular weekly ads emphasizing specials to encourage customers to continue to shop with us.

Importantly, while I worked hard to "get my first customers," I worked even harder to keep them, including offering personalized and friendly service. By retaining my customers, I did not have to spend a fortune trying to attract a lot of new customers. In my view, it was no accident that I was able to achieve my sales forecasts for my new stores. I simply understood the value of promotion and worked creatively to coordinate a variety of promotional techniques that paid handsome dividends.

I often hear other entrepreneurs questioning the value of promotion and, in many cases, have watched them try to avoid making the necessary investment in promotion. But in my experience, opening a business and not promoting it is a recipe for disaster. The reality is you need promotion and, importantly, it does not have to cost you a fortune.

I understand that as an entrepreneur, it is highly likely that you will have limited financial resources. But this is not an excuse not to promote your business. Instead, it simply pushes you to find novel ways to leverage promotion that results in doing more with less! The integration and coordination of your promotional efforts will be important for your venture. In fact, smart entrepreneurs coordinate all their promotional activities—advertising, personal selling, sales promotion, public relations, and direct marketing—to provide a consistent message across all audiences, to maximize the promotional budget, and to increase the impact of their promotion. This is referred to as *integrated marketing communications* (IMC). Keep the concept of IMC in mind as we walk through this important chapter, where we discuss promotion and how to put together a successful promotional program for your business and its products/services.

Promotion

Promotion is an important element of your entrepreneurial marketing mix. As you know from Chapter 1, promotion is the means of communication between you and your customer. More specifically, **promotion** is marketer-initiated communications activities directed to target customers (target audiences) to influence their attitudes and behaviors. Five major promotional techniques are available to you to communicate with your target customer: advertising, public relations (PR), sales promotion, personal selling, and direct marketing. Your **promotional mix** is the combination of the promotional techniques you intend to use to complete the communications task.

The Role of Promotion

The role of promotion is quite simple: to influence and affect the behavior of the intended target audience. In general, promotion is used to achieve three broad objectives: (1) create brand awareness, (2) build favorable brand attitudes, and (3) encourage brand action—get the customer to buy. This is sometimes referred to as "achieving the 3As," which we will discuss further later in the chapter.

As an entrepreneur, you are a new player in the market, and your first task is to use promotion to make customers aware of your business and your products/services (brand awareness). As you have already learned, getting into the customer's brand awareness set is a fundamental requirement if you hope to win the customer's business. While it is required, it is not sufficient. You must also be able to communicate why the customer should buy from you. In other words, build favorable brand attitudes toward your company and its products/services to get in the customer's brand consideration set. Then, you must be able to persuade the customer to actually make the purchase (brand action). If successful, your work is still not completed. You must keep using promotion to remind customers to continue to buy from you!

The Promotional Mix

As mentioned earlier, your promotion mix can consist of a combination of advertising, PR, sales promotion, personal selling, and direct marketing.

Each of these promotional techniques has particular strengths and weaknesses, and each can play particular roles in achieving your basic promotional objectives. Figure 10.1 shows the basic strengths and weaknesses of these promotional techniques.

Figure 10.1   Strengths and Weaknesses of the Basic Promotional Techniques

Technique	Strengths	Weaknesses
Advertising	Efficient in achieving broad reach, quickly; attention getting	High costs; difficult to measure effectiveness; customers skeptical
Public relations	Has credibility; provides more information than ads	Difficult to obtain PR; need media cooperation
Sales promotion	Stimulate sales in short run; very flexible	Can be abused by customers; can cheapen product in the minds of customers if used too often
Personal selling	Personal feedback; persuasive; control over audience selection	Can be very expensive per exposure; message may be inconsistent
Direct marketing	Can provide direct, measurable results; precision targeting; customization	Customer may not buy unless he or she knows the company; database management can be expensive

Advertising

Advertising is the use of paid media by an identified sponsor to communicate information about a company, product, or service to specific target customers.[1] Advertising gives you the ability to reach a broad audience quickly and to do so in an attention-getting manner. But, in general, the costs to produce and place advertising can be high. Still, as an entrepreneur, you must also recognize that some advertising media can be used at a reasonable cost. For example, while national television ads can be very expensive, local television advertising can be significantly cheaper. Your job is to examine the relative costs of advertising (each medium and compared to other promotional techniques) and its ability to reach and influence your potential customers. If advertising is going to be part of your promotional mix, you will have many specific advertising media to consider (see Figure 10.2).

Figure 10.2 Strengths and Weaknesses of Major Advertising Media

Medium	Strengths	Weaknesses
Television	Broad reach; visual	High cost; short exposure time
Radio	Low cost; targeted	No visuals; short exposure time
Magazines	Very targeted; long life	Long lead time to place; cost
Newspapers	Good local market coverage	Short life span; crowded medium
Yellow Pages	Good geographic coverage; long life	Tough to keep up to date
Direct mail	Very targeted; personalized messages; customization	High cost per contact; poor image (junk mail)
Internet	Interactivity	Cost to develop; difficult to track effectiveness
Outdoor	Targeted; repeat exposure	Message must be simple
Consumer-generated media	Customers generate the promotion	Lack of control of what is promoted

For example, television advertising is a possible option for your venture. While national television advertising can be expensive, you could select local TV advertising or advertising on cable channels. In fact, in addition to lower costs, many cable channels such as The Comedy Network or the Food Network deliver very specific audiences, audiences that may include your customers. Another TV advertising option is the *infomercial*—program-length (often 30 minutes) advertisements designed to educate the customer about your company and its products/services.

If your venture is located in a specific community and targets customers in that community, the local newspaper may be a good advertising option for you. It can provide excellent local market coverage at reasonable costs. In fact, if you are a local retailer, the newspaper may be a key medium for you. For example, my food stores ran a full-page ad every Thursday featuring many food specials. And many of our customers clipped out the ad and brought it with them while they shopped!

Yellow Pages advertising is also a good medium for local businesses. *Yellow Pages* directories reach almost every household, and customers use them when searching for providers of particular products/services. With the advent of the Internet, you also have the option of using online *Yellow Pages.*

One of the fastest growing advertising mediums is Internet advertising. Many entrepreneurs are taking advantage of this medium, particularly as part of their integrated promotional efforts. Internet advertising is similar to print advertising, but it has additional advantages because it can incorporate the audio and visual capabilities of the Internet. It also has the unique feature of being interactive. There are also a variety of venues to advertise online, including portal sites, individual sites, and search engines. For example, with search advertising (e.g., Google Adwords), you would pay for the chance to have your ad displayed when a user searches for a given keyword. In most cases, you only pay when the user clicks on your ad or link (a pay-per-click—PPC model). Finally, you can also develop your own website and integrate a variety of advertising and other promotional techniques within the site.

A new and novel form of advertising that entrepreneurs are taking advantage of is called *consumer-generated media.* This is also sometimes called *user-created media.* This is media generated by consumers/users and disseminated via various media channels, particularly the Internet. As an entrepreneur, you can interface with such media in a number of ways. You might advertise on consumer-generated media sites such as YouTube. You could allow users to create content and then sponsor that content and allow it to be shared on consumer-generated content sites. You could sponsor a contest encouraging users to create content or partner with the user to co-create the media and the message and then disseminate it. The bottom line is you can allow your user to help promote your business and your products/services and do so very inexpensively. For example, one new resort I know of asks its guests to prepare a video of their stay, which is posted to the resort website and then picked up by travel review sites on the Internet. Occupancy rates at the resort have risen as a result of this user-generated media activity.

An important consideration for entrepreneurs is the emphasis that should be placed on corporate advertising versus product advertisements.[2]

The objective behind *corporate advertising* is to build awareness of the company and establish goodwill for the company rather than advertising specific products or services. Many customers consider the company behind the products/services and want to have confidence when doing business with the company. So, when launching a business, many entrepreneurs will focus on corporate advertising that tells the story of the company, what it does and what it sells.

Of course, *product advertising* is also important, so entrepreneurs should also invest in efforts to tell customers about their products and where they can be found. It is important for the entrepreneur to stress the brand's features and benefits and persuade the customer to select the venture's brand rather than the competitors' brands. In many cases, the entrepreneur will attempt to thread the needle and promote both the company and the product in the same advertisement. In other words, with limited resources, the entrepreneur must find ways to promote both the company and its products.

Finally, also important when considering advertising is whether the entrepreneur is seeking a direct or delayed response from the advertising. *Direct-response advertising* seeks to motivate the customer to take immediate action. For example, a television ad wanting you to call a 1–800 number and order a product right now is a direct-response ad.

Delayed-response advertising, however, presents information about the company and/or its products designed to influence the customer in the near future when making purchases. For example, a furniture store might advertise the quality furniture it sells but may not expect you to drop everything and run to your car to visit the showroom. Instead, it is planting a seed in the hope that when you are considering a new furniture purchase, you might consider visiting this store. Many entrepreneurs who want immediate and measured responses to their advertising emphasize direct-response advertising. Thus, you will often find direct-response advertising being leveraged as part of the entrepreneur's direct marketing efforts.

Public Relations

There is an old saying in the entrepreneurship field: "While you have to pay for advertising, you can pray for PR!" But today, many entrepreneurs don't just simply pray for **public relations** (PR); instead, they actively plan and execute well-controlled PR programs that are often part of integrated promotional plans. PR is a type of communication designed to create a positive image about a company, its products/services, or people via the use of nonpaid forms of communication.[3]

One of the most frequently used PR tools is **publicity**—the practice of creating and disseminating information about a company, its products/services, people, or company activities to secure favorable news coverage in the media reaching identified target audiences.[4] Publicity typically takes the form of a news release. In short, you craft a story and encourage the media to tell it! Another popular way to garner free publicity is by using online review sites such as Gizmodo and Lifehacker.

But in addition to publicity, there are many other public relations tools available to you. These include sponsorships and collateral materials such an annual reports, brochures, newsletters (print and/or electronic), corporate Web sites, or videos. Event or cause sponsorship is a very popular choice among startup ventures. The goal of sponsorships is to create a way to disseminate company and/or product information, create brand awareness, and connect your company and/or its product to the event being sponsored. You might, for example, sponsor a sports team competing in a league or tournament or sponsor a community event. Through your sponsorship, you can reach your target audience and build goodwill toward your company and its products/services.

Sales Promotion

Another promotional technique is **sales promotion,** a short-term inducement of value offered to arouse customer interest in buying a product or service. Used in conjunction with advertising or personal selling, sales promotions can be offered to intermediaries (channel members) as well as to your end-customers. If you are considering the use of sales promotion, you have plenty of options. See Figure 10.3 for an overview of the types of sales promotions you can use as well as their strengths and weaknesses.

Couponing is often a quick and inexpensive way to get your first customers to try your products/services. The key is to use them correctly. This means targeting new customers and not just rewarding customers who are already loyal to your business. Sampling is also an effective sales promotion for most new ventures. You are simply putting the product into the customer's hands for free with the hope that if the customer likes the sample, he or she will purchase the product in the future. For example, sampling was the key to the success of one of my clients who produced a premium yogurt.

Figure 10.3 Strengths and Weaknesses of Sales Promotion Techniques

Technique	Strengths	Weaknesses
Coupons	Obtains retailer support	Customer may delay purchase
Deals	Reduces customer risk	May reduce perceived value of product
Premiums	Customers respond to free merchandise	Customer wants the premium, not the product
Contests	Build customer involvement	Requires creative or analytical skills
Sweepstakes	Encourages increased consumption	Sales drop after program ends
Samples	Encourages trial	High cost to company
Loyalty programs	Creates loyalty	High cost to company
Point-of-purchase displays	Improves product visibility	Hard to obtain/place and increased cost
Rebates	Stimulates demand	Reduces perceived product value
Product placement	Positive message in noncommercial setting	Little control over presentation

She did extensive in-store sampling, and customer reaction was overwhelmingly positive and led to tremendous sales success.

Another sales promotion tool that a new venture should consider is a loyalty program. Loyalty programs encourage and reward repeat purchases. Loyalty programs such as frequent-flyer, frequent-traveler, and frequent-purchase programs at the retail level are very common today. But there is room for new ventures to begin their own loyalty programs. When Second Cup, a retail coffee shop, opened its doors, it offered customers a loyalty program where every tenth cup of coffee was free. Customers simply presented their loyalty card every time they purchased a cup of coffee. The card is scanned and the purchase is recorded by the point-of-sale system, and every tenth cup of coffee is automatically provided free to the customer.

For many years, sales promotion was considered by many as a supplemental ingredient of the promotional mix. But more recently, its use and importance has increased. Why? Well, many entrepreneurs are now looking for measureable results from their promotional efforts. Sales promotion is an effective tool in this regard. In addition, many customers have become more value conscious and thus are more responsive to sales promotion activities. Finally, information technology has helped in the planning and execution of sales promotion activities.

Still, sales promotion should not be used as a stand-alone promotional technique and should not be overused. If used too often, sales promotions can lose their effectiveness (e.g., customers may delay purchase until you use a sales promotion, or they might begin to question the value of your product).

In addition to sales promotions directed toward your customers, you also have the option of using sales promotions (called trade promotions) that are directed toward your intermediaries or channel members. Three common trade promotions are allowances and discounts, cooperative advertising, and training of channel members' sales forces. To encourage channel members to maintain or increase inventory, you can offer discounts or price reductions or offer allowances such as case allowances, merchandise allowances, or finance allowances. If you have channel members who are engaged in actively promoting your products/services, you can also consider a cooperative advertising/promotion program where you will pay a percentage of the promotion expenses incurred by the channel member. Finally, you can offer training to your channel members' sales forces to increase sales performance. Often, this training is accompanied by incentive programs to help motivate the sales forces.

Personal Selling

Many new ventures will find it necessary to use personal selling as a major component of their promotional mix. **Personal selling** is the two-way flow of communication between a buyer and seller, designed to influence a person's or group's purchase decision. Unlike advertising, personal selling is usually face-to-face communication between the sender and receiver (although telephone and electronic sales are growing).

There are important advantages to personal selling. A salesperson can control to whom the presentation is made and can immediately see or hear the customer's reaction. If the feedback is unfavorable, the salesperson can modify the message. However, the flexibility of personal selling can also be a disadvantage. Different salespeople can change the message so that no consistent communication is given to all customers. The high cost of personal selling is also another major disadvantage. On a cost-per-contact basis, it is generally the most expensive of the five major promotional techniques.

As an entrepreneur, what you must remember is that you may have to be the most important salesperson for the venture. You may have to sell yourself and your company effectively to obtain financing, to secure channel arrangements, and to instill customer confidence in the enterprise. In many ways, it will be difficult for the customer to separate you, as the venture founder, from the enterprise itself. Thus, it will be very important for you to be your venture's best cheerleader and champion, and this will require effective personal sales skills.

Direct Marketing

Another promotional technique, **direct marketing,** uses direct communication with consumers to generate a "measurable" response in the form of an order, a request for further information, or a visit to a retail outlet. In other words, it is designed to create direct orders, generate leads, or build traffic. The communication can take many forms, including face-to-face selling (personal selling, already discussed), direct mail, catalogues, telephone solicitations, direct-response advertising (on television and radio and in print), online marketing, e-mail marketing, and mobile marketing. Like personal selling, direct marketing often consists of interactive communication. It also has the advantage of being customized to match the needs of specific target markets. Messages can be developed and adapted quickly to facilitate one-to-one relationships with customers. Importantly, it is its emphasis on a measurable customer response that distinguishes direct marketing from other promotional techniques.

Some of the most inexpensive and often very effective forms of direct marketing that entrepreneurs can use include e-mail marketing, e-zines, direct promotion on social networking sites, and mobile marketing. E-mail marketing is a fast, easy, and relatively inexpensive way to promote your business and its products/services. It is particularly useful in promoting special offers and inducing trial. In addition to e-mail marketing, some entrepreneurs have introduced the concept of e-zines (electronic magazines) and/or electronic newsletters to promote their businesses.

Many entrepreneurs are also directly promoting their companies and their products and/or services via social media. As you have learned in previous chapters, social media is changing the way customers behave and how business is done. In fact, social media now offers entrepreneurs a tremendous opportunity to promote their ventures very, very cost-effectively. In fact, social media is the brave new world for entrepreneurs. A small startup company, for example, the Smart Cookie Company, started with just $2,000 and promotes the sale of its home-baked cookies using the social media platform Facebook. The social networking and microblogging site Twitter is also being used by entrepreneurs to sell their products and services. Finally, direct "mobile marketing" is exploding in terms of its usage by entrepreneurs. Entrepreneurs are using text messaging, short message service (SMS), and common short codes (CSC) to connect directly with customers and asking for their business. In fact, some experts suggest that mobile marketing is becoming a foundational pillar for entrepreneurs when it comes to promoting their ventures.

When it comes to doing more with less, entrepreneurs have to embrace using social media as a critical component of their promotional plans. However, you have to know how to use social media appropriately to promote your products/services.[5] When it comes to social media, remember these basic tenets:

1. Leverage social media to create positive word-of-mouth promotion.

2. Netizens (online users) will talk about your venture whether you have a presence there or not. So, have a presence—don't ignore this vehicle.

3. Do not annoy or irritate your customers—involve them, communicate with them, collaborate with them.

4. Make certain the content you present is important and relevant to your customers.

5. Have solid, measureable objectives and metrics for measuring those metrics.

6. Use social media not to just inform, but to listen to your customers and competitors.

7. Build trust between you and your customers—avoid dishonesty at all costs. Importantly, make sure you can deliver on your promises. In other words, link your operations to your social media—have differentiated offerings and get them to the customers when and where they want them.

While direct marketing has been one of the fastest growing forms of promotion, it has several disadvantages. First, many forms of direct marketing require a comprehensive and up-to-date database with information about the target market. Developing and maintaining the database can be expensive and time consuming. In addition, growing concern about privacy has led to a decline in response rates among some customer groups. Finally, some customers are becoming very annoyed by direct marketers who contact them without permission, and such unsolicited communication can lead to a negative perception of your business. If you decide to use direct marketing, you should use a permission-based approach—gaining the customer's consent before engaging in this activity.

The Integrated Promotion Plan

A good marketing plan (see Chapter 11) will also contain a detailed and integrated promotion plan. Because of resource scarcity, a new venture must emphasize the integrated nature of the promotion plan. As mentioned earlier in this chapter, this means coordinating all promotional activities—advertising, personal selling, sales promotion, public relations, and direct marketing—to provide a consistent message across all audiences, to maximize the promotional budget, and to increase the impact of their promotion; this is also referred to as integrated marketing communications (IMC). The basic anatomy of the integrated promotion plan is shown in Figure 10.4. We will now discuss the details of each element contained in the plan.

Figure 10.4   The Integrated Promotion Plan

1. Target audience
2. Promotion objectives
3. Promotion budget
4. Promotional theme and message
5. Promotional mix
6. Execution
7. Control and evaluation

Target Audience

An effective promotion plan begins with a well-defined target audience. In short, you must know who you wish to communicate with and why. For a new venture, the focus will be on attracting your first customers and/or those who influence those customers' buying decisions. This is why you must know, in detail, who your most likely customers are. Also, your channel members may also be a distinct target audience. If you have done an effective job at segmenting the market and selecting your target segments/markets, your task of determining the target audience for your promotion will be much easier. But it is important to note that your target audience may not be the same as your target segments. For example, you may have two to three distinctive segments but may choose to promote your product/service to only one of those segments (your target audience). And if you intend to target channel members, this is your target audience and not your end-customer.

Promotion Objectives

As we discussed earlier in the chapter, the role of promotion is quite simple: to influence and affect the behavior of the intended target audience. In general, promotion is used to achieve three broad objectives: (1) create brand awareness, (2) build favorable brand attitudes, and (3) encourage brand action—get the customer to buy. This is referred to as achieving the 3As.[6]

These 3As are used to help shape the nature and scope of more specific and measurable objectives that will form the basis of your promotion plan. For example, after careful consideration of the 3As, the entrepreneur must establish several different and specific promotion objectives such as establishing a strong brand image, encouraging product trial, developing sales leads, stimulating impulse purchasing, or developing repeat purchase behavior. Regardless of what the specific objective might be, from building awareness to increasing repeat purchases, promotion objectives should possess three important qualities. They should (1) be designed for a well-defined target audience, (2) be measurable, and (3) cover a specified time period. For example, you cannot state an objective such as "increase brand awareness." A better stated objective would be "increase brand awareness from 5 percent to 10 percent in the first quarter of 2011."

Promotion Budget

After setting the promotion objectives, you have to determine how much you have to spend on promotion to achieve those objectives. Determining the ideal amount for the budget is difficult because there is no precise way to measure the exact results of spending promotion dollars. However, several methods are used to set the promotion budget.[7]

In the *percentage of sales* approach, funds are allocated to promotion as a percentage of anticipated sales, in terms of either dollars or units sold (e.g., our promotion budget for this year is 3 percent of forecasted sales). The advantage of this approach is obvious: It is simple and provides a financial safeguard by tying the promotion budget to sales. However, there is a major fallacy in this approach, which implies that sales cause promotion. Using this method, a company may reduce its promotion budget because of a downturn in past sales or an anticipated downturn in future sales—situations where it may need promotion the most.

A second common method is a *competitive parity* approach—matching the competitor's absolute level of spending or the proportion per point of market share. It is important to consider the competition when setting the promotion budget since customer responses to promotion are affected by competing promotional activities. For example, if your competitor runs 30 radio ads each week, it may be difficult for you to get your message across with only five messages. The competitor's budget level, however, should not be the only determinant in setting a company's budget. The competition might have very different promotional objectives, which require a different level of promotion expenditures.

Common to many new ventures is the *all-you-can-afford* approach. In other words, money is allocated to promotion only after all your other budget items are covered. Using this approach, the entrepreneur is acting as though he or she does not know anything about a promotion-sales relationship or what the venture's promotion objectives really are.

The best approach to setting the promotion budget is the *objective and task* approach, whereby the company (1) determines its promotion objectives, (2) outlines the tasks to accomplish these objectives, and (3) determines the promotion cost of performing these tasks. This method takes into account what the company wants to accomplish and requires that the objectives be specified. Strengths of the other budgeting methods are often integrated into this approach because each previous method's strength can be tied to the objectives. For example, if the costs are beyond what the company can afford, objectives are reworked and the tasks revised. The difficulty with this method is the judgment required to determine the tasks needed to accomplish objectives.

Promotional Theme and Message

The position you wish to occupy in the marketplace must be communicated effectively to your target audience. Your positioning is brought to life in the marketplace through the establishment of a creative "positioning theme." This positioning theme is the umbrella from which all your other specific promotional messages are created. This includes all your advertising, public relations, sales promotion, direct marketing, and personal selling messages. The theme is used in all promotional activities, while the specific message content may vary depending on the promotional techniques. Still, all messages will be consistent with the general positioning theme.

For example, a startup meat shop specializing in premium meats and exceptional customer service established its positioning theme as "You're going to love us and our meat." In radio ads, the company would promote specials and invite customers to shop there, and each commercial would end with the positioning theme (i.e., "You're going to love us and our meat"). The television ads would show happy customers interacting with very friendly staff while selecting fine cuts of meat. This ad would strictly reinforce the basic positioning theme, and each would end with the positioning theme tagline. The same was true for their newspaper ads and their direct-mail programs. The company reinforced this positioning consistently, even if the message content varied somewhat depending on the objective of the promotional activity or the technique used.

So, once your basic positioning theme is established, you must design specific messages to communicate effectively with your target audience. Again, remember that the message content and the appeal you use are driven by your positioning theme. Every promotional message consists of both informational and persuasive content. For example, informational and persuasive elements include the company name, product (brand) name, and where to buy, as well as product benefits presented in a way to attract attention and encourage purchase. Once you determine the specific message content, you must determine how it will be said—the message appeal. You can make many different types of appeals, but the most common ones include sex appeals, humor appeals, and fear appeals.

A sex appeal suggests to the target audience that the product will increase the attractiveness of the user. Sex appeals are commonly found in many product categories, from automobiles to toothpaste. Unfortunately, sex appeals may only be successful at gaining the audience's attention but may not affect how the customer thinks or feels toward the product. Fear appeals suggest to the target audience that they can avoid some negative experience through the purchase and use of a particular product or brand. Food producers who market low-fat, low-sodium products often tell their audiences that they can avoid heart attacks by eating healthier. Finally, humor appeals are widely used and infer the product is more fun than the competitors'. However, humor appeals tend to wear out quickly.

In short, it is your basic positioning theme that drives the nature and scope of the specific promotional messages you will use. Once you establish the positioning theme, you must go to work to determine the specific message content and the message appeal, and both must reinforce the positioning theme you have established.

Promotional Mix

You must select the right promotional mix that is both affordable and effective in achieving your stated objectives. And again, it is critical to remember that the mix must be carefully integrated and mutually reinforcing. Many factors influence the composition of your promotional mix, including the characteristics of each technique, the target audience, characteristics of the product/service, and the purchase decision stage of the customer.

As mentioned earlier in the chapter, each promotional technique has its own characteristics, including particular strengths and weaknesses (see Figure 10.1). Your specific promotion objectives will largely determine the type of promotional technique you will use since particular promotional techniques are better suited to achieve particular objectives than others. For example, if you wish to reach a wide target audience very quickly to build brand awareness, advertising may be the best option. If you wish to induce customers to try your product/service, sales promotion might be the best choice.

Your choice of target audience will also drive the composition of your promotional mix. To the extent that time and money permit, the target audience for your promotion program is likely to be the prospective customers for your firm's product. If this is the case, you might rely more heavily on advertising and sales promotion. If your customer is the target, you will be emphasizing a **pull strategy,** directing your promotional mix toward the customers to induce them to demand the product from the channel members (assuming you are using an indirect channel). In essence, with a pull strategy, the customer "pulls" the product through the channel.

On the other hand, your channel members might be the focus of your promotional efforts. In this situation, personal selling may be the major promotional element of your mix. If the target audience is your channel members, then you are focusing on a **push strategy,** directing your promotional mix toward the channel members to encourage them to order and stock your product. Using a push strategy, the channel member "pushes" the product to the customer. If you wish to reach both your customers and channel members, a combination of pull-push will be used. The mix will be developed and the budget allocated to reflect the relative importance of the target audiences (customer and channel member).

The proper promotional mix also depends on the type of product you are marketing. For example, the more complex the product, the greater the emphasis will be on personal selling. If the customer perceives there is risk in buying the product/service, the greater the need for personal selling.

The purchase decision stage the customer is in can also affect the promotional mix. In the prepurchase stage, advertising and public relations are more helpful than personal selling because advertising and public relations inform the potential customer of the existence of your product and your company. Sales promotion in the form of free samples also can play an important role to gain low-risk trial. When the salesperson calls on the customer after heavy advertising or public relations, there is some recognition of what the salesperson represents. This is particularly important in business-to-business marketing in which sampling of the product is usually not possible. Direct marketing such as direct mail or direct-response advertising could also be used to encourage customers to seek more information or request a sample.

At the purchase stage, the importance of personal selling is highest, whereas the impact of advertising and public relations is lowest. Sales promotion in the form of coupons, sampling, and rebates can be very helpful in encouraging demand. In this stage, although advertising is not an active influence on the purchase, it could be the means of delivering the coupons, deals, and rebates. Direct marketing can also be useful at this stage.

In the postpurchase stage, the salesperson is still important. In fact, personal contact after the sale increases customer satisfaction. Advertising is also important to reassure the customer that he or she has made the right purchase decision. Sales promotion in the form of coupons and direct marketing reminders can help encourage repeat purchases from satisfied first-time users. Public relations plays a small role in the postpurchase stage.

Execution

The central element of a promotion program is the promotion itself. Advertising consists of advertising copy, the artwork, or the video that the target audience is intended to see, read, or hear. Personal selling efforts depend on the characteristics and skills of the salesperson. Sales promotion activities consist of the specific details of inducements, such as coupons and samples. Public relations efforts are readily seen in tangible elements, such as news releases, and direct marketing actions depend on written, verbal, and electronic forms of delivery. The design of the promotion will play a primary role in determining the message that is communicated to the audience. This design activity is frequently viewed as the step requiring the most creativity. In addition, successful designs are often the result of insight regarding consumers' purchasing behavior. All of the promotion tools have many design alternatives. Advertising, for example, can use fear, humor, or other emotions in its appeal. Similarly, direct marketing can be designed for varying levels of personal or customized appeals. One of the challenges in executing the promotion plan is to design each promotional activity to communicate the same message.

Once the designs of all the promotional program elements are complete, it is important to determine the most effective timing of their use. The promotion schedule describes the order in which each promotional tool is introduced and the frequency of its use during the campaign. Several other factors, such as seasonality and competitive promotion activity, can also influence the promotion schedule. For example, seasonal businesses such as ski resorts are likely to reduce their promotional activity during the "off" season. Similarly, restaurants, retail stores, and health clubs are likely to increase their promotional activities when new competitors enter the market.

One thing that smart entrepreneurs do is to map out in detail, by day, by week, and by month, the entire promotion plan and all its executional elements. In doing so, the entrepreneur knows exactly what must be accomplished at any given time throughout the year.

Control and Evaluation

You must also establish ways to control and evaluate the success or failure of your promotional plan. Having well-defined objectives allows for proper control and evaluation. To evaluate the success of your advertising, you can run tests to determine if the target audience noticed the ads. You can monitor your sales promotion activities by counting the number of coupons redeemed. You can assess the effectiveness of direct marketing by measuring the number of calls received in response to a direct-response ad. You can measure the effectiveness of personal selling efforts by examining the number of new accounts opened. You can evaluate the effectiveness of your use of social media by measuring the numbers of visitors to your website and the chatter on social networks about your brand. You could also test the impact of your public relations activities by asking customers about their attitudes toward your company both before and after the PR program to gauge its effectiveness. But whatever the control and evaluation procedures are, they should be spelled out in the promotional plan. And if results are not as predicted, you must take corrective actions and make appropriate adjustments.

In the end, you must recognize the need for promotion. Importantly, you will find that it does not necessarily require a substantial investment. In fact, you will find some good advice in the Entrepreneurial Marketing Spotlight from Eileen Gunn, Founder of FamiliesGo!, a travel website for busy parents planning family vacations; Kim Bhasin, reporter for the Business Insider; and Susan Ward, founder of Cypress Technologies, an information technology (IT) consulting business.

Entrepreneurial Marketing Spotlight

Eileen Gunn, Founder of FamiliesGo!, a travel website says it is very important to talk up your venture before you even launch. She suggests using social media including Twitter to start some buzz. She also suggests reaching out to the media—getting a media list and work it to let your customers know that your business is coming. Kim Bhasin, reporter, also advises entrepreneurs to embrace social media. He suggests tie-in ads and offers to your Facebook page and have a direct channel with your customer via Twitter. He also suggests to start a blog—it gets your name out and keeps you connected to your customers. Bhasin also says to put up multimedia on YouTube and Flickr, and this technique will not cost you much but may deliver a big audience. Susan Ward, founder of Cypress Technologies, also offers some good advice.

(1) Use every outgoing piece of paper and every electronic document to promote your venture. This includes your business cards, business stationery, faxes, e-mails, receipts, and so on. Make sure you business name, contact information, and company message are on everything.

(2) Write articles to gain exposure and build positive word of mouth. Place these articles in publications that reach your target audience. Electronic e-zines are always looking for content (see the Internet's Best E-zine Directories).

(3) Send out press releases on a regular basis. But make them newsworthy; talk about business developments, new products/services, awards, sponsorships, and so on.

(4) When online, use some time to promote your business. Post messages on forums or bulletin boards, or use your own blog.

(5) Use buddy marketing. If you send out a business brochure, include a leaflet and/or business card of another business that has agreed to do the same.

(6) Give away freebies (e.g., in an ad, say the first 50 people who respond will receive a free X).

(7) Promote your venture on a talk show. Many local radio or cable TV stations have programs on business. Approach them and offer to be a guest, or try being an expert on a call-in program!

(8) Promote by giving a free seminar. Share your expertise with others. For example, a nursery owner gives seminars at his local community center on the proper care of plants and has increased his customer base.

(9) Use your vehicle to promote your venture. For about $100, you can buy magnetic signs that you can place on your vehicle to display your business name and phone number.

(10) Promote your business through your leisure activities. Always bring your business cards with you when engaging in leisure activities. Even wear your company's T-shirt or jacket that displays your company's name and logo. Use every opportunity to get your name in front of prospective customers.[8]

Key Takeaways

- If you want your venture to succeed, you must invest in promoting your business. Promotion is an investment and not just an expense!
- Promotion is marketer-initiated communications activities directed to target audiences to influence their attitudes and behaviors.
- There are five major promotional techniques available: advertising, public relations, sales promotion, personal selling, and direct marketing. Your promotional mix is the combination of these techniques you intend to use.
- Promotion is used to achieve three broad objectives: create brand awareness, build favorable brand attitudes, and encourage brand action—get the customer to buy!
- If you intend to use advertising, you must be aware of the strengths and weaknesses of the major advertising media.
- With a venture startup, you are going to have to promote the business and promote your products/services (e.g., use corporate and product promotion).
- With finite resources, you should leverage public relations whenever possible. Local sponsorship of events or teams is a good way to get your name in front of the customer.
- Sales promotion can be very effective in encouraging customers to try your product/ service. Sampling, for example, is inexpensive and effective.
- Personal selling is going to be important for you to close business. As a founder, you will be the chief salesperson for the venture.
- You can use numerous effective and inexpensive direct marketing techniques to build your business. E-mail marketing and promoting your business via social media is vital. In fact, social media is the brave new world for entrepreneurs when it comes to promotion.
- Your integrated promotion plan must contain the following elements: target audience, promotion objectives, promotion budget, promotional theme and message, promotional mix, execution, and control and evaluation.
- Because of limited resources, you must use an integrated promotional approach—coordinating all promotional activities to provide a consistent message, maximize your budget, and increase the impact of your promotion.

Entrepreneurial Exercise

Knowing your target audience(s), specify two to three specific and measurable promotional objectives you wish to achieve with this audience. In other words, what do you want to have happen as a result of the promotional activity? Next, map out the most effective promotional techniques that you can use to reach the target audience(s) and achieve your objectives. Finally, craft a positioning theme and test it on some prospective customers. What feedback did they provide? Are you on target, or do you now have to rethink the theme?

Key Terms

Promotion 169
Promotional mix 169
Advertising 170
Public relations 173
Publicity 174

Sales promotion 174
Personal selling 174
Direct marketing 177
Pull strategy 184
Push strategy 184

Notes

1. Mark N. Clemente, *The Marketing Glossary* (New York: AMACOM, 1992).

2. F. G. Crane, "The Need for Corporate Advertising in the Financial Services Industry: A Case Study Illustration," *Journal of Services Marketing* 4, no. 2 (1990): 31–37.

3. Clemente, *The Marketing Glossary.*

4. Ibid.

5. For more reading on social media, see Dave Evans, *Social Media Marketing* (Alameda, CA: Sybex, 2008)

6. John R. Rossiter and Larry Percy, *Advertising and Promotion Management* (New York: McGraw-Hill, 1987).

7. E. Bigne, "Advertising Budget Practices: A Review," *Journal of Current Issues and Research in Advertising,* Fall 1995, 17–31.

8. Eileen P. Gunn, "How I Promote My Startup — Even Before I Launch, Inc.," June 7, 2011, Retrieved from http://www.inc.com/eileen-p-gunn/how-i-promote-my-start-up-even-before-i-launch.html; Kim Bhasin, "7 Ways to Promote Your Busines Online for Free," *Homepreneurs*, February 2012. Retrieved from http://homepreneurs.wordpress.com/2012/01/25/7-ways-to-promote-your-business-online-for-free/; and Susan Ward, "Ten Low-Cost Ways to Promote Your Business," 2009. Retrieved from www.sbinfocanada.about.com http://sbinfocanada.about.com/cs/marketing/a/bizpromotion.htm

Eleven

The Entrepreneurial Marketing Plan

I am often asked, "Why should I bother putting together a written marketing plan for my venture?" Well, first, if you ever intend to pursue outside funding for your venture, you have to have a written plan. Otherwise, no one will take you seriously. So, consider your marketing plan as a "selling document." Second, and perhaps even more important, it is through the crafting of the marketing plan that you will be able to see, in a real tangible way, all the necessary ingredients that will be required for venture success. In fact, many successful entrepreneurs suggest that it is critical to have a written plan not just because it provides you a "road map" but that the act of creating the road map forces you to think through the key drivers of the venture's success.[1] Most important, it forces you to address two critical questions about your venture: (1) Do I have the right marketing opportunity, and (2) Can I effectively exploit that opportunity profitably with the right business model? Bill Sahlman at the Harvard Business School suggests that the plan does not have to be elaborate with a decade of month-by-month financial projections. But what it should do is outline, thoroughly and with clarity, the situation, the opportunity, the business model, the people (your team), and the reward.[2] And, in my view, it is the act of preparing the plan that provides vital direction for the venture. The written plan will not guarantee venture success, but without a well-crafted plan, you do increase the risk of venture failure! So, my suggestion is that you commit your plan to paper. You do not necessarily stay wedded to the plan, especially in a dynamic market, but it does and should serve as a useful guide as you attempt to start and grow your venture.

Difference Between the Venture's Business Plan and the Venture's Marketing Plan

A written **marketing plan** is a road map for the marketing activities of the venture for a specified period of time (e.g., one, three, or five years). A business plan, on the other hand, is the road map for the entire venture for a specified period of time. The key difference between the two is that the business plan provides details on all the other functional areas of the business beyond marketing, including research and development, operations, production, finance, and so on. Still, for a new venture, it is typical that the bulk of the business plan will be the marketing plan. Moreover, in many cases, it is very possible that the business plan and marketing plan will be virtually identical.

There are many generic marketing plan templates readily available in textbooks and online. But there is no single plan that necessarily applies to all ventures. Instead, the format and content of a marketing plan will depend on a number of issues. For example, you have to consider who is going to be reading the plan and what is the purpose of the plan. If the plan is going to be read by an internal audience, the people working for the venture, the plan is designed to show the direction the venture is heading and to assist those who will be responsible for the implementation of the plan. If the plan is going to be read by an external audience such as a banker or venture capitalist, the purpose of the plan is to secure capital to finance the venture. In this case, the plan will also include details on the management team that would not be included in an internal marketing plan. Also, the financial information would be more detailed when the plan is used to obtain outside financing. Thus, you may find it necessary to craft different versions of the plan depending on the audience and its purpose!

The Critical Questions the Marketing Plan Must Address

If you are seeking outside financing for your venture, the most critical questions the marketing plan must address are as follows:

1. Is there a viable marketing opportunity?

2. Is there something unique and different about the opportunity that differentiates the venture from the competitors?

3. Does the venture have a robust business model?

4. Is there a well-defined target market that has expressed an interest in what you intend to market?

5. Are the revenue/sales and expenses realistic, and is there a healthy profit picture?

6. Is there a management team with the capabilities and experience to execute the plan?

7. Does the plan show how those investing in the venture will get their money back and make a return on their investment?

Rhonda Abrams, author of *The Successful Business Plan,* suggests that within the first five minutes of reading your plan, readers must perceive that the answers to these questions are fully provided and answered in the affirmative.[3] If not, you are not likely to receive financial support for your venture. In addition, your team and employees may be left wondering about the viability of the venture.

The Anatomy of the Marketing Plan

The essential output of the venture planning process is to produce a concrete plan of action that will achieve the venture's objectives. This plan of action should be committed to paper and will be called your marketing plan. The actual format, design, and structure of a marketing plan will vary from venture to venture, but every marketing plan should at least include the following (also see Figure 11.1):

- An executive summary
- A review of the marketing situation
- The marketing opportunity
- The business model
- Specific and measurable marketing objectives
- Marketing strategy, with identified target markets, intended positioning, and detailed marketing mix
- Operations, production, and supply
- Marketing budget/financials, including projected revenue/sales and expenses
- The marketing team
- Evaluation and control mechanisms

Figure 11.1   The Anatomy of a Marketing Plan

Executive Summary

Marketing Situation

- Industry analysis
- Competitive analysis
- Customer analysis
- Company analysis

The Marketing Opportunity

The Business Model

Marketing Objectives

Marketing Strategy

- Target market
- Positioning
- Marketing mix
  Product Price
  Promotion
  Place
  People
  (if a services-based venture, include)
  Physical evidence
  Process
  Productivity

Operations

Marketing budget/financials

Management team

Evaluation and control

The Executive Summary

The executive summary should provide a succinct overview of the entire marketing plan in two to three pages. However, it should not be a simple listing of all the topics contained in the body of the marketing plan. Instead, it should emphasize only the key elements/issues presented in the plan. These include the marketing situation, the marketing opportunity, the business model, the marketing objectives, the marketing strategy, operations, the marketing budget/financials, and the marketing team. A critical aspect of the executive summary is to communicate why your venture will be successful (i.e., a good marketing opportunity, a good business model, the right marketing offer, and a good team to execute).

If the plan is to be submitted to potential investors or to secure financing for the venture, most of these individuals will not read past the executive summary. Therefore, your executive summary must give the reader a good understanding of your venture and a reason why he or she should invest and/or provide capital to fund the venture.

The Marketing Situation

This section of the marketing plan describes, in detail, the marketing situation, including industry analysis, competitive analysis, customer analysis, and company analysis as well as any other factors in the marketing environment that are relevant to the development and execution of the marketing plan.

Industry Analysis

In the industry analysis section, you should provide a description of the primary industry in which you will compete. It is important to outline the size of the total market and the growth rate of the market. You should indicate if there is large addressable market, a rapidly growing market, or a high-growth-potential market. Other industry characteristics such as, historical profit margins, return on investment, or return on assets metrics should also be highlighted. Finally, the life cycle of the industry should also be addressed (e.g., introduction, growth, maturity, decline). In short, show your understanding of the industry ecosystem and your relative system in that system.

Competitive Analysis

In the competitive analysis section, you will detail your competition, from most direct to indirect. You should also provide the strengths, weaknesses, and strategies of the named competitors. In addition, you must outline the competitive advantages of each competitor, the customers they target, the market share they hold, and their financial power. Barriers to entry into the market should also be addressed here. Be sure to highlight the key competitive plays of each competitor and how your play will differ from the competitors and/or how you will best those competitors.

Customer Analysis

In this section, you should paint a thick, rich description of the customers in the market. Remember, there may be several major customer groups target markets or segments, and you must provide a solid analysis of each segment even if you do not intend to target a particular segment. Use the segmentation analysis described in Chapter 5 to provide the details on the various segments, especially those you intend to target, including geographic, demographic, psychological, and behavioral variables.

In particular, it is important to discuss the needs of the customers in the various segments. It is important to discuss customers in terms of what makes them tick and why they would (or would not) buy from you. In addition, you should quantify the segment size, growth rate, and value of the segments. Finally, you should be sure to answer the key questions used in performing good segmentation analysis: Who is buying, where, how, how much, when, and why? You can briefly discuss the "target market(s)" you intend to pursue, but you will provide more detail on this when you discuss your marketing strategy.

Company Analysis

In this section, you offer a detailed description of your venture and provide an analysis of your firm's strengths and weaknesses. You must spell out the exact nature of the venture, including the type of firm (sole proprietorship, LLC, corporation, etc.), the configuration of the company (would key activities you engage in) and the primary factors that will lead to your success. It is also vital to detail your competitive advantage and key personnel working for the venture.

The Marketing Opportunity

After carefully presenting the marketing situation, you will use this section to spell out your marketing opportunity. If the preceding analysis has been well thought out, the marketing opportunity should be self-evident to everyone who reads the plan. Still, do not take this for granted and state your case explicitly. This means defining the nature and scope of the opportunity—"the sweet spot" for your venture. For example, you may have discovered an underserved market segment in a large growing market that is dissatisfied with existing alternatives but inclined very favorably, based on your user research, to purchase your product or service. From an investor's perspective, you need to provide validation for this opportunity and your voice of consumer feedback provides this important validation. Moreover, investors also want to see the "size of prize"—the magnitude of the opportunity in real dollars. So, you need to stress the evidence to confirm the size of prize in this section.

The Business Model

Closely connected to your marketing opportunity is the concept of the business model for the venture. As you know your business model is a framework for making money for the venture. It outlines the set of activities that the enterprise will perform, how it will perform them, and when it will perform them to create customer value and earn a profit. For example, if you are going to design a product, manufacture it, distribute it and market it, spell this out. If you are going to design a product but license it out to another party, map this out. Be specific here and highlight how exactly the enterprise make money; how it will create value; for what specific target market; the precise advantage the enterprise has; and your strategy for getting initial revenue and how you will continue to generate revenue. Remember, recurrent revenue is the lifeblood of an entrepreneurial enterprise, so be sure to hit this hard in this section of your plan.

Marketing Objectives

In this section of the marketing plan, you articulate your **marketing objectives.** The most common marketing objectives include sales, stated in terms of units sold or dollars, and market share. Other, more specific objectives are also defined at the marketing mix level. For example, you might spell out objectives such as brand awareness levels to achieve through advertising, numbers of channel members carrying the product, and exact pricing compared to competitors. And remember, these objectives must be specific and measurable, as well as cover a specified time period.

Marketing Strategy

Your **marketing strategy** is the basic "game plan" or your means for achieving the marketing objectives. It outlines the target markets sought, intended positioning, and specific details of the marketing mix designed to appeal to the target market.

Target Market

The customer analysis section provided details on all the customers (major groups or segments) in the market and indicated your target market selection. Here you provide greater detail regarding your target market in terms of whom the customers are and why you are targeting them. Again, you need to pinpoint the needs of this target market and how you intend to meet those needs. You should quantify the number of customers you are pursuing, share of market sought, and rationale for the market penetration estimates. For example, if you are targeting 18- to 24-year-old women attending college in Boston, you need to spell out the total size of this target market and the percentage of this target market you intend to capture. The market value of the target market should also be spelled out (e.g., annual dollar purchase) and how much of that total market value you intend to obtain.

Positioning

With your target market well defined and specified, you now must detail your intended positioning. Remember, positioning is the place the product or service will occupy in the hearts or minds of the target market in relation to your competitors.

Also remember from Chapter 5 that positioning can be considered your "value proposition" or "marketing promise" to the customer. It is critical to link the needs of your target market to your positioning strategy. Importantly, your positioning must distinguish you from your competitors, and it must be valuable and meaningful to your target market. For example, Wal-Mart positions itself as the low-price leader, Volvo positions itself as the safest automobile, and Diet Coke is positioned as the best-tasting diet cola on the market. Finally, it is also critical that your entire marketing effort (including all elements of the marketing mix—discussed in the next section) be built to support the chosen positioning.

Marketing Mix

With your target market and positioning clearly mapped out, you must now detail your marketing mix. If you have a product-based venture, your mix will consist of product, price, promotion, place, and people. If you have a service-based venture, your mix will include product, price, promotion, place, people, physical evidence, process, and productivity. You must clearly outline the exact configuration of each marketing mix element. For example, for "product," you will outline the product features, brand name, packaging elements, service, warranty, and other components that make up the product. For pricing, provide validation as to why you are pursuing your pricing strategy (e.g., premium pricing for affluent customers with strong felt need for your product who have shown by your voice of consumer research a willingness to pay). For "promotion," you will outline your promotional mix (advertising, public relations, sales promotion, personal selling, and direct marketing) in very specific detail. For place, or channel, outline how you intend to get your product to your customers. You will do the same for all other marketing mix elements. Your goal is to put together a cohesive mix with all elements mutually reinforcing one another.

Operations

In this section of your plan, you will outline the "back end" of your venture. You will provide information as to your strategies with regards to your operations. You will detail what you will do inhouse and what you will outsource (e.g., will you be manufacturing yourself or will you externalize manufacturing? If you are shipping product, will you do it yourself or farm it out to UPS or FedEx?). Remember investors like lean new ventures, so you need to carefully consider what you absolutely must do inhouse and what you can cost-effectively outsource.

Marketing Budget/Financials

In the **marketing budget/financials** section of your marketing plan, you must spell out sales, expenses, and profit levels that can be expected as a result of your marketing efforts. Specifically, you outline your sales forecast, or a series of sales forecasts, indicating what you expect to sell under specified conditions for the marketing mix (e.g., at what price and with what level of marketing effort) and under specified external market factors such as competitive response to your market entry. Your budget should also include a detailed statement of expenses, margins, and profits, at different estimated sales levels, to account for possible changes in the marketing mix or external market-related factors. Here you can also provide what is called your "best estimate" forecast for your financials and one or two other sets of projections based on "what if" scenarios. For example, to construct your financials, you might use the assumption of achieving varying levels of market share capture (e.g., 5, 10, and 15 percent).

You would then show the sales, expenses, margins, and profits based on achieving those various market share levels. You can also present your budgets/financials for various periods (e.g., one to five years); furthermore, you might present the numbers annually, by month, by quarter, and so on.

Figure 11.2 provides an example of five-year financials for a new startup gourmet bakery. It shows just the basics, sales/revenue, costs, and operating profit, but it is sufficient to show the financial health of the venture over this period.

However, these projections in Figure 11.2 are based on the judgment of the entrepreneur, as are most projections for almost every other venture. And this is where problems arise with budgets/financials. I have come to believe that there are simply too many unknowns to accurately predict sales or profits over a five-year period. In fact, after reviewing dozens and dozens of marketing and/or business plans for startups, I have never seen any five-year projections ever pan out! In particular, I see a general tendency to overestimate sales, underestimate expenses, and underestimate the time required to achieve the sales objectives. I also typically see the "time to first dollar" taking much longer than the entrepreneur ever anticipated and the time to break even being chronically underestimated. So, in the end, I tend to see ventures that are underfinanced and suffering cash flow problems very quickly.

Figure 11.2   Five-Year Financial Projections, Gourmet Bakery

	Projections (in $ thousands)				
	2012	**2013**	**2014**	**2015**	**2016**
Number of bakeries	1	1	2	2	3
Sales/revenue, $	300	400	700	800	1,100
Cost of sales, $	111	48	259	296	407
Labor costs, $	93	24	217	248	41
Other costs, $	72	96	168	192	264
Operating profit, $	24	32	56	64	84

I am not dismissing the importance of preparing a marketing budget and financials; this task must be completed. But what I am saying is that there is a tendency for a lot of financial "voodoo" when preparing and presenting the so-called numbers. In fact, most potential investors approached by entrepreneurs question the financials and often discount the numbers they see. In many cases, topline revenue numbers are often generated after costs and break even are established. In other words, once a break even is constructed, magically the revenue streams get created. In other cases, entrepreneurs make wild stabs at forecasting sales by making assumptions such as "the total market size is $1 billion so by obtaining 2 percent of the market we will achieve $20 million in sales." But, when pressed, the entrepreneur generally cannot defend why he or she assumes the venture will obtain that 2 percent market share. That is why earlier in this book (Chapter 2), I urged you to use a better way to forecast sales/revenue—voice of consumer feedback and likelihood of purchase measures. This approach, while still subject to variance, is a much better approach to the other methods just discussed.

So, the message for you is to be creative about different ways to construct your "numbers" and to honestly map out the assumptions made when doing so. For example, I know of one firm that uses five different approaches to develop sales forecasts or projections when opening new outlets for its chain restaurant business. It has found that the weighted average of the numbers produced by these methods most accurately predicts sales, expenses, and profits. Keep this in mind when you have to prepare your numbers and you might find you'll get closer to the "real" numbers your venture is likely to produce.

Management Team

In this section, you will outline and describe your management team—those responsible for developing and converting the marketing plan into reality. You will spell out who is responsible for planning, executing, evaluating, and controlling all the activities that are part of the marketing plan. If you are seeking outside financing, it is also important to provide the background and experience of your team.

Evaluation and Control

The final section of your plan is the evaluation and control that will be used to monitor the process of the marketing plan. Typically, with specific marketing objectives having been spelled out in the plan, the team responsible for the plan will compare the results of the plan with the marketing objectives to identify any deviations, both negative and positive. Then, the team must act on those deviations—correcting negative deviations and exploiting positive ones.

Developing the entrepreneurial marketing plan will take time, energy, and imagination. But it is absolutely necessary. In the Entrepreneurial Marketing Spotlight, you will read why it is necessary and what you must consider when crafting your plan.

Entrepreneurial Marketing Spotlight

It has long been said that "failing to plan is planning to fail." A good marketing plan is the answer to that dilemma. In fact, a study involving successful entrepreneurs revealed that having a viable plan and executing it well is a key imperative for venture success. The entrepreneurs in this study also stressed that the plan does not have to be lengthy or complicated. But it must be built on a solid foundation of facts and valid assumptions. It must also set out realistic and achievable objectives, and it must be shared with everyone in the venture who will be responsible for its implementation.

The marketing plan must contain a clear and concise executive summary and solidly establish your marketing opportunity. Importantly, it must stress execution—how you will exploit your identified marketing opportunity. In addition, it must map out your revenue, costs, and profitability. The marketing plan must also be well written, well presented, well researched, detailed, and complete. Finally, John Jantsch suggests that your marketing plan should simply answer who you are, what you do, who needs what you do, and how you intend to attract their business. After taking the time to craft your plan, you must put it to work. In other words, "Plan the work, then work the plan." Also, remember that the plan is a living document. It is to be used routinely and updated as required.[4]

Key Takeaways

- Consider your written marketing plan as your "road map" that is designed to guide you toward venture success.
- Also consider your written marketing plan as a "selling document" if you intend to seek outside financing for your venture. No plan means no money!

- The process of creating the plan will give you insight as to whether you actually have the right opportunity and if you can exploit it profitably. And, whether or not the venture has a business model to sustain it over time.
- While there are a variety of marketing plan templates, the essential anatomy of a good marketing plan contains an executive summary, a review of the marketing situation, the marketing opportunity, the business model, specific and measurable marketing objectives, marketing strategy, operations, marketing budget/financials, the management team, and evaluation and control mechanisms.
- Be careful when preparing your financials and avoid financial "voodoo." Allow your potential customer to help you drive your numbers, especially your sales forecasts. And, of course, be realistic!

Entrepreneurial Exercise

In very specific terms, map out your marketing opportunity and detail the marketing actions required to exploit this opportunity, effectively and profitably. What are the most important tasks that you must complete to exploit the opportunity?

Key Terms

Marketing plan 203
Marketing objectives 197

Marketing strategy 197
Marketing budget/financials 199

Notes

1. Frederick G. Crane and Jeffrey E. Sohl, "Imperatives for Venture Success: Entrepreneurs Speak," *International Journal of Entrepreneurship and Innovation* 5, no. 2 (2004): 99–106.

2. William A. Sahlman, "How to Write a Great Business Plan," *Harvard Business Review*, July/August 1997, 98–108.

3. Rhonda Abrams, *The Successful Business Plan: Secrets & Strategies* (Grants Pass, OR: Oasis Press, 2000).

4. Crane and Sohl, "Imperatives for Venture Success"; John Jantsch, "7 Steps to the Perfect Marketing Plan," March 18, 2009. Retrieved from www.entrepreneur.com.

Appendix A

Sample Entrepreneurial Marketing Plan

Elizabeth Bunnell, Andrew Han, Angela Kontos, Steve Lubelczyk, and Jennifer Lynch

Table of Contents

1. Executive Summary

PetPulse, a new pet biosensor startup, aims to be the first-mover in the $14B vet-related pet care market in the United States. By licensing proprietary technology from Agenda, Inc. and BIOSENSE, PetPulse provides pet parents 24/7 health monitoring and illness detection. An implantable microchip sensor with handheld scanner works as a virtual veterinarian that provides real-time updates on your pet's ongoing health and wellness needs.

The 2011 U. S. Pet industry expenditure was $51B with $14B just in vet care, up 9 percent from 2010. As the trend for pet owners viewing their pets as valued members of the family increases, the vet care expenditure for 2012 is expected to increase another 8 percent despite the ongoing financial crisis affecting U. S. families.

Primarily targeting experienced pet parents of dogs and cats, PetPulse provides the parent with the ability to check their pets vitals by scanning the microchip implanted in their pet. Once scanned, the microchip runs the analysis chosen by the pet parent and reports the results to our database, which cross-checks the data with a number of metrics such as pet age, breed, preexisting conditions, prior results, and age standards. The results are then e-mailed to the owner and veterinarian on record to ensure proper follow-up and care is provided pending the analysis provided in the report. Our service provides peace of mind to the pet parent and a voice to their beloved pet. We look to be allies with veterinarians to provide the best service possible for the members of our pet family. By providing training and educational materials to the veterinarians, as well as providing a per implantation incentive, we strive to create a symbiotic relationship of knowledge sharing, improved pet health and wellness care, and enhanced customer service for the pet parent.

In terms of validating the marketing opportunity, the American Pet Products Association's National Pet Owners Survey showed 62 percent of U.S. households own a pet, which equates to almost 73 million homes and a total of 165 million dogs and cats. Moreover, our voice of consumer research indicates a strong felt need for our product offering and a substantial percentage of our target market expressing a willingness to purchase. The business model will provide a dual revenue stream comprised of a one-time implantation fee and a reoccurring monthly subscription. At the end of Year 2, we are projecting revenue of close to $50M and an operating profit of $29M. By Year 5, revenue is expected to be almost $200M and operating profit of $170M.

The management team of PetPulse is comprised of passionate pet parents with years of cross-functional experience. Our passion and prior experience, coupled with key advisers ranging from veterinarians to clinicians, provides PetPulse the ability to run a highly talented company driven by our passion for healthy pets.

The team consists of the following personnel: Jennifer Lynch – founder of PetPulse and CEO—brings 12+ years of product management experience in Software and Consumer Goods. She is a lifetime pet parent and current owner of 2 dogs, one of whom suffers from kidney failure and was the inspiration behind PetPulse. Steven Lubelczyk—Chief Financial Officer—brings 12+ years of business analysis and financial planning experience. Current pet parent of Fletcher, a sweet chocolate lab. Elizabeth Bunnell Chief Marketing Officer—brings 9+ years of marketing and brand management experience to the team at PetPulse. She is a current pet parent of Henry, a fun-loving golden retriever. Angela Kontos—Chief Operations Officer—brings 10+ years of project and program management experience to the team at PetPulse. While not a current pet parent, she loves being the aunt to all of the pets in the PetPulse family. Andrew Han—Chief Technology Officer—brings 7+ years of technical knowledge and experience coupled with his MS in Electrical Engineering from Columbia University. While not a current pet parent, he eagerly looks forward to spending time with pets in the future.

2. Marketing Situation

Industry Analysis

Vet care makes up about a third of the overall pet expenditure in the United States; therefore, health care costs for pet owners is a big part of the overall expense. The U.S. pet industry expenditures for 2011 reached almost $50B and vet care accounted for $14B of that total, which was an increase of 9 percent from 2010.[2] In addition to using our purchase intent results from our concept test, we thought it prudent to prove the market existed for microchip implants, so we looked at those that had microchips for identification for comparative purposes. In 2008, 5 percent of the 130 million cats and dogs in the United States were microchipped.[3]

The domestic pet population for dogs and cats is showing steady signs of growth. In 2012, the Humane Society reports there are currently about 165 million dogs and cats in the United States, an increase of 27 percent more than four years.[4] According to the American Pet Products Association, a National Pet Owners Survey showed 62 percent of U.S.

Figure A Total U.S. Pet Expenditures

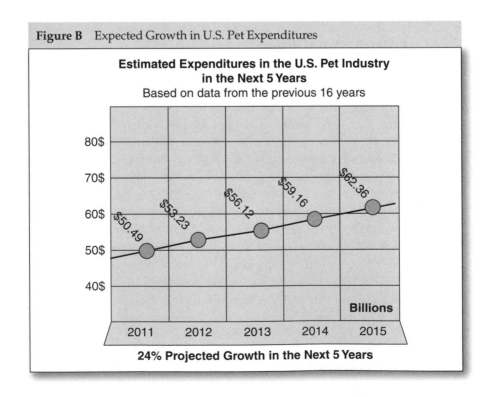

The Total U.S. Pet Industry Expenditures since 1994

$17 $21 $23 $28.5 $29.5 $32.4 $34.4 $36.3 $38.5 $41.2 $43.2 $45.5 $47.7

50$ · 40$ · 30$ · 20$ · 10$

Billions

1998 1999 2000 2001 2002 2003 2004 2005 2006 2007 2008 2009 2010

13% Avg. Annual Growth Rate

Figure B Expected Growth in U.S. Pet Expenditures

Estimated Expenditures in the U.S. Pet Industry in the Next 5 Years
Based on data from the previous 16 years

$50.49 $53.23 $56.12 $59.16 $62.36

80$ · 70$ · 60$ · 50$ · 40$

Billions

2011   2012   2013   2014   2015

24% Projected Growth in the Next 5 Years

households own a pet, which equates to almost 73 million homes. In 1988, the first year the survey was conducted, 56 percent of U.S. households owned a pet as compared to 62 percent in 2008.[5] All of these facts and trends are showing positive growth within the pet industry even in an economic downturn.

In addition, technology trends are moving toward developing chips for monitoring specifically for human use. This demonstrates society will be expecting of these types of medical advancements, not only for themselves, but for their furry friends. PetPulse is planning to be on the cutting edge of this technology advancement, therefore able to benefit from these trends.

Competitive Analysis

While no direct competitors currently exist, Mion is improving their Monitor chip to offer similar capabilities. The challenge we will face is related to the brand recognition and trust Mion has established in the pharmaceutical industry. That being said, our business model provides a competitive advantage by partnering with vets and building a strong relationship. Being an animal healthcare company, we will be able to focus on the pet care industry and build a tight relationship with the vets. Larger pharmaceutical companies face the challenges of having to balance their large portfolio of offerings while trying to focus on a niche market such as pet care. This will make it difficult for Mion and other to penetrate since we plan to be first to market with this offering.

Customer Analysis

According to the 2011–2012 APPA National Pet Owners Survey,[1] nearly all pet owners attribute companionship, love, company, and affection as the top benefits to owning a pet. In addition, three-quarters of dog owners and more than half of cat owners consider their pet a child or family member. Through various surveys and interviews, our research reaffirms these findings, which will drive us to focus on this subset of pet owners we refer to as pet parents, those who view their cats and dogs as family members. These consumers are willing to do what it takes to ensure their pets are healthy, safe, and happy. In addition, PetPulse will target and build relationships with veterinarians, the primary channel of distribution for our product and service.

Experienced pet parents will be our lead users since they have already experienced the loss of a pet and understand the expenses and care necessary for an aging animal. As a result of those past experiences, these consumers would be more likely to seek proactive care. In our voice of consumer sample of 149 respondents, 66 percent had experienced the loss of a pet due to illness in the past. Of that population, 58 percent responded in the top two box based on the description of the product indicating that they were very or somewhat likely to buy the product.

The results also showed the respondents who had not experienced the loss of a pet suffering from illness, 41 percent of them still indicated they were very or somewhat likely to buy the product based on the description. We understand that as pets age, they are more likely to become ill and thus their parents will have a greater desire for our product. Of those we surveyed, 70 percent had pets older than 3 years. This led us to focus on the large older pet population as part of our consumer target segment. The final segment will be first-time pet owners of puppies and kittens. The reason they would be not be the primary focus is because they do not have the experience or understanding of expenses required to provide medical care for a pet since they are still in the infancy stage and require lesser health care monitoring than an adult pet. Communicating the benefits of our product to this segment will be a tougher challenge.

Given the emotional attachment to their pets, owners are seeking alternative therapies to increase the life expectancy of their pets. Some examples include hydrotherapy, massage therapy, chiropractic care, herbs, and homeopathic medicines all of which are not covered by pet insurance and can be costly over time. This indicates to us that pet parents spare no expense when it comes to the well-being and caring of their furry friends. We have also seen a steady increase in the purchase of pet insurance coverage; however, it is still a small percentage of the overall population. All of these signals in the market lead us to believe that target market customers are proactively seeking better care for their pets. We have also found despite an economic downturn since 2008, vet care expenditures are expected to increase 8 percent for 2012.[7] Again this is a solid sign this market is ripe for PetPulse and the innovative solution it can bring to care for a dog's or cat's health.

Company Analysis

PetPulse is an LLC company. The key players involved in the company are passionate pet parents with many years of cross-functional experience. Our passion and prior experience, coupled with key advisers ranging from veterinarians to clinicians, provides PetPulse the ability to run a highly talented company driven by our passion for healthy pets.

The team consists of the following personnel: Jennifer Lynch—founder of PetPulse and CEO—brings 12+ years of product management experience in Software and Consumer Goods. She is a lifetime pet parent and current owner of two dogs, one of whom suffers from kidney failure and was the inspiration behind PetPulse. Steven Lubelczyk—Chief Financial Officer—brings 12+ years of business analysis and financial planning experience. Current pet parent of Fletcher, a sweet chocolate lab. Elizabeth Bunnell—Chief Marketing Officer—brings 9+ years of marketing and brand management experience to the team at PetPulse. She is a current pet parent of Henry, a fun-loving golden retriever. Angela Kontos–Chief Operations Officer—brings 10+ years of project and program management experience to the team at PetPulse. While not a current pet parent, she loves being the aunt to all of the pets in the PetPulse family. Andrew Han—Chief Technology Officer—brings 7+ years of technical knowledge and experience coupled with his MS in Electrical Engineering from Columbia University. While not a current pet parent, he eagerly looks forward to spending time with pets in the future. For more details on the team, see Section 9 of this plan.

3. The Marketing Opportunity

More than $14B was spent on vet care in the United States in 2011 and this expenditure is expected to grow by 8–9 percent per annum. In terms of validating the marketing opportunity, the American Pet Products Association's National Pet Owners Survey showed 62 percent of U.S. households own a pet, which equates to almost 73 million households and more than 165 million dogs and cats. There is also significant growth in the number of people who view themselves as a pet parent and their pet as a valued family number. For example, three-quarters of dog owners view themselves as a pet parent and one-half of cat owners view themselves as a pet parent for a total of more than 54 million households. Moreover, our voice of consumer research with pet parents indicates a strong felt need for our product offering and a substantial percentage of our target market expressing a willingness to purchase. At the end of Year 2, we expect revenue of $50M and an operating profit of $29M. By Year 5, revenue is expected to be $200M with an operating profit of $170M.

4. The Business Model

The business model for PetPulse is relatively simple. The business model will provide a dual revenue stream comprised of a one-time implantation fee ($150) and a recurring monthly subscription for health monitoring ($10 per month for a basic monitoring and $20 per month for premium monitoring). The product will be distributed through veterinary offices, on which they will earn a portion of the profit for implanting the device. With vets beginning to lose out on prescription revenue to big-box pharmacies, they will be looking for additional sources of revenue from nonmedical sources. The consumer can sign up for the appropriate service plan online and their wand will be shipped overnight to them.

Customers pay an initial implant fee and then will pay monthly through their established credit card account for the PetPulse monitoring services with the opportunity to upgrade to a premier service at any point in time. We expect 90 percent of the owners to use the basic service plan, and 10 percent for those with older or sick pets, to use the more advanced plan.

5. Marketing Objectives

Our marketing objective is to capture slightly more than 2 percent of the total U. S. domestic pet parent household segment (dogs and cats only). This is a conservative estimate given our voice of consumer research indicated a significant percentage of pet parents indicated a likelihood to purchase the product. Specifically, 58 percent of pet parents who lost a pet to illness expressed a willingness to purchase and 41 percent of pet parents who had not yet lost a pet to illness expressed a willingness to purchase. At the end of the fifth year, PetPulse will have chips implanted in more than 1.5 million pets.

6. Marketing Strategy

Target Market

There are 73 million household in the United States that own a pet. But our target market consists only of customers who consider themselves as pet parents. In other words, these customers believe their pets are valued family members. Our initial target market will be pet parents of dogs and cats. Three-quarters of dog owners view themselves as pet parents

(34.5 million households) and one-half of cat owners view themselves as pet parents (19.5 million households) for a total of 54 million households. These pet parents are proactively seeking better care for their pets. The core needs of these pet parents are as follows:

- Relieve the anxiety visits to the vet cause for both the pet and owner
- Ability to understand if a change in behavior in the pet is caused by something that requires immediate attention (i.e., diarrhea, pet is lethargic, etc.)
- Reduce number of trips to the vet for pets with a chronic illness that may require frequent monitoring of certain levels such as blood count, protein, etc.
- Proactively detect and treat certain sicknesses/illnesses before they can become life threatening
- Peace of mind for the owner
- Ability to give your pet a "voice" when he/she may not be feeling well

PetPulse is able to meet all the core needs of this target market. Our initial beachhead will be customers in the United States. However, we feel pet parents with the same core needs also exist in global markets and we intend to expand into such global markets over time.

Positioning

Our positioning is a hybrid approach, emphasizing quality for both our product and service as well as an emotional value proposition that we are the vendor of choice for pet parents who really love their pets and want to ensure their good health.

Product Strategy

In Year 1, a standard microchip will be sold that monitors the pet's vital signs including pulse, blood pressure, oxygen levels, and blood analysis. These chips will also contain identification information that links to an online database. A transponder will be housed in a wand-like object that powers the implanted chip wirelessly and receives the appropriate signals. The wand sends the information over a wireless Internet connection or Bluetooth to be displayed on the user's smartphone or computer. Two service packages will be offered: the basic service will provide vital information diagnostic analysis, and the premium service will include blood analysis for worm content and glucose levels. Both packages will link this information to the common database that interfaces with your veterinarian.

In Years 2 and 3, the services will be developed to offer additional diagnostic checks based on the sensor information. Additionally, the service will be upgraded to offer global access by customer and veterinarians. The service will be expanded to offer a direct link to the user's veterinarian, offering remote consultation through transmission of health information from the sensor. We will build up our customer service support to be able to answer calls around the clock, and ensure customer satisfaction in resolving any problems with their pet's health. From the systems perspective, Year 2 will adapt the microchip to be able to enter the bovine, equine, and swine markets. By Year 3, the sensor will be internationally compliant and expand into global markets.

This multiyear rollout also aligns with the Good-Better-Best product layout shown in Figure 1. As PetPulse will be the first to market in the implantable microchip pet health monitoring industry, the initial offering of the Good product will allow us to create an installed-base with pet parent early adopters. As we gain working capital, we will plan to strategically improve the systems and services with the Better and Best offerings each subsequent year while establishing our brand and reputation.

Figure 1   PetPulse Good-Better-Best Portfolio

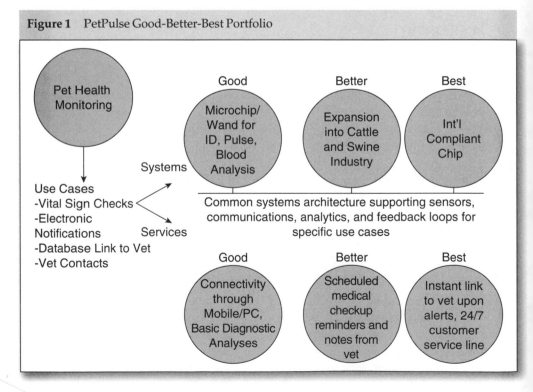

Product/Service Design

The market analysis results indicate that our target user is looking to increase the lifespan of his/her pet, facilitate vet visits from an economic and emotional standpoint, and gain insight into their pet's overall well-being. The PetPulse product addresses these key consumer needs in an elegant and efficient solution. The microchip itself is very small in size, in the tens of millimeters range, as shown in Figure 2. Size is important to maintain the comfort of the customer's pet. Even with additional sensing capabilities, we are able to keep the package size minimized by not using a traditional power source such as a battery. The power is transmitted wirelessly through a wand that the pet owner or veterinarian scans over the pet, as shown in Figure 3. The result is then sent over wireless Internet or Bluetooth to a device at the customer's discretion. This is the minimum level of functionality required, as it is able to address the user needs identified whereas no other product on the market currently achieves this.

In the subsequent year product offerings, features are augmented to increase ease of use for the customer. Additional user needs are addressed by building upon the installed-base of customers as well as participating

Figure 2   PetPulse Implantable Microchip and Sensor

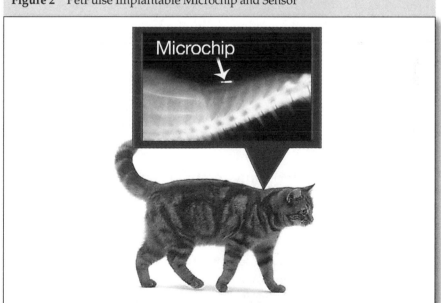

Figure 3   PetPulse Wand Transponder Communicating With a Smartphone

veterinarians. Customer service operators become a convenient resource for consumers to call at any time of day to address emergencies or general questions. The hardware and software architecture is modular and expandable, and eventually marries up with the veterinarian network in providing digital interfaces between customer, pet, and doctor. Additionally, the frequency at which PetPulse will be transmitting will be compliant with International Standards Organization (ISO) regulations and therefore compatible with existing ID tags and readers on the market (125kHz/134.2kHz). This makes it convenient to travel internationally and abide by national and international regulations as a pet owner with a regular implantable microchip would today.

Proprietary Technology, Intellectual Property

The PetPulse product will license the sensor technology from Project, Inc. as they have proven technologies in the implantable microchip space.[8] In addition, we will license the wireless power transmission technology for the microchip and wand from Biosense's Research Center. In order to ensure a competitive advantage, we will negotiate a limited exclusivity agreement in order to have exclusive use of the technology in the pet industry.

Underlying Architecture and Platforms

The hardware and software aspect of PetPulse will have their respective common platforms. As the wireless power and transmission technology will be the same for all chips, only the specific sensors will have to be dropped into the different designs. As for the service and software piece, there will be a common database management system that will coordinate between individual user files and veterinarian files. An additional layer to determine how to push notifications or alerts to the user is then easily integrated.

Development Plan and Key Milestones

As the biosensors are already fabricated and available for prototyping and production, the initial quantities can be packaged with the wireless communication circuit fairly quickly. The wand reader also combines the wireless circuit with commercial-off-the-shelf (COTS) system solutions. The firmware and software execution will be the most time consuming for optimizing. The key milestones and estimated dates are noted below:

Key Milestone	Completion Date
Alpha Version (first prototype)	06/24/12
Beta Version	09/24/12
Final Release for Year 1	11/24/12

Systems Development Cost Plan

The development costs will include multiple phases of product hardware and software prototyping, capital hardware, full-time employee salaries, technology and software licensing fees, testing, and debug. The estimates for these elements are listed in the financial section, and total $200,000 annually.

Pricing

As illustrated in the business revenue model, the initial cost of the implant will be $150 for the first pet along with a monthly fee of $10 for the basic plan or $20 for the premier monitoring plan. The total annual expenditure in the first year is expected to be $270 per pet for a basic plan. According to *Consumer Reports,* this is in line with the average cost of an annual vet visit for a geriatric dog or cat ($330). Other implantable devices, such as Monitor cost $45 to implant and have an annual membership fee of $17.50. However, Monitor only offers a single service, which is to identify a lost pet as compared to PetPulse, which provides an advanced ongoing service allowing it to charge a premium pricing. This is a premium pricing model that is driven by the fact that our voice of consumer research revealed strong felt need for the product as well as an ability and willingness to pay on behalf of the target market.

Promotion

The PetPulse brand was market tested with our target market and was very well received including being selected as the best brand-name option of the several brands tested. The promotional activities we will use to reach our target market include trade shows, advertising in trade publications and on trade websites, and an endorsement from a reputable veterinary doctor for a total cost of $350,000. We will also have a robust website and will leverage social media to build brand awareness and positive attitudes toward the brand.

- *Trade Shows:* There are over eight veterinary trade conference and exhibitions in the United States annually. The largest is the North American Veterinary Conference (NAVC) that occurs in January. Because this conference is also the first one of the year, NAVC is also where new product innovations are announced and the most current medical advances are revealed first. The conference attracts over 16,000 attendees of which one-third of attendees being veterinarians. The other attendees are made up of technicians, veterinary hospital personnel, and students from veterinary and veterinary technician schools. The estimated cost for this event in the first year is $25,000. This covers premium corner space at the conference on the first two days; space in the exhibit hall on the second two days; promotional material handouts including pamphlets and PetPulse branded merchandise; travel and shipping expenses; graphic design and displays for the booth; and branded attire for the sales team.

- *Advertising:* Traditional mass market advertising will not allow the brand to connect without the distribution target, veterinarians, or our consumer target. In order to educate the vet population and ensure consumers are asking for PetPulse, we will launch a Veterinarian Print Publication campaign. The timing will coincide with the product launch. These publications include *Veterinary Practice News* and *Pet Practice News*. The print campaign will be supplemented with a targeted online advertising campaign on the publication websites and through Google targeted ad units. The total cost for the campaign is $200,000.

- *Endorsement:* To reinforce the trust of the PetPulse brand and connect with the decision makers at our main channel of distribution, PetPulse will bring on Dr. Mark D. Connor. Dr. Connor is credited with discovering the cause, cure, and prevention of feline dilated cardiomyopathy (FDC). Dr. Connor is also the president and cofounder of Veterinary Information Network (VIN) that provides online up-to-date information for veterinarians. Dr. Connor will endorse PetPulse as a major new breakthrough in veterinarian medicine that would be instrumental in identifying the medical signs of FDC in cats if they were implanted. Dr. Connor will be featured in the print ad campaign, as part of videos that will be used on the brand website, and will attend industry trade shows with special appearances. The total cost to secure Dr. Connor is $125,000 for the first two years.

Place/Channels

The findings from our original research have indicated that our target consumer would expect to purchase PetPulse from their veterinarian. The reason is because they highly regard medical advice from their veterinarian as a primary driver for purchase. These findings coupled with the requirement for implantation has driven the decision to target veterinary clinics and hospitals as the primary source for distribution to our target consumer. A secondary channel will be developed through breeders and adoption agencies. To reach our distribution channels, we plan to attend trade shows in addition to having field sales team that will market directly to the vets, breeders, and adoption agencies.

7. Operations

Overall, we will be using subcontract manufacturers to supply and produce our products, therefore limiting infrastructure fixed costs and operating on higher variables costs. The supplier and procurement of the microchip will be taken care of by same manufacturer who produced the Agenda biosensors. As there are only a few additional components on the microchip side, this will be the most cost-efficient solution. The wand system, plastic, packaging, and testing will be subcontracted to established connections we have in China. They possess the skills and supply chain to expertly produce this product. We will compare vendor quotes to ensure we are spending our money wisely to get our projected margins.

We will plan to use well-established third-party logistics firms to ship our product back to the United States and transport to our facilities. The microchip will be shipped to veterinarian offices and the wand will be shipped directly to the customer through UPS or FedEx upon activation of the service. Storing the wands at a central location will reduce the amount of inventory required to carry on hand.

In the first year, customer service will be provided for business-related and general questions. We will hire employees in our office to answer these calls or take them ourselves in order to ensure customer satisfaction. This is also a great way to garner direct feedback for our future products and enhancements. The customer service cost model is based on 2 percent of sales and will grow accordingly.

Our office will be leased on an annual basis. It will include a few offices and cubicles, as well as a storage warehouse for our products. During startup when cash is tight, we will not be splurging on extravagant decorations or furnishings, but will ensure that our employees have all the necessary tools to get their job done. From a culture standpoint, we will spend where necessary to ensure happy employees, which we hope will translate to happy customers.

8. Marketing Budget/Financials

The venture team will invest $250,000 of their own resources. This initial investment will be earmarked for 10 quarterly payments for the upfront licensing agreement necessary for the technology. The business will run fairly lean in the first few months, employing two full-time officers, as well as two full-time computer programmers to develop the back-end systems for the PetPulse, and slowly ramping up the staffing needs.

PetPulse is seeking $3M dollars to support its startup in operations to be supplied in Month 2 of the venture. The company is forecasted to burn cash for the first 14 months of operation, though have a gross margin of about $841K to help support operations. Over the 14 months, the cash is expected to be allocated as follows:

- $450,000 in salary for the company officers—Assumes two officers will be on board from Day 1, a third officer will join in Month 5 and the final two in Month 7.
- $456,250 will be to support two IT programmers (from the start) and five regional sales people to join in Month 8.
- $158,000 for the creation and staffing of a call center
- $156,000 for T&E and tradeshows
- $185,000 for advertising and endorsements
- $153,000 for rent and office expenses
- $200,000 for systems and equipment
- $73,000 for legal and liability insurance
- $900,000 in inventory

The forecast projects the lowest cash level on hand in Month 14 to be $775,000, allowing for flexibility in unforeseen events. Key revenue events assumes the first sale in Month 9 and operational breakeven in Month 13. PetPulse becomes cash flow positive in Month 15. At the end of two years, PetPulse is forecasted to have $18M in cash on the books. At this point, the investor can opt to sell its shares back to the company for $5.8M (annualized return of 40 percent), or they can hold on until the possible liquidation event around the end of the fifth year.

This plan is very conservative with a five-year target of 2 percent of all domestic dog and cat pet parents buying the product and service. Even so, the $3.25M startup costs will be fully recouped before the end of the second year. The first eight months of the venture will be nonrevenue generating, and the company will have an operating loss of $1.4M in Year 1. However, in Month 13, the company will show its first operating profit and profitable by Month 16—wiping out Year 1 losses. Revenues are expected to grow from $98K in Year 1 to $49M in Year 2, $101M in Year 3, and nearly $200M by Year 5.

With two revenue streams, one for the chip and wand (lower margin), and one for the monthly services (higher margin), the net profit improves over time. In Month 13, the first profitable month, the net profit is 17 percent of revenue. As the services become a larger portion of the revenue, that quickly builds with Year 2 having a net income of 39 percent of revenue and Year 5 around 56 percent of revenue.

Financial Exhibit A—Income Statement

Income Statement Summary
$(000)

YEAR 1	Month 1	Month 2	Month 3	Month 4	Month 5	Month 6	Month 7	Month 8	Month 9	Month 10	Month 11	Month 12	Year 1
Revenue Sale of Goods	-	-	-	-	-	-	-	-	5	7	9	62	83
Revenue Sale of Services	-	-	-	-	-	-	-	-	1	1	3	11	15
Total Revenue	-	-	-	-	-	-	-	-	5	8	12	73	98
COGS	-	-	-	-	-	-	-	-	3	4	5	35	47
Gross Margin	-	-	-	-	-	-	-	-	3	4	7	38	52
Operating Profit	(64)	(64)	(64)	(60)	(68)	(68)	(100)	(255)	(170)	(138)	(199)	(132)	(1,383)
EBITDA	(58)	(58)	(58)	(48)	(57)	(57)	(88)	(243)	(158)	(127)	(187)	(120)	(1,258)
EBITDA Cumulative	(58)	(115)	(173)	(221)	(278)	(334)	(422)	(666)	(824)	(951)	(1,138)	(1,258)	(1,258)

YEAR 2	Month 13	Month 14	Month 15	Month 16	Month 17	Month 18	Month 19	Month 20	Month 21	Month 22	Month 23	Month 24	Year 2
Revenue Sale of Goods	515	724	996	1,349	1,805	2,440	3,211	4,195	5,449	3,941	2,549	2,566	29,739
Revenue Sale of Services	77	171	300	474	708	1,018	1,424	1,955	2,644	3,135	3,444	3,753	19,106
Total Revenue	593	895	1,296	1,823	2,513	3,458	4,635	6,151	8,093	7,076	5,993	6,319	48,845
COGS	290	408	563	764	1,024	1,384	1,823	2,384	3,098	2,264	1,492	1,378	16,873
Gross Margin	303	486	733	1,059	1,489	2,073	2,812	3,767	4,995	4,812	4,502	4,941	31,972
Operating Profit	154	290	565	897	1,256	1,855	2,552	3,491	4,651	4,511	4,200	4,617	29,038
EBITDA	166	302	576	914	1,273	1,872	2,570	3,509	4,668	4,528	4,217	4,634	29,228
EBITDA Cumulative	(1,092)	(791)	(214)	700	1,973	3,845	6,414	9,923	14,591	19,119	23,336	27,970	27,970

YEAR 3 to 5	Yr3 Q1	Yr3 Q2	Yr3 Q3	Yr3 Q4	Year 3	Yr4 Q1	Yr4 Q2	Yr4 Q3	Yr4 Q4	Year 4	Year 5
Revenue Sale of Goods	7,798	7,949	8,100	8,251	32,099	8,403	8,556	8,708	8,861	34,528	36,983
Revenue Sale of Services	13,118	15,911	18,711	21,518	69,257	24,333	27,155	29,985	32,823	114,296	159,815
Total Revenue	20,916	23,859	26,811	29,769	101,356	32,736	35,711	38,693	41,684	148,824	196,798
COGS	4,222	4,352	4,482	4,612	17,667	4,743	4,874	5,006	5,138	19,760	20,027
Gross Margin	16,695	19,508	22,329	25,157	83,689	27,993	30,837	33,688	36,546	129,064	176,771
Operating Profit	15,706	18,431	21,117	23,874	79,127	26,628	29,436	32,267	35,091	123,422	170,747
EBITDA	15,757	18,499	21,184	23,941	79,382	26,695	29,504	32,334	35,158	123,691	171,013
EBITDA Cumulative	43,727	62,226	83,410	107,351	107,351	134,046	163,550	195,884	231,042	231,042	402,056

Financial Exhibit B—Cash Flow

Cash Flow ($000)

YEAR 1	Month 1	Month 2	Month 3	Month 4	Month 5	Month 6	Month 7	Month 8	Month 9	Month 10	Month 11	Month 12
Beginning Cash	-	163.2	3,102.0	2,853.2	2,787.8	2,738.8	2,689.7	2,582.4	2,342.6	2,186.3	2,023.4	1,688.7
Cash Flow From Operating	(59.3)	(59.7)	(59.7)	(50.2)	(58.5)	(58.5)	(91.5)	(248.5)	(164.1)	(145.0)	(341.2)	(446.2)
Cash Flow from Investing	(25.0)	-	(200.0)	(25.0)	-	-	(25.0)	-	-	(25.0)	-	-
Cash Flow from Financing	247.9	2,998.6	10.9	9.8	9.6	9.4	9.2	8.7	7.8	7.1	6.5	5.1
Ending Cash	163.2	3,102.0	2,853.2	2,787.8	2,738.8	2,689.7	2,582.4	2,342.6	2,186.3	2,023.4	1,688.7	1,247.5

YEAR 2	Month 13	Month 14	Month 15	Month 16	Month 17	Month 18	Month 19	Month 20	Month 21	Month 22	Month 23	Month 24
Beginning Cash	1,247.5	805.8	775.1	919.8	1,057.2	1,145.9	1,414.4	1,867.6	3,466.1	7,167.0	11,601.8	15,128.0
Cash Flow From Operating	(219.9)	(32.1)	143.4	160.4	86.2	265.6	474.2	1,592.6	3,688.3	4,431.8	3,479.7	2,874.6
Cash Flow from Investing	(225.0)	-	-	(25.0)	-	-	(25.0)	-	-	(25.0)	-	-
Cash Flow from Financing	3.2	1.4	1.3	1.9	2.5	2.9	4.0	5.9	12.6	28.0	46.5	61.2
Ending Cash	805.8	775.1	919.8	1,057.2	1,145.9	1,414.4	1,867.6	3,466.1	7,167.0	11,601.8	15,128.0	18,063.8

YEAR 3 to 5	Yr3 Q1	Yr3 Q2	Yr3 Q3	Yr3 Q4	Year 3	Yr4 Q1	Yr4 Q2	Yr4 Q3	Yr4 Q4	Year 4	Year 5
Beginning Cash	18,063.8	28,311.7	40,685.2	54,992.2	18,063.8	71,278.2	89,364.7	109,713.1	132,154.6	71,278.2	156,965.7
Cash Flow From Operating	10,212.4	12,000.1	13,745.8	15,537.6	51,495.9	17,327.8	19,153.1	20,993.1	23,052.8	80,526.8	110,918.2
Cash Flow from Investing	(225.0)	(25.0)	-	-	(250.0)	(200.0)	-	-	-	(200.0)	(200.0)
Cash Flow from Financing	260.5	398.4	561.3	748.4	1,968.5	958.8	1,195.2	1,458.4	1,748.3	5,360.7	10,452.3
Ending Cash	28,311.7	40,685.2	54,992.2	71,278.2	71,278.2	89,364.7	109,713.1	132,154.6	156,965.7	156,965.7	278,136.2

9. Management Team

The management team of PetPulse is comprised of passionate pet parents with years of cross-functional experience. Our passion and prior experience, coupled with key advisers ranging from veterinarians to clinicians, provides PetPulse the ability to run a highly talented company driven by our passion for healthy pets.

PetPulse Inc. Organizational Chart

Management Team

The PetPulse management team consists of a CEO, CFO, CMO, COO, CTO, and a board of advisers.

Jennifer Lynch—Founder and CEO

Jennifer Lynch has been working in product management for consumer products and software for over 10+ years. Her expertise is running strategic business units for global brands as well as developing strategic business partnerships. Prior to founding PetPulse, she managed key business units for Runner Shoe Company, worked on a joint product creation process with Mountain Climb Inc. and City Sportwear, and worked in software management implementing content into web portal applications with key Global Fortune 500 companies.

Steven Lubelczyk—CFO

Steven Lubelczyk has 12+ years of working experience in data/ financial analysis and financial budgeting and sales forecasting. Working broadly in the global steel industry, Steve has a solid understanding of cost structures for importing goods from around the world, with a focus on China. His experience across all departments in his current organization has built a solid base in understanding the complete workings of a company and different departments' financial impact on the bottom line. Steve is financially conservative and ready to launch PetPulse as a stable and successful company. He is also the proud pet parent of Fletcher, a rescued chocolate lab that bounces around when Steve comes home from work.

Elizabeth Bunnell—CMO

Elizabeth Bunnell has 9+ years of working experience in the consumer products marketing industry. She began her career in brand development and marketing for a women's startup fashion company and, most recently, led the global consumer marketing strategies and execution for Fluffy Friends, a Toys Brand-owned Fun Plush brand for girls. Elizabeth's foundation in entrepreneurial environments, brand development experience, and passion for animals will prove to be a great asset to the PetPulse brand.

Angela Kontos—COO

Angela has been working in the financial services industry for 10+ years. She has implemented multimillion-dollar projects and is currently responsible for managing a $40M technology budget. Given the recent economic downturn, she has gained firsthand experience and knowledge of cost pressures in an operational environment. She has had to implement lean and six-sigma processes, manage cross-functional teams and an increasingly larger global footprint due to the push for off-shoring. She is also the proud parent of a 17-year-old daughter and while not currently a pet parent, her passion for improving health care for animals has been a key driver for her joining the PetPulse team.

Andrew Han—CTO

Andrew has 7+ years working with electrical systems, ranging from RADAR on government contracts to consumer electronics in the toys/games industry. His technical experience has been in the prototyping and development of integrated circuits (ICs) and systems-level designs.

Board of Advisers/Directors

Tanya Decker, DVM

Dr. Decker was born and raised in Spain and immigrated to Israel at the age of 19. She studied a bachelor degree in Animal Sciences at Cornell University and then received her doctorate at the Koret School of Veterinary Medicine. In Israel, Dr. Decker has dedicated her time to work as a zoo keeper and a veterinary technician, and she volunteered with disabled adults and low-income immigrants. Dr. Decker moved to Boston with her husband in 2005. She worked as an oncology technician at Angell Animal Medical Center until she got her veterinary license in the United States. She started working as a general practitioner at Boston Medical Animal Clinic in August 2006 and she left in June 2007 to complete a one-year medical and surgical internship at Angell Memorial Animal Hospital. After her internship, she returned to VCA in July 2008 and had worked with us since then. Dr. Decker speaks fluently English, Spanish, Hebrew, and Russian. Dr. Decker currently resides with her husband and her daughter in Boston.

Amanda Smith, DVM

Dr. Smith was born and raised in Ithaca, NY. She received a BA in Psychology from Yale University in 1995. She worked in both nonprofit and education before moving out to Northern California in 1999 to return to school to finish her veterinary school prerequisites. She earned her DVM from the University of California, Berkeley in 2006. She then completed a yearlong internship at a small animal specialty and emergency practice in San Francisco before finally moving back to the northeast to Boston to join Massachusetts Animal Hospital. Dr. Smith's veterinary interests include cardiology, ophthalmology, soft tissue surgery, and diagnostic ultrasound. In her free time, Dr. Smith enjoys travel, music, yoga and dance, spending time with friends, eating good food, and exploring Boston and the surrounding area. She shares her home with her dog Sparky, a lab/hound mix, and two cats, Fluffy and Max.

Staffing Plan

Two company officers will be on staff at startup along with two technology developers/programmers. A sales team will be hired at Month 8 and a call center will be ramped based on 2 percent of sales revenue. The expectation is that the company officers will be able to handle all incoming calls in the beginning stages along with building the relationships with the distribution channels. By the end of the first year, all five company officers will be onboard.

10. Evaluation and Control

PetPulse will be carefully evaluating, monitoring, and controlling its performance with regard to effectively executing its strategies as well as meeting its marketing and financial objectives. The company has the in-house talent to use appropriate metrics (e.g., market share achievement, customer acquisition costs, etc.) and to review such via marketing dashboard technology. Any deviations including shortfalls will be promptly diagnosed and corrected by the team.

References

1. http://www.fetchpetcare.com/industry_overview/page/142/-/page.php
2. Source: American Pet Products Association
3. McGrath, Jane. "How Pet Microchipping Works," 21 April 2008. HowStuff Works .com. http://science.howstuffworks.com/innovation/everyday-innovations/pet-microchip.htm 27 January 2012.
4. http://www.humanesociety.org/issues/pet_overpopulation/facts/pet_ownership_statistics.html
5. http://www.americanpetproducts.org/press_industrytrends.asp
6. http://www.aspca.org/about-us/faq/pet-statistics.aspx
7. Source: Laura Bennett, CEO of Embrace Pet Insurance
8. http://www.agenda.com/products.html
9. https://technology.grc.biosense.gov/tech-detail-coded.php?cid=GR-0025&mini=y

Index

About the Author

Frederick G. Crane is an Executive Professor of Entrepreneurship & Innovation at the College of Business at Northeastern University, Editor of the *Journal of the Academy of Business Education*, and cofounder of Ceilidh Insights LLC, an innovation management training, intellectual property consulting, and consumer-insight company. He was formerly a professor of marketing and entrepreneurship at the University of New Hampshire and a chair and full professor at Dalhousie University. He currently teaches courses in entrepreneurship, innovation, and entrepreneurial marketing.

Dr. Crane grew up in a family business and also founded and operated several of his own businesses. In addition to being a serial entrepreneur, he has also been an investor in several startups, served on the advisory boards of entrepreneurial firms, and worked as a consultant for angel investors, venture capitalists, and government agencies on venture funding projects. In addition, he has developed and delivered numerous training programs and workshops for entrepreneurs and small-business owners.

His academic research activities have resulted in more than 100 publications, including 15 books, and he currently sits on the editorial boards of several academic journals. His current research stream intersects the domains of marketing, entrepreneurship, corporate venturing, and innovation, and he is conducting ongoing research on the psychology of entrepreneurship, entrepreneurial education, entrepreneurial branding, and innovation readiness. Dr. Crane is also an award-winning educator who has received numerous honors for teaching excellence over the past 20 years.

⑤SAGE research**methods**

The essential online tool for researchers from the
world's leading methods publisher

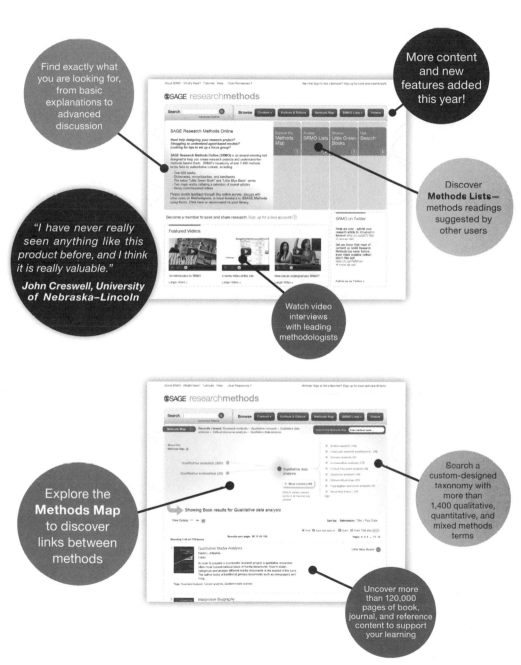

Find exactly what you are looking for, from basic explanations to advanced discussion

More content and new features added this year!

Discover **Methods Lists**— methods readings suggested by other users

"I have never really seen anything like this product before, and I think it is really valuable."

John Creswell, University of Nebraska–Lincoln

Watch video interviews with leading methodologists

Explore the **Methods Map** to discover links between methods

Search a custom-designed taxonomy with more than 1,400 qualitative, quantitative, and mixed methods terms

Uncover more than 120,000 pages of book, journal, and reference content to support your learning

Find out more at
www.sageresearchmethods.com